Law Question

EQUITY & TRUSTS

Questions and Answers Series

Titles in the Series

Other titles in preparation

Law Questions & Answers

EQUITY & TRUSTS

Third Edition

MARGARET WILKIE

Visiting Lecturer in Law, University of Sheffield

ROSALIND MALCOLM

Barrister, University Director in Law, University of Surrey

PETER LUXTON

*Solicitor, Professor of Property Law,
De Montfort University, Leicester*

OXFORD
UNIVERSITY PRESS

OXFORD

UNIVERSITY PRESS

Great Clarendon Street, Oxford OX2 6DP

Oxford University Press is a department of the University of Oxford.
It furthers the University's objective of excellence in research, scholarship,
and education by publishing worldwide in

Oxford New York

Auckland Bangkok Buenos Aires Cape Town Chennai
Dar es Salaam Delhi Hong Kong Istanbul Karachi Kolkata
Kuala Lumpur Madrid Melbourne Mexico City Mumbai Nairobi
São Paulo Shanghai Singapore Taipei Tokyo Toronto

and an associated company in Berlin

Oxford is a registered trade mark of Oxford University Press
in the UK and certain other countries

Published in the United States
by Oxford University Press Inc., New York

A Blackstone Press Book

British Library Cataloguing in Publication Data

Data available

Library of Congress Cataloging in Publication Data

Data available

ISBN 1-84174-097-7

3 5 7 9 10 8 6 4 2

Typeset by Montage Studios Limited, Tonbridge, Kent
Printed in Great Britain
on acid-free paper by
Antony Rowe Limited, Chippenham and Reading

Contents

Preface

This is the third edition of the first book in this series. We are delighted that the book has sold so well, and assume that this is a testimony to its usefulness to students of this difficult and academic subject. The feedback from lecturers is that it is generally considered as a good revision aid and a support to tutorial work — no doubt particularly so where tutorials involve large numbers of students and are infrequent, as on distance learning courses.

The law of equity and trusts continues to develop through the cases, and we have of course updated the book taking these into account, amending and substituting questions where appropriate. The most important developments for this edition, however, are in the statute law. The Trustee Act 2000 has had a significant impact on trustees' duties and powers, particularly with regard to investment and delegation. The constitution of trusts has also been affected by the Contracts (Rights of Third Parties) Act 1999, although to what extent has yet to be clarified by judicial interpretation.

The purpose of the book remains unchanged — it is intended as a student aid in structuring an answer to examination-type problems, and in elucidating some of the more difficult areas of the subject.

The law is stated as at February 2002.

Margaret Wilkie
Rosalind Malcolm
Peter Luxton
February 2002

Table of Cases

Table of Statutes

1 Introduction

This book has been written by three lecturers with many years' experience of researching and teaching equity and trusts on different law degree courses at various universities. It is an attempt to give guidance to students on what is expected in the answer to typical questions on the topic (and also, in some instances, on what is superfluous and irrelevant!). We have, in places, pointed out what might distinguish a good answer (class 2(i) or better) from one of a lower quality.

We are acutely aware that many institutions are now adopting assessed coursework as part of their total mark for a subject at the end of the year. Where we feel that the topic is one which might lend itself to this type of coursework, we have included, in the introduction to the question, references to academic articles and further cases which would assist in a deeper study of the area. Very often, assessed coursework will stipulate a maximum limit on the number of words you should write. If this is the case, then you should keep within such limits. This may well require careful planning and balancing of the material in your answer, part of the exercise being to test your ability to write clearly and concisely.

Although the material in all equity and trusts courses will have a large part in common, individual lecturers may accord parts of the subject more extensive treatment. It would be a foolish student indeed who did not heed the emphasis given by his or her lecturer to any particular parts of the course. If your lecturer has, for instance, written a book on charities, it is likely to be a subject dear to the heart and one which will be taught and examined.

Many of the questions on equity and trusts are likely to be problem questions. In dealing with a problem-type examination paper in particular, it is wise to spend a good few minutes at the beginning carefully reading the questions. Ignore the student next to you with a scratchy pen who turns over the first page of the answer book while you are still thinking. There is nothing more deflating than realising, on an examination post mortem, that there was a question on the paper in which you could have done well ... much better than one you did attempt!

Equally important for essay and problem questions is to spend a few minutes, before you actually embark on writing your answer, in jotting down a rough plan of what should be included. This should be brief — perhaps just a few key words or case names, which you can then expand to a paragraph in your answer. You will have been intelligent enough to calculate the time available for each question (after allowing time for reading the paper thoroughly at the beginning) and you should then keep to your plan: avoid writing excessively on a point which interests you to the detriment of other parts of the question. It is a common experience for examiners to find that the first two or three pages of some examination scripts contain nothing of relevance at all. We suspect those are the scripts of candidates who start writing from the first moment, without allowing prior pause for thought.

There are a few other obvious techniques which will endear you to your examiner. Leave the margins on your answer book clear — they are for your examiner's use and not yours. Start each question on a new page and number not only the question clearly, but also the different parts of it. Leave a line between each part. Illegible writing is a handicap in life, but especially so in the examination room. It may not in itself lose you marks, but it will irritate your examiner. Also, an examiner whose attention is directed to deciphering a barely legible script is less likely to be able to follow the argument you are putting forward, which could possibly result in lost marks. Spelling has been called a low form of cunning, but it is important and if it is not your forte, it is worth working on it. This is especially so with legal terms and judges' names. If you do not wish to give the impression you have never opened a law book in your life, you should try to avoid crass errors. (Candidates attempting charity answers, please note: the judge who laid down the four heads of charity was Lord Macnaghten — there is no 'u' in the name and the 'n' is not capital.)

If you suffer from dyslexia, or have an impairment which might affect your ability to write, you might consider it a good idea to mention it to your tutor in advance of your examination. Most institutions are willing to make allowances for this. Some, for example, are prepared to give extra time at the examination, or extra facilities such as the provision of an amanuensis.

The most important point of all is to be sure to ANSWER THE QUESTION YOU ARE ASKED rather than the question you would like to have been asked (perhaps because you revised it in detail the night before). You are unlikely to get marks for irrelevant material and you risk trying the patience of your examiner, which may be wearing thin by the hundred and first script — which just happens to be yours. Avoid writing a treatise on the law on the subject raised by the question — seldom do questions say, 'Write all you know about . . .' Above all, assume that all legalities relating to the problem are in order, unless the question specifically suggests otherwise: do not look a gift horse in the mouth. For example, it is not necessary to set out the requirements for a valid will or a valid trust if the question simply states that a will or a trust was made with no indication of any flaws.

Good reading, and good luck!

2   The Nature of Equity and the Law of Trusts

INTRODUCTION

The topics covered by this chapter are, by their very nature, bound to be broad and discursive. If you took the opportunity at the beginning of your course (or even during the preceding summer vacation) to undertake some of the general reading recommended by your lecturer, you will reap your reward here. Success in answering these questions depends on a broad reading of the available literature and an historical, even philosophical, approach. You may largely ignore the minutiae of the law reports in favour of a jurisprudential understanding of the development of equity and its doctrinal bases.

The relevant literature includes: Maitland, F. W., *Equity*, 2nd edn, Cambridge University Press, 1936; Holdsworth, W., *History of English Law*, 7th edn, London: Sweet & Maxwell, 1966; Snell, E., *Principles of Equity*, 29th edn, London: Sweet & Maxwell, 1991; Pollock, F., *Jurisprudence and Legal Essays*, London: Macmillan, 1961; Ashburner, *Principles of Equity*, 2nd edn, 1933.

Check your own reading list for additional material recommended by your lecturer.

The chapter contains four essay questions. The usual principles apply in tackling such questions in exam conditions: draw up a plan in rough and stick to it; do not ramble; make a series of points; write a conclusion.

However, there is a difference in answering essay questions of this type and some of the essay questions covered in the rest of the book. Essays that require discussion of substantive law do, at least, start with something on which to hang your hat. An essay, for example, on the development of the search order, or on the constructive trust, requires an analysis of a sequence of case law. If you know half a dozen cases on the point, then the art is to angle them at the question. Different essay titles on the same area of substantive law usually require the same case law but with a different nose! Essay questions on highly theoretical subjects do require a different style. They require a factual base and plenty of examples of the points you are making, but for high marks they need a touch of original thinking. Even if your thinking is not original, they require a thoughtful intellectual analysis of other people's thinking. If you have not thought about the issues raised by these questions before you enter the examination room, then you are not going to achieve high marks on these questions. If you have the makings of a highly practical lawyer, then select a problem question!

It is quite likely that these topics could crop up as assessed essay questions. If so, then a long session in the library is the starting point. Conduct your preparation for the essay as if you were undertaking a piece of research. Survey the literature noting carefully your sources. Then think over your arguments. Do you agree with X that there has been a fusion of law and equity or do you agree with Y that there has not? Why do you agree or disagree? Do you see both sides of the argument? Argue the case with your friends then write it up while the adrenaline is flowing.

QUESTION 1

The innate conservatism of English lawyers may have made them slow to recognise that by the Judicature Act 1873 the two systems of substantive and adjectival law formerly administered by courts of law and courts of equity ... were fused. As at the confluence of the Rhone and the Saone, it may be possible for a short distance to discern the source from which each part of the combined stream came, but there comes a point at which this ceases to be possible. If Professor Ashburner's fluvial metaphor is to be retained at all, the confluent streams of law and equity have surely mingled now. (Lord Diplock in *United Scientific Holdings Ltd* v *Burnley Borough Council* [1978] AC 904.)

Discuss.

Commentary

The reference is to Ashburner, *Principles of Equity*, 2nd edn, 1933, at p. 18. Further useful references are Lord Evershed MR, (1954) 70 LQR 326; V. Delaney, (1961) 24 MLR 116; and T. Watkin, (1977) 6 AALR 119. It is interesting to note that there are several statements from judges of the highest seniority which concur with the statement of Lord Diplock quoted above, at least to the extent that they consider that this issue is redundant and the combined effect of the systems should be considered. See, for example, Lord Evershed, (1948) JSPTL 180, Lord Denning, (1952) CLP 1, and in *Landmarks in the Law* (Butterworths, 1984). Academic writers seem, in general, to take a different view. So, the question is provocative, even controversial. A good modern example of the conflict is provided by the House of Lords' decision in *Tinsley* v *Milligan* [1994] 1 AC 340 and the ensuing case law. For a criticism of this decision, see R. Buckley, (1994) 110 LQR 3.

Suggested Answer

The statement by Lord Diplock was accepted unanimously by the judges in the House of Lords. The case concerned the timing of the service of notices triggering rent-review clauses. The notice to trigger a rent review had been served late by the landlord and the question arose as to whether time was of the essence. The Law of Property Act 1925, s. 41 provides that 'stipulations in a contract, as to time or otherwise, which according to rules of equity are not deemed to be or to have become of the essence of the contract, are also construed and have effect at law in accordance with the same rules'. The section clearly states that a rule of equity is to be adopted within the body of legal rules. Lord Diplock proclaimed that the systems had, quite simply, become fused and that no distinction was to be drawn between law and equity.

This view is at the most extreme, yet it is one apparently shared by other eminent judges. Lord Denning, in *Landmarks in the Law*, states that 'the fusion is complete'. Sir George Jessel MR in *Walsh* v *Lonsdale* (1882) 21 ChD 9, one of the first cases on this issue to be heard subsequent to the Judicature Acts 1873–1875, said 'there are not two estates as there were formerly, one estate at common law by reason of the payment of rent from year to year, and an estate in equity under the agreement. There is only one court, and the equity rules prevail in it'. In *Tinsley* v *Milligan* [1994] 1 AC 340, Lord Browne-Wilkinson said that English law was now a single law which was made up of legal and equitable interests, and a person owning either type of estate had a right of property amounting to a right in rem not merely a right in personam. The approach of Lord Goff in *Napier and Ettrick (Lord]* v *Hunter* [1993] AC 713 is in accord with this: 'No doubt our task nowadays is to see the two strands of authority, at law and in equity, moulded into a coherent whole.'

The difficulty originates from the early development of equity as a separate system from the common law. The common law courts emerged in the centuries following the Norman conquest. Intervention by the Lord Chancellor gradually developed into a separate body of law, known as equity, which had, by the fifteenth century, become well established. The Chancellor's jurisdiction was exercised through what became the Court of Chancery. The two systems were sometimes in conflict. Parties seeking common law relief would need to seek the jurisdiction of the common law courts. If they wanted equitable relief they would go to the Court of Chancery. This might occur during the course of the same litigation. The common law courts only had limited jurisdiction to grant equitable relief. The Common Law Procedure Act 1854, s. 79, gave the common law courts a limited power of granting injunctions; the Chancery Amendment Act 1858 gave power to the Court of Chancery to award damages instead of (or in addition to) injunctions or specific performance.

The problem became acute in the nineteenth century, and a series of Parliamentary reports led eventually to the Judicature Acts 1873 and 1875. These Acts amalgamated the superior courts into one Supreme Court of Judicature. The Courts of Queen's Bench, Exchequer and Common Pleas and the Court of Chancery, the Court of Exchequer Chamber and the Court of Appeal in Chancery, were all replaced by the Supreme Court. The Supreme Court consisted of the Court of Appeal and the High Court, which originally had five divisions (subsequently reduced to three). The Supreme Court could administer both rules of common law and equity. Thus, there is no question as to the fusion of the courts. The two distinct sets of courts fused on 1 November 1875. Sir George Jessel MR, who, as Solicitor-General, was the government officer largely responsible for the Judicature Acts, said in *Salt* v *Cooper* (1880) 16 ChD 544, that the main object of the Acts was not the fusion of law and equity, but the vesting in one tribunal of the administration of law and equity in all actions coming before that tribunal.

Yet it is difficult to pursue Lord Diplock's dictum further to the point of saying that the substantive rules of law and equity are themselves indistinguishable. In trusts there is a distinction between legal and equitable interests and the right to trace property in equity depends on the existence of a fiduciary relationship. In property law the equitable doctrine of part performance was only enforceable by an equitable remedy. Except where statute has intervened, legal and equitable interests are distinguishable in that legal interests are rights *in rem* that bind the whole world whereas equitable rights are lost against equity's darling (the bona fide purchaser of a legal estate for value without notice). In land with unregistered title, the Land Charges Act 1972 makes a number of equitable interests registrable (and one legal interest — the puisne mortgage) and indeed has the effect of determining that such interests which are not registered are void against certain types of purchasers. Nevertheless, a group of equitable interests still fall outside the ambit of the statute and are subject to the equitable doctrine of notice. Equitable interests behind a trust, pre-1926 equitable easements and restrictive covenants fall into this category.

It is possible to cite examples, however, where the distinction has become irrelevant. In registered land, the categories of registered, minor and overriding interests imposed by the Land Registration Act 1925 cut across the distinction between legal and equitable interests. Statute has rendered the distinction redundant.

In general, legal rights and remedies remain distinct from equitable ones. Some overlap does, however, occur; for example, an injunction, an equitable remedy, can be sought for an anticipatory breach of contract, or to stop a nuisance, both common law claims. In *Seager* v *Copydex Ltd* [1967] 1 WLR 923, CA, an action was brought for breach of confidence in respect of confidential information revealed by the defendants about a carpet grip. Such a claim is equitable and normally the equitable remedies of injunction and account are available. However, an injunction would have been ineffective and the judge awarded damages. It would seem, therefore, that a common law remedy is available for an equitable claim for breach of confidence. See, for example, the *Spycatcher* case, *A-G* v *Guardian Newspapers Ltd (No. 2)* [1990] 1 AC 109 (p. 286 per Lord Goff).

In *Tinsley* v *Milligan* [1994] 1 AC 340, it was held that the equitable principle governing when title to property was affected by illegality had now merged into the rule of common law. A claimant can therefore enforce a property right acquired pursuant to an illegal contract, provided that he does not need to bring evidence of the illegality to establish his title.

In *Tinsley* v *Milligan*, the conflict between law and equity became apparent in a modern setting. Two women agreed that a house they shared should be held in the name of one so that the other could fraudulently claim housing benefit. When they later disagreed, the legal owner sought to evict her partner. The defendant claimed that she had an equitable interest. The House of Lords held that the defendant had a right to assert her equitable ownership. The principle that a litigant cannot rely on an illegal purpose to rebut the presumption of advancement was confirmed, but, in this case, the equitable presumption of the resulting trust was held to apply. Thus, the defendant did not need to rely on her own illegal conduct and the equitable maxim that 'he who comes to equity should come with clean hands' did not have to be invoked. This case, seeking to balance illegality and unjust enrichment, has created difficulties in application. In *Tribe* v *Tribe* [1996] Ch 107, a case concerning a transfer of shares from father to son, the matter was complicated by the effect of the presumption of advancement. *Tinsley* v *Milligan* had confirmed the principle that a litigant cannot rely on his or her own fraud or illegality to rebut this presumption except where there is some act of repentance. But in *Tribe* v *Tribe*, the Court of Appeal held that, in the circumstances of this particular case, the father would be able to rely on an illegal purpose to rebut the presumption of advancement because the illegality (the avoidance of the cost by the tenant of a schedule of dilapidations) had not proved necessary and had not been carried out. This result meant that the two cases were consistent: the defendant (Miss Milligan) had recovered her interest in the house even though she had acted fraudulently; the father (David Tribe) had also recovered his shares although he had planned a fraudulent act. To have come to a different result simply because the relationship between the parties in *Tribe* v *Tribe* gave rise to the presumption of advancement, was not considered appropriate by the Court of Appeal. This area of illegal transactions is currently under review by the Law Commission (Law Com Consultation Papers No. 154 (1999) *Illegal Transactions: The Effect of Illegality on Contracts and Trusts*).

Thus, the systems are administered in the same courts, but in general the distinction remains relevant and continues to produce conflicts.

QUESTION 2

Equity is not past the age of child bearing. (per Lord Denning MR, *Eves* v *Eves* [1975] 1 WLR 1338, CA)

Discuss.

Commentary

This question may sometimes appear as an assessed essay. Confronted in the examination room, it may seem daunting. What should be included? Clearly the source of the quotation should be considered. In context, it is being used to justify a new development in equity; in the particular case cited, the new model constructive trust. It would be justifiable to limit the answer to this particular topic, but, on the other hand, it could be broadened to include all the new developments over recent years in the field of equity. To select one or the other approach cannot be wrong. However, as in many situations, in attempting to produce the answer the examiner wants, you should consider the approach in lectures. Did the lecturer use this as a general theme throughout the course? This might indicate the wide ranging approach. Or was particular attention paid to the novelty of the new model constructive trust?

If the question is set as coursework there is a greater argument for adopting the broad approach. There is scope for a powerful dissertation. In the examination room it may be safer to adopt the narrow approach rather than attempt to be too ambitious. It could, of course, be a gift of a question if you know a little about everything, rather than a lot about a limited subject.

The answer suggested here takes the broad approach.

Suggested Answer

When equity originally developed as a gloss to the common law it was innovative; it developed new remedies and recognised new rights where the common law failed to act. The efficacy of equity was largely due to its ability to adapt and innovate, yet inevitably, this development itself became regulated in a similar way to the development of the common law. There are maxims of equity which may determine the outcome of disputes. Although the judge has a discretion in the granting of an equitable remedy, that discretion is exercised according to settled principles. Thus, it might be said that equity can develop no further; the rules of precedent predetermine the outcome.

Yet, this is belied by a number of new developments in equity, for example, the recognition of restrictive covenants, the expansion of remedies, the development of doctrines such as proprietary estoppel, the enhanced status of contractual licences and, as referred to in the quotation from the judgment of Lord Denning MR, the new model constructive trust, are all illustrations of developments in equity.

There is an attempt, however, to justify these new developments, which are all examples of judicial creativity, by precedent. As Bagnall J said in *Cowcher* v *Cowcher* [1972] 1 WLR 425 at p. 430: 'This does not mean that equity is past childbearing; simply that its progeny must be legitimate — by precedent out of principle. It is well that this should be so; otherwise no lawyer could safely advise on his client's title and every quarrel would lead to a law-suit'.

Equity developed the remedies of the injunction, specific performance, account, rectification and rescission. The injunction has been a growth area. The search order (developed in the case *Anton Piller KG* v *Manufacturing Processes Ltd* [1976] Ch 55), reflects the growth of new technology and the need to protect ownership rights in that property. Intellectual property such as video and audio tapes and computer programs can easily be destroyed before an action for breach of copyright can be brought. Confidential information relating to industrial processes can disappear leaving a claimant with no means of proof. The search order developed to allow a claimant to enter a defendant's premises to search for and seize such property where there was a clear risk that such property would be destroyed before trial. As an area of equitable creativity, it is still being refined by the judges, with cases such as *Columbia Picture Industries Inc.* v *Robinson* [1986] 3 All ER 338 and *Universal Thermosensors Ltd* v *Hibben* [1992] 1 WLR 840 laying down guidelines for the exercise of such a Draconian order.

The freezing injunction is another example of a refined application of an established remedy developed in the case of *Mareva Compania Naviera SA* v *International Bulk Carriers SA* [1975] 2 Lloyd's Rep 509 following *Nippon Yusen Kaisha* v *Karageorgis* [1975] 1 WLR 1093. While a claim may succeed, if it is impossible to enforce a judgment because there are no assets, then the judgment is worthless. In international disputes, assets may be transferred abroad to make the judgment debt impossible, or at least, very difficult, to follow. Recognising this dilemma, the judges in the *Mareva* case were prepared to grant an order freezing the defendant's assets. Further cases have now demonstrated that the courts are prepared to make this order available world-wide in certain circumstances (see, for example, *Derby & Co. Ltd* v *Weldon (No. 3 and No. 4)* (1989) 139 NLJ 11 and *Republic of Haiti* v *Duvalier* [1990] 1 QB 202).

Equity initially recognised the trust. This was one of the original developments of equity. However, the protection granted to equitable owners behind a trust has developed significantly over the last 30 years with the new model constructive trust, the contractual licence and the doctrine of proprietary estoppel.

The constructive trust of a new model developed largely because of the creative activity of Lord Denning MR. In *Hussey* v *Palmer* [1972] 1 WLR 1286, CA, Lord Denning described the constructive trust as one 'imposed by law wherever justice and good conscience require it'. Cases such as *Eves* v *Eves* [1975] 1 WLR 1338, CA, where the woman was given an equitable interest in the property representing her contribution in terms of heavy work, and *Cooke* v *Head* [1972] 1 WLR 518, CA, a similar case, took this development further. However, it may be that this development has halted since the retirement of Lord Denning. Several cases, including *Lloyds Bank* v *Rosset* [1991] 1 AC 107, have re-established earlier principles in this field relating to the existence of a common intention that an equitable interest should arise, and the existence of a direct financial contribution. These principles are more akin to those relating to the establishment of a resulting trust.

The new model constructive trust has been most alive in the field of licences. At common law, a contractual licence was controlled by the doctrine of privity of contract, and failed to provide protection against a third party. Equitable remedies have been made available to prevent a licensor breaking a contractual licence and to enable a licence to bind third parties. It has been accepted that certain licences may create an equitable proprietary interest by way of a constructive trust or proprietary estoppel. In *Binions* v *Evans* [1972] Ch 359, CA, it was held by Lord Denning MR that purchasers were bound by a contractual licence between the former owners and Mrs Evans, an occupant. A constructive trust was imposed in her favour as the purchasers had bought expressly subject to Mrs Evans' interest and had, for that reason, paid a reduced price. Also in *Re Sharpe* [1980] 1 WLR 219, a constructive trust was imposed on a trustee in bankruptcy in respect of an interest acquired by an aunt who lent money to her nephew for a house purchase on the understanding that she could live there for the rest of her life.

The fluidity of these developing areas is again shown in recent case law which appears to hold back from a development which may have pushed the frontiers too far. Obiter dicta by the Court of Appeal in *Ashburn Anstalt* v *W. J. Arnold & Co.* [1989] Ch 1, approved in *Habermann* v *Koehler* (1996) 73 P & CR 515, suggest that a licence will only give rise to a constructive trust where the conscience of a third party is affected. It will be imposed where their conduct so warrants. Judicial creativity in equitable fields is thus made subject to refinements by judges in later cases.

Proprietary estoppel is another example of an equitable doctrine which has seen significant developments in the interests of justice since its establishment in the leading case of *Dillwyn* v *Llewelyn* (1862) 4 De GF & J 517. The doctrine is based on encouragement and acquiescence whereby equity was prepared to intervene and adjust the rights of the parties. Its application has been further enhanced by the Court of Appeal in *Gillett* v *Holt* [2001] Ch 210, where a broader approach to the doctrine was taken that depended, ultimately, on the unconscionability of the action. Again, it is a development which stands outside the system of property rights and their registration established by Parliament.

Cases such as *Matharu* v *Matharu* (1994) 68 P & CR 93, *Costello* v *Costello* (1995) 70 P & CR 297 and *Durant* v *Heritage* [1994] EGCS 134 show that the doctrine of proprietary estoppel and the protection of licences by estoppel remain an effective method used by the judges for the protection of licences and equitable rights. The degree to which the right receives protection is variable depending on the circumstances of the particular case. For instance, in *Matharu* v *Matharu*, the licence did not confer a beneficial interest but gave the respondent a right to live in the house for the rest of her life. In *Durant* v *Heritage* the court ordered the house to be transferred to the applicant under the doctrine of proprietary estoppel.

The most recent development in equity, however, has resulted from the decisions of the House of Lords in *Barclays Bank plc* v *O'Brien* [1994] 1 AC 180 and *CIBC Mortgages plc* v *Pitt* [1994] 1 AC 200. These two cases have heralded the re-emergence in a broad sense of the equitable doctrine of notice. They provide that, where there is undue influence over a co-mortgagor or surety, this may give rise to a right to avoid the transaction. This right to avoid the transaction amounts to an equity of which the mortgagee may be deemed to have constructive notice. This resurrection of the equitable doctrine of notice in a very modern context demonstrates clearly the flexibility of equity. A number of cases followed these two decisions. In *Royal Bank of Scotland* v *Etridge (No. 2)* [2001] 4 All ER 449(a case in which eight conjoined appeals were heard), the House of Lords laid down general guidelines for the application of the doctrine of notice in this context.

So, although there may be setbacks and refinements in the development of new doctrines when later judges seek to rationalise and consolidate new principles, nevertheless it is clear that equity maintains its traditions.

QUESTION 3

Explain and discuss the maxim, 'equity looks upon that as done which ought to be done'. To what extent (if any) does this maxim operate to impose a trust on any person?

Commentary

This discussion question requires an examination of the various applications of the maxim. It touches upon a number of different fields. In relation to trusts of land, its operation has been affected by the Trusts of Land and Appointment of Trustees Act 1996. On the application of the doctrine in the context of *Williams & Glyn's Bank Ltd* v *Boland* [1981] AC 487, HL, see Stuart Anderson (1984) 100 LQR 86.

Some aspects of this are esoteric, for example, the rule in *Lawes* v *Bennett* (1785) 1 Cox 167. Many lecturers do not cover this rule in their courses. If that is the case then you may not be expected to deal with it in a question of this sort. The guidance on the suggested content of this answer offered here must be tempered by what you have been expected to cover in your syllabus.

Suggested Answer

The maxims of equity operate as guidelines for the exercise of judicial discretion. Although equity did not acquire the rigidity of the common law, it did develop a body of principles. An equitable remedy is available at the discretion of the judge. The judge is assisted in the exercise of this discretion by these principles. They provide, for example, that for claimants to be granted equitable remedies, they must come to court with clean hands; they must have behaved equitably and must not have delayed in seeking the intervention of equity. These principles, known as maxims, do not operate as binding precedent but provide a basis for the development of equity. Some of them have, however, formed the basis for certain rules which are binding. There are 12 maxims in addition to some general principles.

The maxim 'equity looks upon that as done which ought to be done' demonstrates the principle that, where there is a specifically enforceable obligation, equity will enforce it as though the obligation had been carried out. The common law is rigid in that, if the proper formality has not been carried out (for example, the execution of a deed for the transfer of an interest in land) then it will not recognise the interest. Equity is prepared, nonetheless, to enforce the obligation as though all due formalities are present.

For example, a contract for the sale of land is specifically enforceable if it has been effected in accordance with the rules laid down in the Law of Property (Miscellaneous Provisions) Act 1989, s. 2. It is an estate contract which creates an equitable interest in favour of the purchaser, and is binding on third parties if protected by registration. Until completion, the vendor holds the legal estate upon constructive trust for the purchaser.

It is arguable, on the authority of *Oughtred* v *IRC* [1960] AC 206, HL, and *Re Holt's Settlement* [1969] 1 Ch 100, that, once an agreement has been entered into which is specifically enforceable, then the equitable interest passes without the need for formalities, as provided by the Law of Property Act 1925, s. 53(2). This view was held to be sound in *Neville* v *Wilson* [1997] Ch 144, CA.

A contract for a lease, provided it complies with the contractual requirements, is enforceable in equity under the rule in *Walsh* v *Lonsdale* (1882) 20 ChD 9. Although the due formality of a deed required at law has not been complied with, equity sees as done that which ought to be done, and enforces the contract for the lease.

The maxim underlies the doctrine of conversion. Before the implementation of the Trusts of Land and Appointment of Trustees Act 1996, this doctrine stated that where there was a trust for the sale of land, equity assumed that the sale had already taken place. This meant, therefore, that the beneficiaries' interests were deemed to have been converted into personalty already, even if the land had not been sold. Since many trusts for sale arose where couples purchased a home for their joint occupation, their interests were frequently held in this manner long before the property was sold. The problem was considered in *Williams & Glyn's Bank Ltd* v *Boland* [1981] AC 487, HL. Mrs Boland was deemed to have an interest behind a trust for sale. The contest arose between her equitable interest and the interest of the bank, as mortgagee of the legal estate. If Mrs Boland had an interest in land then she would have an overriding interest under the Land Registration Act 1925, s. 70(1)(g). However, if her interest had already been converted into personalty, she would not have an overriding interest since the subsection only protects rights in land. It was held that the purpose of the doctrine was to simplify conveyancing in cases where the intention was to sell the land immediately. The doctrine should not be extended beyond that to a case where it was clearly a fiction.

The Trusts of Land and Appointment of Trustees Act (TLATA) 1996 now provides that trusts for the sale of land are replaced by trusts of land with the power of sale. This means that the interest behind the trust is an interest in land until the power is exercised (s. 3(1)). This applies to trusts for sale arising before or after the commencement of the TLATA 1996, except in relation to trusts created by will where the testator died before commencement (s. 3(2), (3)).

A more obscure application of the doctrine is the rule in *Lawes* v *Bennett* (1785) 1 Cox 167, which applies to the exercise of an option. If a leaseholder is granted an option to purchase the freehold and the freeholder dies before the option is exercised, then the disposition of the rents pending the exercise of the option, and the eventual purchase price, must be determined. The rents will go to the person entitled to the freehold. This would be either a residuary or a specific devisee. The proceeds of sale, however, which are payable when (and if) the option is exercised, pass to the residuary legatee as conversion into personalty is deemed to have taken place.

The maxim was applied to conditional contracts in *Re Sweeting (deceased)* [1988] 1 All ER 1016. A contract for the sale of land, subject to conditions, was not completed until after the vendor's death. It was held that the proceeds of sale went to the residuary legatee as the interest had already been converted into personalty.

The maxim also underlies the rule in *Howe* v *Earl of Dartmouth* (1802) 7 Ves 137, which relates to the duty to convert (*inter alia*) wasting assets. The rule is limited in that it only applies to residuary personalty settled by will in favour of persons with successive interests. The duty is that, where there are hazardous, wasting or reversionary assets they must be converted into authorised investments. Where there is a duty to convert, there is also a duty to apportion between the life tenant and remainderman until sale. The scope of the rule in *Howe* v *Earl of Dartmouth* is now of more limited significance, however, as the Trustee Act 2000 has greatly widened the range of investments that are available to trustees.

So, the maxim applies to a variety of cases where equity is prepared to act as though the common law requirements had been fully complied with, or to convert property where it is equitable to do so.

QUESTION 4

What is equity?

Commentary

This question requires an historical and jurisprudential analysis of the meaning and position of equity in the legal system.

It is important to use examples to avoid an undirected discussion. The approach suggested here is to deal with the historical side first, using this as a vehicle for a discussion of the contribution which equity has made to the legal system.

Suggested Answer

Equity to the layman means fairness and justice, but in the legal context its meaning is much more strictly defined. There are rules of equity; it must obey the rules of precedent as does the common law, and its development may appear equally inflexible and rigid.

Yet, because of its historical development and the reasons underlying this, there does remain an element of discretion and the potential for judges to retain some flexibility in the determination of disputes.

There are well-established principles which govern the exercise of the discretion but these, like all equitable principles, are flexible and adaptable to achieve the ends of equity, which is, as Lord Selborne LC once remarked, to 'do more perfect and complete justice' than would be the result of leaving the parties to their remedies at common law: *Wilson v Northampton and Banbury Junction Railway Co.* (1879) LR 9 Ch App 279, 284 (and see Lord Hoffmann, *Co-operative Insurance Society Ltd v Argyll Stores (Holdings) Ltd* [1998] AC 1).

Equity developed as a result of the inflexibility of the common law; it 'wiped away the tears of the common law' in the words of one American jurist. When the common law developed the strictures of the writ system through the twelfth and the thirteenth centuries and failed to develop further remedies, individuals aggrieved by the failure of the common law to remedy their apparent injustice petitioned the King and Council. The King was the fountain of justice and if his judges failed to provide a remedy then the solution was to petition the King directly. The King, preoccupied with affairs of state, handed these petitions to his chief minister, the Chancellor. The Chancellor was head of the Chancery, amongst other state departments. The Chancery was the office which issued writs and, therefore, when the courts failed to provide a remedy, it was appropriate to seek the assistance of the head of the court system. Originally the Chancellor was usually an ecclesiastic. The last non-lawyer was Lord Shaftesbury who retired in 1672. Receiving citizens' petitions, the Chancellor adjudicated them, not according to the common law, but according to principles of fairness and justice; thus developed equity.

Early on, each individual Chancellor developed personal systems of justice giving rise to the criticism that equity had been as long as the Chancellor's foot. The Lord Chancellor did indeed sit alone in his court of equity, or Chancery, as it became known. It was not until 1813 that a Vice-Chancellor was appointed to deal with the volume of work. Equity began to emerge as a clear set of principles, rather than a personal jurisdiction of the Chancellor, during the Chancellorship of Lord Nottingham in 1673. By the end of Lord Eldon's Chancellorship in 1827 equity was established as a precise jurisdiction.

But the development of a parallel yet separate system of dispute resolution was inevitably bound to create a conflict. An individual aggrieved by a failure of the common law to remedy a gross injustice would apply to the court of equity. The Chancellor, if the case warranted it, would grant a remedy preventing the common law court from enforcing its order.

The catharsis occurred in the *Earl of Oxford's Case* (1615) 1 Rep Ch 1, where the court of common law ordered the payment of a debt. The debt had already been paid, but the deed giving rise to the obligation had not been cancelled. The court of equity was prepared to grant an order preventing this and rectifying the deed.

The clash was eventually resolved in favour of equity; where there is a conflict, equity prevails. This rule is now enshrined in the Supreme Court Act 1981, s. 49.

A series of maxims underlies the operation of equity, establishing a series of principles. For example: 'equity looks upon that as done which ought to be done'; 'he who comes to equity must come with clean hands'; 'equity will not allow a statute to be used as a cloak for fraud', are all examples of the maxims.

The remedies developed by equity, such as injunctions and specific performance, are, unlike the common law remedy of damages, subject to the discretion of the judge. Thus a judge may decide that, although a breach of contract has been established, the conduct of the claimant is such that an equitable remedy should not be granted. In addition, if damages are an adequate remedy, then there is no need to substitute an equitable remedy.

In substantive law, equity has frequently reflected the reality of transactions between private citizens. It recognised the trust when the common law had refused to acknowledge the existence of a beneficiary and provide remedies for breach of trust against a defaulting trustee. The concept of the trust has been the vehicle for much creative activity on the part of the courts of equity. The trust has developed from an express agreement between parties to situations where the conduct of parties has led the courts to infer or to impose a trust.

So, equity remains a separate system of rules operating independently of the common law. Until the late nineteenth century it operated in a separate set of courts. So, a plaintiff seeking both legal and equitable remedies would be obliged to pursue an action in separate courts. Much delay and expense ensued. The position was eventually resolved in the Judicature Acts 1873 and 1875 which established a system of courts in which both the rules of equity and common law could be administered. The position had already been ameliorated to some degree by the Common Law Procedure Act 1854, which gave the common law courts power to grant equitable remedies, and the Chancery Amendment Act 1858 (Lord Cairns' Act), which gave the Court of Chancery power to award damages in addition to, or in substitution for, an injunction or a decree of specific performance. A claimant can, therefore seek both damages and an injunction in the same court.

The equitable jurisdiction is, in fact, a personal jurisdiction operating against the conscience of the individual, whereas the common law jurisdiction operates against real property. Thus, an order from a court based on equitable principles preventing a legal order being enforced operates against the conscience of the defendant. In theory, therefore, there is no clash between the jurisdictions. In practice, there is a significant constraint on the common law jurisdiction.

The historical distinction does remain, however, in the existence of separate divisions of the High Court, viz, the Chancery Division (which deals primarily with matters which involve equitable rights and remedies) and the Queen's Bench Division (which deals primarily with matters involving rights and remedies at common law).

So, equity represents a later development of law, laying an additional body of rules over the existing common law which, in the majority of cases, provides an adequate remedy: 'Equity, therefore, does not destroy the law, nor create it, but assists it' (per Sir Nathan Wright LJ in *Lord Dudley and Ward* v *Lady Dudley* (1705) Pr Ch 241 at p. 244).

3 The Three Certainties and Section 53 of the Law of Property Act 1925

INTRODUCTION

Questions on certainties are usually problem-type questions. Frequently all three of the certainties — intention, subject-matter and objects — will be included in one question. The classic form of a question in this area involves a will with a series of gifts, each of which raises a separate issue on certainty; the testator will have just died and you will be asked to advise the executors.

The question may be confined to certainty within trusts. However, you may be expected to make a comparison with the rules for certainty for powers, particularly if the question also concerns certainty of objects (see question 3(c)). If you intend to answer a question on certainty therefore, you should also know the distinction between trusts and powers.

A wide knowledge of case law is essential for answering these problems. Frequently, parts of the question may appear to be based directly on one case. Avoid the temptation to start your answer with a reference to the case. Establish the general principle, apply it to the particular problem, and then support it with a reference to the particular case.

Sometimes there is a trap in these apparently straightforward questions. If the question seems to fit very obviously into a particular precedent, look out for a later precedent which may distinguish it. See question 1(a) for an example of this. Apart from this possibility, these problem questions are usually plain sailing if you know the basic principles and some of the cases. It is more important to remember the wording used in a case than the name. If you find names difficult to memorise, you can always write: 'In a decided case . . .'.

When dealing with different parts of the question avoid repeating yourself. If you have dealt with certainty of intention in part (a), for example, then do not run through the points again for part (b). The examiner would not want more than a brief reference to the point if it occurred in a different form in part (b) and would not give you marks for regurgitating the same law again. Part (b) will invariably involve a different issue, perhaps another certainty, and you should deal with this at more length. If you think both parts are on certainty of intention and nothing else, then you are probably in trouble and should choose another question.

Problem questions are relatively easy to devise and discussion questions are quite rare in this field — unless your examiners happen to be gifted creative writers. We have therefore included three problem-type questions in this chapter. Any essay question which your examiner devised is likely to be straightforward and you could use the material in these problem questions for it.

Generally, these problem questions are gifts to the reasonably well prepared examinee. No such person should get less than a 2(ii) on such a question. Conversely, it is quite difficult to get a first. You would really need to impress the examiner with a detailed knowledge of the cases, perhaps even referring to distinguishing judgments (as in question 1(a) with the reference to *Comiskey* v *Bowring-Hanbury* [1905] AC 84).

Not infrequently, examiners have been known to include certainty in 'pick 'n' mix'-type questions. Tread warily! Certainty could be mixed in with questions on topics such as constructive trusts, charities or trusts of imperfect obligation. For an example, see question 4 in chapter 9.

For further reading on s. 53 and the cases on it discussed in question 4, see 'Formalities for the disposition of equitable interests under a trust' by Professor Graham Battersby (1979) 43 Conv 17, a case note by J.W. Harris 'The case of the slippery equity' (1975) 38 MLR 577, and 'Mr Vandervell again' by P. J. Clarke (1974) 38 Conv 405.

QUESTION 1

Lucien, who died recently, left a will appointing Bill and Ben his executors and trustees. The will contained the following dispositions:

(a) 'My freehold house to my wife Harriet absolutely in full confidence that she will hold it for either my daughter Tessa or my son James as she sees fit.'

(b) 'The income from my blue-chip shares to my trustees Bill and Ben from which they must ensure that my old Uncle Tom has a reasonable standard of living.'

(c) 'Three of my five Van Gogh paintings to my trustees to hold one of them in trust for my sister Pearl, whichever she may choose, and the other two in trust for my sister Jewel.' Pearl died before the testator.

Advise Bill and Ben as to the validity of these dispositions.

Would your answer in (c) differ if Pearl had survived the testator but died before choosing?

Commentary

This question is an example of how two parts of a question, (a) and (b), may both include different examples of uncertainty as to words or intention. You should therefore state the general law on this subject fairly fully in your answer to (a), but merely refer to it briefly and apply it in your answer to (b).

Both parts (b) and (c) include uncertainties as to subject-matter, and again any general statement of law on this should be made under (b) and avoid repetition of this under (c).

It may be appropriate to mention some cases briefly in (a) and discuss them further in (b) and (c), but make sure that they are relevant ones, e.g., *Mussoorie Bank* v *Raynor* (1882) 7 App Cas 321, where the words 'feeling confident that she will act justly to our children in distributing the same' were held not to create a trust. However, as well as looking for an understanding of the requirement of certainty of intention, the examiner will be looking for a proper application of the law to the problem set and not a general discussion of cases which are dissimilar. Remember that there are three parts to the question and you should not spend an undue amount of time on one part at the expense of the other parts.

Suggested Answer

(a)   In *Knight* v *Knight* (1840) 3 Beav 148, Lord Langdale MR said that three certainties were required to establish a valid trust, namely, certainty of words (or intention), subject-matter and objects. The essence of a trust is that it imposes a binding obligation on the trustees, and the question to consider here is whether the words used are sufficiently obligatory to impose a trust. Until the Executors Act 1830, courts were very ready to find a trust, as property to which a trust was not attached would remain in the hands of the executors. The Executors Act 1830 changed this, however, and from then on the courts were less willing to find a trust where words which could be construed as merely precatory were used. *Lambe* v *Eames* (1871) 6 Ch App 597 is generally regarded as the turning-point, where the court refused to construe merely precatory words as creating a trust. In *Re Steele's Will Trusts* [1948] Ch 603 it was said that the exception to this would be where a testator had used identical wording to that previously held to create a trust. This case has been criticised, however, for replacing a search for the testator's intention with a mechanical application of legal rules; furthermore it ignores the fact that the meaning of words can change over time.

There are two conflicting cases where words used were similar to those found here. In *Re Adams & Kensington Vestry* (1884) 27 ChD 394 a gift 'to the absolute use of my wife ... in full confidence that she will do what is right as to the disposal thereof between my children' was held not to impose any trust upon the wife but was construed by the court to be an absolute gift to her. In *Comiskey* v *Bowring-Hanbury* [1905] AC 84, however, the House of Lords (Lord Lindley dissenting) considered a bequest to the testator's wife of 'the whole of my real and personal estate absolutely in full confidence that she will make use of it as I should have made myself and that at her death she will devise it to such one or more of my nieces as she may think fit and in default to my nieces equally'. This was held to create a trust for the widow for life, remainder to the nieces as she might by will appoint, but otherwise equally.

In *Re Hamilton* [1895] 2 Ch 370 it was said by Lindley LJ that each disposition must be construed on its own merits. The disposition in this problem appears to be nearer to *Re Adams & Kensington Vestry* than to *Comiskey* v *Bowring-Hanbury* on the ground that there is no gift over in default. Nevertheless it may be possible to distinguish the disposition in (a) from *Re Adams & Kensington Vestry* on the specificity of the ultimate beneficiaries — in which case it could be construed as imposing a trust.

If there is a trust, it is a discretionary trust for either Tessa or James, and there is therefore no uncertainty of objects. If the words are held not to impose a trust, then the disposition operates as an absolute gift to Harriet.

(b)   For a trust to be valid, the subject-matter must also be certain. This includes both the property and the beneficial interests which the beneficiaries are to take. If either of these is uncertain, the trust will fail. In this case, it is possible that both are uncertain.

In *Re Kolb's Will Trusts* [1962] Ch 531 it was said that a reference to stocks and shares 'in the blue-chip category' was insufficiently certain because the term 'blue chip', whilst used to indicate a very good share, has no precise meaning. If so, the trust will fail for uncertainty of subject-matter, which means that all Lucien's shares (and the income therefrom) not otherwise validly and specifically bequeathed, will form part of Lucien's residuary estate. If, however, the reference to blue-chip shares is held sufficiently certain it becomes necessary to consider other parts of this disposition.

The wording 'they must ensure' might well be sufficiently obligatory to impose a trust on the income in the hands of the trustees, as it indicates that the trustees were not intended to enjoy the whole of the income beneficially. It would appear, however, that they are not to use the whole of the income for Uncle Tom. Sufficient income for a reasonable standard of living might appear to be uncertain, but in *Re Golay's Will Trusts* [1965] 1 WLR 969 it was held that 'a reasonable income' was capable of being quantified objectively in relation to a person's lifestyle. Presumably, therefore, a sufficient income relating to Uncle Tom's lifestyle could be ascertained.

(c)   The problem in this part of the question is again to determine the subject-matter of the trust. There is an initial uncertainty as to the subject-matter of the trust as a whole, that is, as to which three of the five Van Gogh paintings is to be held on trust for Pearl to choose from. This is similar to *Palmer v Simmonds* (1854) 2 Drew 221, where a gift of 'the bulk of my estate' failed for uncertainty. Additionally, the interests of Pearl and Jewel are uncertain until Pearl has made her choice; death means that no choice can now be made. In *Boyce v Boyce* (1849) 16 Sim 476, a testator left three houses in his will, 'one to Maria, which she may choose; the others to Charlotte'. Maria predeceased the testator, and the trust for Charlotte, which was dependent upon Maria's choice, was held to fail for certainty of subject-matter. Pearl having predeceased the testator, it is impossible to determine which paintings should be held in trust for Jewel. All three paintings will therefore fall into residue. In the absence of a residuary gift, they will pass, as on intestacy, to Lucien's next-of-kin.

If Pearl had survived the testator but died before making a choice, although prima facie there is still an uncertainty of subject-matter, it is possible that this would enable the circumstances to be distinguished from *Boyce* v *Boyce*. The *Boyce* v *Boyce* situation has an element of ademption about it as the testator is presumed to know that Pearl has predeceased him and is therefore unable to make a choice. However, if the testator has no reason to suppose that Pearl will not choose, and dies in the belief that he has set up a valid trust, it might be possible for equity to intervene, although it is not clear how. The maxim 'Equity is equality' would not reflect the testator's intentions.

One tenuous argument might be that Lucien intended to make Pearl a trustee of the power of selection, i.e., that it is a trust power to select. This would mean that the maxim 'Equity will not allow a trust to fail for want of a trustee' could be applied, and someone else (or even the court) could make the choice. On the wording of the disposition, however, there seems little to favour such a construction.

QUESTION 2

Clockwise Ltd is a mail-order company selling a particularly popular line of talking alarm clocks. It received numerous orders with accompanying cheques but, because of difficulties with the suppliers of certain components, was unable to dispatch the orders. On the advice of the company's accountants, the cheques were paid into a separate bank account which the bank was instructed to call the 'Customers' Trust Deposit Account'. Owing to an error by the bank clerk, the account was called instead 'Clockwise No. 2 Account'.

Clockwise Ltd also wished to purchase some new machinery, and one of its business associates, Ticktock plc, agreed to lend the company the sum of £10,000 solely for this purpose. This money was paid into another separate account called 'Clockwise No. 3 Account'. Clockwise Ltd signed an agreement for the purchase of the machine and paid a deposit of £3,000 from this account, leaving in it £7,000.

Unfortunately, the problems with Clockwise's suppliers became more acute and Clockwise Ltd has now gone into liquidation. The bank (which is owed money by the company) and the liquidator are claiming the monies in the No. 2 and No. 3 accounts.

(a)   Advise the bank and the liquidator.

(b)   Would your answer differ if the monies paid by the customers, and lent by Ticktock plc had, by an error of Clockwise Ltd, been paid instead into Clockwise Ltd's general trading account?

Commentary

This question on certainties is based on a number of commercial cases where the existence of a trust has been pleaded successfully to prevent money paid to a company for a particular purpose being available for distribution generally to its creditors. The cases have been criticised in academic articles (see, for example, Goodhart and Jones, 'The Infiltration of Equitable Doctrine into English Commercial Law' (1980) 43 MLR 489 and P. J. Millett, 'The Quistclose Trust: Who Can Enforce It? (1985) 101 LQR 266). They are, however, defensible on the practical grounds that if potential customers or lenders who are helping a company to survive are not allowed to protect their property, they will not be prepared to deal with the company at all. In *Re Kayford Ltd* [1975] 1 WLR 279, where Megarry J found that a trust had been created, he made the point in his judgment that, although it was quite proper for the mail order company to have done what it did with money received from members of the public, he was not so sure that the same considerations should apply to commercial creditors. The distinction has not been drawn in subsequent cases, however, where the courts have found trusts in favour of commercial creditors also (see *Carreras Rothmans Ltd* v *Freeman Matthews Treasure Ltd* [1985] Ch 207 and *Re Lewis's of Leicester* (1995) 1 BCLC 428).

Suggested Answer

(a)   One of the three certainties essential to establish a valid trust is the certainty of words or intention. Words are not themselves necessary: the person in whom the property is vested may manifest a clear intention to create a trust by actions.

In *Paul* v *Constance* [1977] 1 WLR 527 a man said on several occasions that funds in a deposit account in his name belonged both to himself and his mistress. Section 53 of the Law of Property Act 1925 does not require any formality for the creation of a trust of personalty, and these oral statements were held to be sufficient to create a trust for his mistress of half of the money in the account.

In *Re Kayford Ltd* [1975] 1 WLR 279, a mail order company, which was experiencing financial difficulties, paid cheques received from customers into a separate dormant account which only at a later date was called 'Customers' Trust Deposit Account'. Megarry J held that this appellation was a sufficient manifestation of intention to create a trust of the monies therein for the customers. Being a trust of personalty, no written formalities were required by the Law of Property Act 1925, s. 53, for its creation. The monies having been kept separately meant that there was certainty of subject-matter; the objects of the trust (the customers) were also certain.

Although in the question the account into which the monies have been paid does not bear the name 'Trust Account', the fact of segregation of the money received from the customers may be sufficient evidence of certainty of intention to create a trust. As the money has been kept separately there is also certainty of subject-matter; the beneficiaries are the customers. The money would not therefore be available to the bank or the liquidator.

Similarly, where property is handed over for a particular purpose only, this may be sufficient to impress it with a trust for that purpose. In *Barclays Bank Ltd* v *Quistclose Investments Ltd* [1970] AC 567, Quistclose lent some £200,000 to Rolls Razor Ltd (which was in financial difficulties) for the sole purpose of paying a dividend on its ordinary shares. The money was paid into a separate bank account. Rolls Razor went into liquidation before the dividend was paid. It was held that the money was not available to the bank with whom the account was opened, nor for distribution by the liquidator to the general creditors of the company. It had from the start been impressed with a trust for a particular purpose (the payment of a dividend) and had therefore never belonged to Rolls Razor beneficially. When the trust failed because the liquidation prevented the payment of the dividend, the money was held on a resulting trust for Quistclose.

Applying these principles to the question, it would seem that the money paid by Clockwise Ltd into a separate account for the purpose of purchasing machinery would similarly be impressed with a trust for that purpose, and again would not be available to the bank or the liquidator. As mentioned in the Commentary on this Question, Megarry J's distinction between the money of members of the public and trade creditors has not been observed in subsequent cases.

Does the fact that part of this money has already been appropriated for the purpose affect the trust as to the remainder? In *Re EVTR Ltd* [1987] BCLC 646, money lent for the purchase of a machine was paid to the borrower company's solicitors. When the borrower company went into liquidation, it had already paid part of the money to the suppliers under a contract of purchase. The Court of Appeal found no reason to distinguish between the resulting trust, which would have arisen if the purpose for which the money was paid had failed initially, and the failure of the purpose only subsequently. Money returned by the suppliers was held to go on a resulting trust for the lender. In the question it is likely that the £7,000 still held by Clockwise Ltd, and any money repayable to them from the £3,000 deposit paid, will go on a resulting trust for Ticktock plc.

(b)   What if the monies in either case are paid into Clockwise Ltd's general trading account by error? In such circumstances, although the necessary intention to create a trust might be there, there would be no certainty or segregation of the subject-matter and it would almost certainly be impossible to find a trust. In the case of the customers' cheques, presumably if a trust were intended, it would affect only funds paid into the designated account. Payment into a different account would therefore prevent the trust being constituted. In the case of Ticktock's money, although the money would be impressed with a trust from the start, there would be the practical problem that money paid into the general trading account might not be traceable. The case of *Hunter* v *Moss* [1994] 1 WLR 452 (referred to in the answer to **Question 3(d)**) suggests that segregation of the subject-matter of a trust is not essential if the subject-matter is all identical. It might be argued on behalf of the customers of Ticktock plc that Clockwise Ltd has done everything in its power to constitute a trust so that the principle in *Re Rose* [1952] Ch 499 should apply. If it is possible to establish a trust in favour of the customers and Ticktock plc then they may be able to trace the trust monies into Clockwise Ltd's general trading account. They will only have a claim however to the extent that their monies are still in the account and not deemed to have been paid out under the rule in *Clayton's Case* (*Devaynes* v *Noble* (1816) 1 Mer 572). If the account has been overdrawn at any time since the monies were paid in, then their claim will be defeated. (For a more detailed explanation of the rules relating to tracing see **Chapter 12**).

QUESTION 3

Consider whether a trust has been created in the following circumstances:

(a)   Eliza orally declared herself a trustee of her house, Dunroamin, for her son Percy. She subsequently wrote a letter to Percy informing him that she had done so.

(b)   Oliver, on visiting his only niece, Alison, aged 10, handed her an emerald ring which had belonged to her grandmother. As he handed it over, Oliver told Alison that she was to have the ring. When Oliver left, he took the ring with him, and when he died shortly afterwards, it was found among his effects.

(c)   Simon, who died recently, made a will leaving, *inter alia*, 'the residue of my estate to my dear wife Sarah trusting that she will dispose of whatever she does not want between such of my relatives and friends as she shall select'.

(d)   One Friday, Paul bought ten tickets in the National Lottery. He immediately declared himself a trustee of nine of them for his son Steve, and of the remaining one for his girlfriend Gladys, but without indicating which of the ten was to be held for Gladys. The following day, when the draw was made, one of Paul's tickets won the top prize of £40 million. Advise Gladys.

Commentary

This is a certainty question mixed with other areas of trust law. In (a) all three certainties are satisfied, but you are required to consider whether the necessary formalities for the creation of a trust of land have been complied with. Part (b) raises the question of the constitution of a trust and the difference between a trust and a gift. Part (c) raises doubts about all three certainties, but also requires a knowledge of the test for certainty of objects for discretionary trusts and powers, and some of the cases on this. In part (c) you will probably consider certainty of words and subject-matter first. If you come to the conclusion that the trust would fail on either or both of these, do not of course be deterred from discussing certainty of objects also. The examiner will undoubtedly be looking for a discussion of all three certainties. Part (d) deals with certainty of subject-matter in the light of *Hunter* v *Moss* [1994] 1 WLR 452.

Suggested Answer

(a)   The three certainties for a trust are satisfied, but the Law of Property Act 1925, s. 53(1)(b), requires that 'a declaration of trust respecting any land or any interest therein must be manifested and proved by some writing signed by some person who is able to declare such trust or by his will'. Although the oral declaration of trust by Eliza is therefore ineffective, the subsequent letter testifying to the oral declaration would be sufficient for the purpose of s. 53. The section does not require that the trust should be created in writing, but merely that its creation should be evidenced in writing.

(b) If Oliver had declared himself to be a trustee of Alison's ring, this would have been effective as it is possible to create a trust of personalty by words alone. As the ring is still in his possession, he would have held it as trustee and the trust would have been fully constituted. His words would have had the effect of severing the beneficial ownership in the ring, thereby creating the duality of ownership essential to a trust.

However, Turner LJ stated in *Milroy* v *Lord* (1862) 4 De GF & J 264 at p. 274 that the court will not allow a purported gift which is ineffective because there is no delivery of the subject-matter to take effect as a trust. In *Jones* v *Lock* (1865) LR 1 Ch App 25, a father put a cheque into the hand of his nine-month-old son saying, 'I give this to baby for himself'. When he later died and the cheque was found among his effects, it was held that there had been no effective gift; nor had any effective trust of the cheque been created.

If Oliver's words on handing over the ring to Alison indicate an intention to make a present gift, the gift is thereby perfected and his taking back the ring cannot recall such gift. In such circumstances, he would, at most, be a bailee of the ring for Alison.

On the other hand, Oliver's words on handing over the ring might indicate merely an intention to make a gift of it in the future. In these circumstances, Alison has merely custody or bailment of the ring, and Oliver is free to take it back (which he does).

If Oliver had made it clear when he left that he was taking the ring with him for safe-keeping but he regarded it as belonging to Alison, this might have been sufficient intent to create a trust of it for Alison with himself as trustee, or else merely a bailment with himself as bailee. However, there is no evidence to support such interpretation, and it is therefore probable that there will be an ineffective gift and an ineffective trust.

(c) First, it might be argued that the word 'trusting' in this context is a more colloquial expression than the legal words 'on trust for', implying merely reliance upon Sarah's integrity rather than imposing an obligation on her. If this is argued successfully, then the words are precatory in nature and fail to satisfy the certainty of words necessary to create a trust.

Secondly, 'the residue of my estate' is sufficiently capable of ascertainment to form the subject-matter of a trust (the residue being the remainder of a person's estate not specifically disposed of). Nevertheless there is uncertainty of subject-matter here because the share which the friends and relatives are to receive ('whatever she does not want') is necessarily uncertain. In *Sprange* v *Barnard* (1789) 2 Bro CC 585, a gift to the testatrix's husband with a provision that 'at his death, the remaining part of what is left, that he does not want for his own wants and use' was to be divided between the testatrix's brother and sisters, failed as a trust for uncertainty of subject-matter.

The third certainty, that of objects, also has to be considered here. If the requirements of certainty of words and subject-matter were satisfied, there might still be a problem with regard to certainty of objects. This would be a discretionary trust and the test for certainty of objects is that laid down by the House of Lords in *McPhail* v *Doulton* [1971] AC 424, namely, can it be said of any given postulant that they are, or are not, within the scope of the discretion? When the Court of Appeal considered the application of this test to the word 'relatives' in *Re Baden's Deed Trusts (No. 2)* [1973] Ch 9, the Court of Appeal decided that the expression 'relatives' was conceptually certain enough to satisfy the test, although the judges had differing reasons for deciding this. We therefore have high judicial authority that the word 'relatives' is conceptually certain.

In *Re Barlow's Will Trusts* [1979] 1 WLR 278, the testatrix directed that 'any friends of mine' might buy a painting from her collection at a reduced price. This was held valid, but only because the court interpreted this as a series of individual gifts to apply conditionally to anyone who was able to satisfy the trustees that he or she was a friend. The test for certainty of objects of conditional gifts is, however, more relaxed than that applicable to certainty of objects of discretionary trusts. Had the provision been construed as a discretionary trust (or fiduciary power) to select amongst the testator's friends, it would not have satisfied the test in *McPhail* v *Doulton*. If part (c) involves a discretionary trust, the disposition might well fail the *McPhail* v *Doulton* test for conceptual certainty.

(**d**)   A declaration of trust relating to property other than land may be made orally, so that the declaration of trust made by Paul does not offend the Law of Property Act 1925, s. 53. It would seem however that the purported declaration of trust is void for uncertainty of subject-matter, in that the interests of the intended beneficiaries, Steve and Gladys, have not been specified. In other words, Paul has not indicated which tickets he is holding for which beneficiary.

In *Hunter* v *Moss* [1994] 1 WLR 452, the Court of Appeal held that a declaration of trust of 50 shares from a holding of 950 did not fail for uncertainty of subject-matter, even though the settlor had not specified which particular shares out of his holding were to be subject to the trust. A different result had been reached in the earlier decision of *Re London Wine Co. (Shippers) Ltd* (1975) 126 NLJ 977, where a purported allocation of some bottles of wine in a wine cellar was held insufficient to confer a property interest, since no bottles had actually been segregated and set aside for a particular customer. *Re London Wine Co.* was applied by the Privy Council in *Re Goldcorp Exchange Ltd* [1995] 1 AC 74, where it was affirmed that on the purchase of unascertained goods, there was no fixed and identifiable bulk created by a deemed appropriation, and therefore no property to which any tracing claim could apply. The purchasers of unascertained goods may now have a better claim as against creditors in a liquidation (as in *Goldcorp*) under the Sale of Goods (Amendment) Act 1995, which provides that purchasers who have paid for such goods acquire property rights as tenants in common in them. This would not of course affect a declaration of trust of identifiable and ascertained goods.

The *London Wine Co.* case was distinguished in *Hunter* v *Moss* on the ground that the bottles of wine might not be of equal quality, whereas the shares were all of the same class and carried the same rights. This is not true of tickets in the National Lottery, since the particular number selected for each ticket is an intrinsic part of its potential value. *Hunter* v *Moss* is therefore distinguishable. The suggestion in *Hunter* v *Moss* that the tracing remedy could be used to cure uncertainty of subject-matter has been criticised: Luxton, 'Certainty of subject-matter: a problem shared?' (1994) 28 *Law Teacher* 312. In any event, it is difficult to see how the tracing rules could be used to identify which beneficiary is entitled to the winnings.

Therefore, the only way in which certainty of subject-matter could be satisfied would be if the declaration could be construed as creating not one trust for Steve of nine tickets and another for Gladys of one ticket, but rather a single trust of all ten tickets under which Steve and Gladys share the beneficial interest in the ratio of 9:1 in Steve's favour. The winnings would then be held in trust for them both in the same ratio. This does not seem, however, to be what Paul intended. The trust is therefore probably void for uncertainty of subject-matter, and Paul is entitled to keep the winnings for himself.

QUESTION 4

Last year, as part of his estate planning, Wurzel, a wealthy farmer, wished to dispose of some of his property for the benefit of his family. His first step was to set up a family trust, of which his friends, Oats and Rye, agreed to be the trustees and to hold any property which Wurzel might transfer to them upon any trusts that Wurzel might declare.

Wurzel transferred the freehold title to six holiday cottages in Wales into the names of Oats and Rye, and sent them the deeds.

Two years ago, Wurzel transferred his holding of 5,000 shares in Racine Ltd into the name of the Cube Bank plc as security for a loan which the bank made to him. Six months ago, Wurzel repaid all sums due under the loan, and at the same time wrote to the bank instructing it to transfer the shares into the names of Oats and Rye.

Upon Wurzel's oral instructions, his solicitor wrote to Oats and Rye directing them to hold the cottages and the shares in trust for Wurzel's two grandchildren, Turnip and Carrot, in equal shares.

Last month Wurzel orally declared himself a trustee for his son, Spinach, of his (Wurzel's) beneficial interest under the Root Trust.

Consider the validity and consequences of Wurzel's actions.

Commentary

The Law of Property Act 1925, s. 53, specifies certain formalities relating to the declaration of trusts and the disposition of beneficial interests. The section has been interpreted on a number of occasions in the House of Lords, namely in *Grey* v *IRC* [1960] AC 1, *Vandervell* v *IRC* [1967] 2 AC 291 and *Oughtred* v *IRC* [1960] AC 206, and, in the Court of Appeal, in *Re Vandervell's Trusts (No. 2)* [1974] Ch 269. In each of these cases it fell to be determined whether a particular transaction attracted *ad valorem* stamp duty or income tax.

Stamp duty is a tax on documents only; it has in recent years been restricted in scope, but it still applies to transfers of land and to sales of shares. The consequence of failure to have a document stamped is that it cannot be produced as evidence in court.

Ad valorem duty is duty which varies according to the value of the property transferred. Such duty is payable on a conveyance or transfer on sale. Until 1985, *ad valorem* duty was payable on a voluntary disposition as if it were a transfer on sale, which meant that stamp duty was frequently payable on the creation of a trust. Prima facie, *ad valorem* duty (as opposed to a fixed duty of 50p) was payable only if the document was effective to dispose of the beneficial interest. No *ad valorem* duty was payable, therefore, if only the legal interest passed on a transfer, e.g., on a change of trustees. On the other hand, *ad valorem* duty was payable on a transfer of shares to a donee by a full (i.e., legal and beneficial) owner, because the transfer passed the beneficial interest as well as the legal title.

A donor or settlor might therefore have attempted to avoid stamp duty by effecting a transfer of the beneficial interest without having to use a document. Unfortunately for the taxpayer, many of those schemes which involved a disposition of a subsisting equitable interest were held to be ineffective to avoid *ad valorem* duty because of the Law of Property Act 1925, s. 53(1)(c). The effect of that subsection requiring a disposition of an equitable interest to be effected in writing was that there was a document on which *ad valorem* duty was payable. Taxpayers sometimes argued that s. 53(2) dispensed with the need for writing; but this did not assist the taxpayers in either *Grey* v *IRC* (discussed in the answer) or *Oughtred* v *IRC*.

In *Oughtred* v *IRC*, it was argued that no *ad valorem* stamp duty was payable on a transfer of shares (in that case an exchange) on the ground that the equitable interest had already passed under the prior contract for sale by virtue of a constructive trust, for which no writing was required because of s. 53(2). The majority of the House of Lords held that, in any event, *ad valorem* duty was payable on the share transfer because it ranked as a transfer on sale. This was sufficient to dispose of the case, so that the views expressed on s. 53 were *obiter*. Lord Radcliffe accepted the taxpayer's argument on s. 53(2); and Lord Radcliffe's view was adopted by Megarry J in *Re Holt's Settlement* [1969] 1 Ch 100. In *Neville* v *Wilson* [1997] Ch 144, the Court of Appeal applied Lord Radcliffe's dissenting judgment and held that an oral agreement between the shareholders of a company to divide between themselves the shares of another company, which were held beneficially for them, created constructive trusts between them. The agreements were therefore valid under s. 53(2) of the Law of Property Act 1925 and did not need to be in writing to comply with s. 53(1)(c). (The shareholders also agreed to strike the company off the register, so that had the agreement been void, the shares would have gone to the Crown as bona vacantia.)

If a settlor retains any beneficial interest under a trust, or any possibility of benefiting under a trust, the income arising under it is treated as the settlor's for income tax purposes (see Income and Corporation Taxes Act 1988, Part XV, which replaces earlier similar statutory provisions). In some cases the Revenue have argued that the settlor retains a beneficial interest through having failed to dispose of it in writing as required by s. 53(1)(c). This was the point at issue in both *Vandervell* v *IRC* (which was a victory for the Revenue) and *Re Vandervell's Trusts (No. 2)* (which was a victory for the taxpayer).

The scope of s. 53(1)(c) as explained by these decisions seems, therefore, to reflect the courts' need to interpret the section so as not to allow too broad a circumvention of the taxing statutes.

For a further consideration of these difficult cases, see the articles and case note referred to at the end of the Introduction to this chapter.

Suggested Answer

When Wurzel transferred the legal title to the six cottages to his trustees without informing them of the names of the beneficiaries, the trustees would have held the legal title to them on a resulting trust for Wurzel: *Grey* v *IRC* [1960] AC 1. A resulting trust arises whenever there is a gap in the beneficial ownership: as there was with the option to purchase back the shares given to the Vandervell Trustee Co. in *Vandervell* v *IRC* [1967] 2 AC 291.

Wurzel's declaration of the trusts of the cottages is subject to the Law of Property Act 1925, s. 53.

Section 53(1)(b) applies if Wurzel's equitable interest under the resulting trust ranks as an interest in land. It requires a declaration of a trust of land or any interest in land to be manifested and proved by some writing signed by some person who is able to declare such trust or by his will. The expression 'some person who is able to declare such trust' must be intended to include some person other than the settlor.

The question is whether the letter that Wurzel's solicitor sent to Oats and Rye could satisfy para. (b). There is no authority on this point; but the express inclusion of signature by agent in paras (a) and (c) of s. 53(1) might suggest that signature by agent does not satisfy para. (b): *expressio unius exclusio alterius*. It would appear, however, that the transferee can sign: *Gardner* v *Rowe* (1828) 5 Russ 258. It would also appear that, unlike paras (a) and (c), para. (b) is merely an evidential requirement, i.e., non-compliance does not invalidate the declaration but merely means that, without signed writing, it cannot be proved: *Gardner* v *Rowe*. On this basis, Oats and Rye hold the cottages on a valid trust for the grandchildren, and are therefore, as trustees, obliged to provide the signed writing of the trusts in accordance with para. (b).

It is more likely, however, that the interest of which Wurzel is disposing is not an interest in land but a beneficial interest under a trust. It was held by the House of Lords in *Grey* v *IRC*, that an instruction by a beneficiary to the trustee to hold his interest in trust for a third party is in substance a disposition, and must therefore comply with s. 53(1)(c). Paragraph (c) states that a disposition of an equitable interest or trust subsisting at the time of the disposition must be in writing and signed by the disponor or by his agent thereunto lawfully authorised in writing. As the solicitor is Wurzel's agent, provided his letter to Oats and Rye complies with para. (c), there is a valid disposition of the beneficial interest.

If the solicitor's letter does not comply with para. (c) (if, for example, it is not signed), there is probably no valid disposition. It is not exempted from para. (c) by s. 53(2), i.e., it does not involve the 'operation of a resulting ... trust': see *Grey* v *IRC*, which itself concerned a direction to trustees to hold for a third party an interest under a resulting trust. Lord Denning MR's statement in *Re Vandervell's Trusts (No. 2)* [1974] Ch 269 that a resulting trust dies without the need for any writing at all is difficult to reconcile with *Grey* v *IRC*, but is perhaps distinguishable on the special facts: the option to purchase (which was the subject-matter of the resulting trust) ceased to exist when exercised, and a new beneficial interest arose in respect of the shares which were thereby purchased.

Wurzel's repayment of sums due under the loan from the Cube Bank plc means that the bank's legal mortgage of the shares comes to an end, and the bank holds the legal title to the shares on a bare trust for Wurzel. In *Vandervell* v *IRC*, Vandervell's bank held the legal title to shares on a resulting trust for him and, upon his instructions, transferred them to the Royal College of Surgeons. The House of Lords held that Vandervell's beneficial interest passed to the College contemporaneously with the legal title without the need for compliance with para. (c).

The decision in that case means that a direction by a beneficiary under a bare trust to the trustee to transfer the trust property beneficially to a third party is not a disposition within para. (c) because the direction does not itself dispose of the beneficiary's interest. Furthermore, the trustees' transfer pursuant to such direction, although effective to vest a full title (both legal and equitable) in the third party, is not a disposition for the purposes of para. (c) either. The explanation seems to be that, when the legal and equitable titles pass together, the equitable interest is not separately disposed of, but is subsumed in the passing of the legal title. There is, therefore, no disposition of a 'subsisting equitable interest'.

For these reasons, if the Cube Bank plc has transferred the shares in Racine Ltd to Oats and Rye, the gift is perfect both at law and in equity, and Wurzel cannot recall it. If, however, the bank has not yet effected the transfer, Wurzel can revoke his instructions to the bank and prevent the gift from being completed.

If the effect of Wurzel's declaration of trust in favour of Spinach would be that Wurzel would drop out of the picture (*Grey* v *IRC*) and the trustees of the Root Trust would hold the trust property in trust for Spinach instead (*Grainge* v *Wilberforce* (1889) 5 TLR 436), the declaration would rank as a purported disposition of a subsisting equitable interest. As such, because it is made only orally, it would be void for non-compliance with para. (c).

If, however, the declaration gives rise to a sub-trust, there is no disposition for the purposes of para. (c) because Wurzel retains his equitable interest under the Root Trust and a new beneficial interest is created in favour of Spinach.

It appears that the declaration will be treated as a purported disposition if no additional duties are imposed on the trustees; but otherwise, it will give rise to a sub-trust. Wurzel's declaration does not impose any express duties. If, however, Spinach is a minor, a sub-trust will be created because otherwise the trustees would be subject to additional duties, e.g., those imposed by the Trustee Act 1925, s. 31. If construed as a sub-trust, therefore, the declaration will be valid.

4   Constitution of Trusts

INTRODUCTION

Constitution of trusts is a fascinating area of equity which has produced a welter of academic discussion in articles and elsewhere: it is therefore a popular topic with examiners. Since, moreover, it naturally falls within the earlier part of a course on trusts, it is one which the student should have plenty of time to absorb. This is generally a good area in which hard-working students can gain high marks. Since constitution of trusts is an aspect of the creation of trusts, this topic may well be combined in an examination question with one or more of the three certainties and with formalities. But watch out for other combinations!

QUESTION 1

Equity will not assist a volunteer.

Explain and discuss.

Commentary

Superficially this may appear a simple question, but there is considerable opportunity for a student prepared to draw on their knowledge and understanding of different parts of the subject. The area is vast, but the secret is in selecting the material which most directly addresses the question. Note carefully that you are required not merely to explain the maxim, but to discuss it.

Suggested Answer

The quotation is one of the maxims of equity. It is a pithy way of stating that, where a trust is incompletely constituted or a gift is imperfectly made, equity will not give its remedy of specific performance to an intended beneficiary who is a volunteer, or to the intended donee. In the context of gifts, the maxim is often expressed in the form 'equity will not perfect an imperfect gift': see *Milroy* v *Lord* (1862) 4 De GF & J 264. A volunteer is a person who has not furnished consideration for the creation of the trust. Consideration in equity consists of both common law consideration (money or money's worth) and (in certain instances) marriage. It is clear that a covenant (although it may be enforceable at common law) does not comprise consideration in equity.

If marriage is to constitute consideration, the trust must be made either before and in consideration of a particular marriage, or (if made after the marriage) in pursuance of an ante-nuptial agreement to make such a trust. Furthermore, only certain persons within a marriage settlement are treated by equity as providing consideration: these are the spouses to the marriage and their issue. Issue of a former marriage and illegitimate children will prima facie fall outside the marriage consideration: *Re Cook's Settlement Trusts* [1965] Ch 902. But they may come within it if their interests are so closely intertwined with those of the issue of the marriage in question that they cannot be separated: *A-G* v *Jacobs-Smith* [1895] 2 QB 341, CA. Next-of-kin are outside the marriage consideration: *Re Plumptre* [1910] 1 Ch 609.

The quotation needs to be treated with care, as equity will protect a beneficiary's interest under a completely constituted trust even if that beneficiary is a volunteer (as in *Paul* v *Paul* (1882) 20 Ch D 742, where the settlor, having completely constituted the trust, was not permitted to reclaim the property on the ground that the beneficiaries were volunteers). The maxim also means that where a trust is completely constituted in regard to certain items of property, but incompletely constituted in regard to other items, volunteer beneficiaries cannot compel the settlor to transfer the latter into the trust: *Jefferys* v *Jefferys* (1841) Cr & Ph 138. However, if some of the would-be beneficiaries under an incompletely constituted trust have provided consideration for its creation, they may obtain specific performance. The consequence will be that the trust becomes completely constituted, thus also benefiting the volunteers, who could not have sued personally: *Davenport* v *Bishopp* (1843) 2 Y & C Ch Cas 451.

The modern approach has been expressed as being that 'Although equity will not aid a volunteer, it will not strive officiously to defeat a gift': *T. Choithram International SA* v *Pagarani* [2001] 2 All ER 492, PC, at p. 501, per Lord Browne-Wilkinson. However, in some older cases it appears that equity went further than merely not assisting a volunteer, and would frustrate an action brought at common law to aid a volunteer. Thus, the court has directed covenantees of a voluntary covenant not to sue the covenantor for damages at common law since this would give the volunteers indirectly what they were not entitled to obtain directly: *Re Kay's Settlement* [1939] Ch 329. In principle, however, such a claim should be denied the covenantees only when they hold the benefit of the covenant on a resulting trust for the covenantor. A claim by them ought to be available if the covenant is itself the subject-matter of the express trust, as it was in *Fletcher* v *Fletcher* (1844) 4 Hare 67. In such a case the trust is completely constituted vis-à-vis the covenant, even though it is incompletely constituted as regards the property to which such covenant relates. Thus, although equity will not give specific performance vis-à-vis such property, it will not frustrate a claim brought by the trustee-covenantees for damages for breach of covenant at common law. Indeed, in such circumstances, equity will (if necessary) compel the covenantee to lend his name to a claim at common law against the covenantor. This problem does not arise in relation to covenants entered into at least six months after the passing of the Contracts (Rights of Third Parties) Act 1999, which enables a third party to enforce a contract in his or her own right, thus enabling the volunteer to sue for damages.

Equity recognises three so-called exceptions to the maxim that it will not assist a volunteer. The first is the rule in *Strong* v *Bird* (1874) LR 18 Eq 315 whereby, if the intended donee of an *inter vivos* gift becomes the executor, or even the administrator, of the intending donor upon the latter's death, the legal title passes to him. This, together with a continuing intention to make a gift on the deceased's part, perfects the gift. Arguably, however, this is not so much an exception to the maxim as an illustration of the means by which a gift can be perfected. This principle has been extended to trusts: *Re Ralli's Will Trusts* [1964] Ch 288.

The second exception is *donationes mortis causa*. Equity's assistance is not needed (and therefore the maxim is inapplicable) if the subject-matter of the gift is transferred to the intended donee during the donor's lifetime, albeit subject to the usual conditions to which such gifts are subject. If, however, the intended donee's title remains imperfect at the donor's death, equity's assistance will be required, and this constitutes a genuine exception to the maxim. This will be the case, for instance, if the subject-matter of the *donatio mortis causa* is a chose in action, and the donor hands over merely the indicia of title: *Birch* v *Treasury Solicitor* [1951] Ch 298.

A third exception is proprietary estoppel. If A encourages, or even acquiesces in B's acting to his detriment in the belief that he has rights in the property of A, equity may protect B should A act inconsistently with such rights. This is the principle which can be traced back to *Dillwyn* v *Llewelyn* (1862) 4 De DF & J 517. A modern (and perhaps startling) instance is *Pascoe* v *Turner* [1979] 1 WLR 431, where the Court of Appeal held that the equity raised by the estoppel could be satisfied only by a conveyance of the fee simple. Equity was there assisting a volunteer, but it is unclear whether the remedy in such a case is always commensurate with the extent of the promise: i.e., whether proprietary estoppel is here a means by which imperfect gifts are rendered perfect (see Cooke, 'Estoppel and the protection of expectations' (1997) 17 LS 258; Robertson, 'Reliance and expectation in estoppel remedies' (1998) 18 LS 360).

QUESTION 2

In 1996, A secured B's undertaking to hold any property which A might thereafter transfer to B in trust for A's niece, N. In 1997, A showed B a painting which was hanging on the wall in A's home, and told B that this was to be held on the trusts which he (A) had declared. A was owed the sum of £20,000 by C, and in 1998, A wrote to B saying: 'I hereby assign to you the debt owed to me by C.' A was himself a beneficiary under the FGH Trust, and in 1999, A orally directed the trustees of that trust to hold his interest thereunder in trust for B. In September 2000, A covenanted with B to transfer to B in trust for N any property which A might receive under the will of D, who was then still alive. D died early in 2001, bequeathing to A shares in XYZ Ltd.

A died last month, leaving all his property to E. At the date of his death, he had not transferred either the painting or the shares to B, and he had not notified C of the intended assignment of the debt.

Advise N which of the foregoing items (if any) are held in trust for her, and what steps (if any) she might take to enforce the covenant.

Commentary

This is a typical examination question on volunteers and incompletely constituted trusts. The student needs to identify the requirements for transferring different sorts of property into a trust. The area of the law relating to trusts of covenants is complex and involves apparently conflicting decisions upon which a variety of academic views has been expressed. It seems likely that much of the fire has gone out of this debate, however, with the enactment of the Contracts (Rights of Third Parties) Act 1999, which enables a third party to sue on a contract.

Suggested Answer

Since A intended to create a trust by transferring property to another person, B, as trustee, a trust will arise in favour of the intended beneficiary, N, only if there is a valid declaration of trust and an effective transfer of the property to the trustee: *Milroy* v *Lord* (1862) 4 De GF & J 264, per Turner LJ. The terms of the undertaking which A secured from B are a clear declaration of trust. As regards transfer, however, it is necessary to take each item of property in turn.

The painting is a chattel, which is transferred either by delivery or deed. There is no evidence of a deed here. Delivery requires a physical handing over; merely showing the painting to B does not comprise a delivery: *Re Cole* [1964] Ch 175. The painting has therefore not been transferred into the trust, and will pass under A's will to E.

The benefit of the debt could not be assigned at common law, but under s. 136 of the Law of Property Act 1925, the benefit of a debt can be assigned so as to enable the assignee to sue the debtor in his own name. For such a legal assignment to occur, the assignment must be in writing under the hand of the assignor, it must be absolute, and written notice must be given to the debtor. In the problem, it appears that the assignment was absolute, in that it was intended to be an unconditional assignment of the entire debt. Furthermore, it appears to have been in writing under the hand of the assignor, since A instructed B in a letter. There can be no statutory assignment, however, unless written notice (whether by A or somebody else) has been given to C. As A gave no such notice, it may be that no such notice has been received by C.

Even if C has not been notified, there will have been an assignment in equity. By executing an absolute assignment in writing, A has done all he needs to do; s. 136 does not require that notice to the debtor be given by the assignor. The assignment is therefore perfect in equity as soon as A executes the assignment: *Holt* v *Heatherfield Trust Ltd* [1942] 2 KB 1. The benefit of the debt in equity is therefore held by B in trust for N. In these circumstances, even after A's death, the assignment can become a statutory assignment if a third party (e.g., B) gives notice to C: *Walker* v *Bradford Old Bank Ltd* (1884) 12 QBD 511.

An instruction by a beneficiary to trustees to hold his interest in trust for a third party comprises a disposition of a subsisting equitable interest for the purposes of s. 53(1)(c) of the Law of Property Act 1925: *Grey* v *IRC* [1960] AC 1. It must therefore be in writing signed by the disponor or his agent. Since A's direction to the trustees of the FGH Trust was merely oral, the purported assignment is void. A's beneficial interest under that trust will therefore pass to E under A's will.

Lastly, as A did not transfer the shares in XYZ Ltd to B, the shares are not subject to the trust in favour of N. Equity does not regard a voluntary covenant as consideration, so B cannot compel A's estate to transfer the shares to him. It might, however, be argued that, by covenanting with B to transfer any property he might acquire under D's will, A has vested the benefit of the covenant in B. If this is so, it would seem to follow that N would be the beneficiary of a fully constituted trust of the benefit of the covenant, so that B would have to sue to enforce the covenant by suing for damages for breach of covenant, or else be liable to compensate N for breach of trust.

Whether the benefit of a covenant can comprise the subject-matter of a trust has been the subject of some judicial and much academic debate. The courts have shown their unwillingness to permit covenantees to sue on a covenant for the benefit of volunteers: *Re Kay's Settlement* [1939] Ch 329, *Re Cook's Settlement Trusts* [1965] Ch 902. In the latter case, Buckley J suggested that there can be no trust of the benefit of a covenant concerning future property. If this is correct, B cannot be holding the benefit of the covenant on trust for N, and the only possibility would be that B holds the benefit of the covenant on trust for A's estate. On the other hand, it has been argued that the benefit of a covenant will be held on trust for the intended beneficiaries where the covenantor makes it clear that this is his intention: see Hayton, *Underhill and Hayton, The Law of Trusts and Trustees*, Butterworths, 1995, at p. 155. Such an intention might also be inferred, as where all the intended beneficiaries are volunteers, as in *Fletcher* v *Fletcher* (1844) 4 Hare 67, since otherwise there would be no point in entering into the covenant in the first place: Hornby (1962) 78 LQR 228.

Much of the significance of this argument would now appear to have been rendered obsolete by the Contracts (Rights of Third Parties) Act 1999, which applies to contracts entered into (like the covenant in the problem) at least six months after its enactment. Even a purely voluntary covenant (such as that in the problem) is a contract, and, under s. 1, a person who is not a party to a contract (N) may enforce a term of the contract in her own right if the contract expressly provides that she may, or if the term purports to confer a benefit on her (unless it appears that the parties did not intend the term to be enforceable by the third party). For the purpose of enforcing a term of the contract, the third party has the same remedies as would have been available to her in an action for breach of contract had she been a party to the contract: s. 1(5). Since the covenant was purely voluntary, N could not obtain specific performance to compel A's estate to transfer the shares to B, so that the shares would pass to E under A's will. However, N could sue A's estate for damages, the measure of the damages being the value of the shares that A failed to transfer.

Against this it might be argued that, even if N had been a party to the covenant, if the court were to follow the approach of Eve J in *Re Kay's Settlement*, she would not be entitled to damages. In that case, it appears that the court held that the benefit of a voluntary covenant was held on a resulting trust for the covenantor's estate. If the court took the same view in the question, so that the benefit of the covenant was held in trust for A's estate, this circumstance might indicate that the parties to the covenant did not intend it to be enforceable by the third party. This would effectively remove purely voluntary covenants for the benefit of third parties from the scope of the Contracts (Rights of Third Parties) Act 1999, since the Act would be available only in the very circumstance in which it is not needed, i.e., when equity treats the third party as a beneficiary under a trust of the covenant.

While this is a tenable argument, it is more likely that the courts will reject it and will use the opportunity afforded by the 1999 Act to abandon these refinements of equity, which were essentially designed for the now outmoded era of marriage settlements. The modern approach was expressed recently by Lord Browne-Wilkinson (albeit in a different context), when he said 'Although equity will not aid a volunteer, it will not strive officiously to defeat a gift': *T. Choithram International SA* v *Pagarani* [2001] 2 All ER 492, PC, at p. 501. Long before the 1999 Act was passed, it was held that where the third party volunteer was herself a party to the covenant, she could recover substantial damages for breach of covenant in respect of her own loss: *Cannon* v *Hartley* [1949] Ch 213. It would therefore appear that, unless the covenantor indicates otherwise, the effect of the 1999 Act is to put every intended beneficiary under a voluntary covenant into the position of the covenantee in that case. On this footing, N could sue A's estate for damages to the value of the shares.

QUESTION 3

In 1996, Acute handed his share certificate in respect of his shareholding in Diacritical Ltd to Cedilla, together with a share transfer form which Acute had completed in favour of Cedilla. As he handed these documents over, Acute instructed Cedilla to hold the shares in trust for Acute's nephew, Grave. Cedilla agreed. Shortly after, Cedilla attempted to obtain registration of the shares in her own name, but was defeated by the exercise by the directors of Diacritical Ltd of a power contained in the company's articles to refuse registration.

In 1997, Acute received back the share certificate from Cedilla. He handed it to his cousin, Umlaut, informing him that the shares were a gift to him.

Last month, Acute died with the shares still standing in his name. In his will he appointed Umlaut his executor and gave all his property to Cedilla.

Discuss who is entitled to the shares.

Commentary

This is a complex question, both because the relevant law itself is difficult, and also because you need to sort out in your mind the priorities of several claimants — never the easiest thing in the examination room. There is a lot to write so you will need to be economical with the facts of the cases. Cases should be cited to support legal principle; facts can be given sparingly in order to distinguish one case from another. See, for instance, the treatment in the suggested answer of the authorities which support, or which appear to conflict with, the principle of *Re Rose* [1952] Ch 499, CA. If you have a good understanding and keep a clear head, this is the sort of question where you could score very heavily.

Suggested Answer

Grave is beneficially entitled to the shares if he can establish that he is a beneficiary under a fully constituted trust of them. A trust is completely constituted only if there is compliance with the requirements laid down in *Milroy* v *Lord* (1862) 4 De GF & J 264. Where, as here, the settlor seeks to confer the benefit of property on a person by vesting it in a trustee, two things must be done. First, there must be a clear declaration by the settlor of the terms of the trust. Here, the instructions to Cedilla suffice. Secondly, the settlor must do all he can to vest the property in the intended trustee. The legal title to the shares will not pass to Cedilla unless and until the company registers Cedilla's name in its register of members. Since this has not been done, the legal title to the shares has not passed. The share transfer may nevertheless be perfect in equity if, in accordance with *Milroy* v *Lord*, the settlor has done everything necessary to be done by him to transfer the shares. In *Re Rose* [1952] Ch 499, the Court of Appeal held that a gift of shares was perfect in equity as soon as the donor had put the donee into the position of being able to take steps to complete the transfer: i.e., when the donor had handed to the donee the share certificate and executed share transfer form.

On this basis, the trust in favour of Grave would have been completely constituted from the date in 1996 when these documents were delivered to Cedilla. If so, from that date, Acute would have held the legal title to the shares in trust for Cedilla, who would herself have held the equitable interest thereunder on a sub-trust for Grave. This makes Cedilla a trustee of a completely constituted trust for Grave. She is therefore under a duty to ensure that the trust property is safeguarded — by taking steps to bring in the legal title to the shares (as she did attempt to do), and (if necessary) by compelling Acute to transfer to her any dividends he receives in respect of that holding.

The transfers in *Re Rose* were registered, but there is nothing in the case to suggest a different result where registration is refused. The principle in *Re Rose* has been attacked for thus saddling an intended donor with an unintended and potentially permanent trusteeship: see McKay (1976) 40 Conv (NS) 139. This objection carries some force; moreover a permanent trusteeship in this context contrasts sharply with a contract for the sale of shares where (if the company refuses to register the purchaser) the vendor cannot be fixed with a permanent trusteeship: see *Stevenson* v *Wilson* 1907 SC 445, considered (without criticism) by the House of Lords in *Scott Ltd* v *Scott's Trustees* [1959] AC 763.

A case difficult to reconcile with *Re Rose* is *Re Fry* [1946] Ch 312; but that case may be considered, perhaps, to turn on the effect of relevant Defence Regulations. Apart from that decision, the principle of *Re Rose* is consistent with a range of authorities: see, particularly, *Mallott* v *Wilson* [1903] 2 Ch 494 and *Mascall* v *Mascall* (1985) 49 P & CR 119. The principle was assumed correct by the House of Lords in *Vandervell* v *IRC* [1967] 2 AC 291, HL and it also operates in the case of equitable assignments of legal choses in action: *Holt* v *Heatherfield Trust Ltd* [1942] 2 KB 1.

If *Re Rose* applies, Grave is a beneficiary under a trust of the shares, and is entitled to the dividends which Diacritical Ltd will continue to pay to Acute (and, after Acute's death, to Acute's personal representative). On this basis, the purported gift of the shares to Umlaut, even if ultimately perfected (as discussed below) is later in time, and is therefore subject to the rights of Grave. Similarly, Acute cannot by his will give to Cedilla property which he does not own beneficially. Thus the gift of all his property to Cedilla does not include the shares.

If, however, a court were to distinguish or overrule *Re Rose* and hold that the trust was incompletely constituted, then, unless Grave had provided consideration for the creation of the trust, he could not (as a volunteer) gain the assistance of equity: *Re Plumptre* [1910] 1 Ch 609. Since, however, Acute gave all his property in his will to Cedilla, the intended trustee of the shares, it is arguable that the trust in favour of Grave is completely constituted on Acute's death, since Cedilla then has a right as beneficiary under the will to see that the property is properly distributed: *Re Diplock* [1948] Ch 465, CA. She will ultimately obtain the legal title to the shares when the executor, Umlaut, transfers the shares into her name. It makes no difference that the legal title comes to Cedilla, the intended trustee, in a different capacity: *Re Ralli's Will Trusts* [1964] Ch 288.

There is, however, one further twist: Umlaut's appointment as executor. If it can be shown that Acute had a continuing intention to give the shares to Umlaut from 1997 until his death, the imperfect gift to Umlaut might be perfected under what is known as the rule in *Strong* v *Bird* (1874) LR 18 Eq 315 (i.e., by the acquisition by Umlaut of the legal title to the shares as executor). In principle, this would seem to postpone the equity of the beneficiaries under the will to that of the executor. It was upon this basis that Walton J in *Re Gonin* [1979] Ch 16 objected to the decision in *Re James* [1935] Ch 449, which had extended the rule to administrators. This objection may carry less weight where the intended donee becomes executor, since such appointment results from the testator's own voluntary act. The objection may not be entirely overcome, however, since an executor does stand in a fiduciary relationship to the beneficiaries under the will, and to permit him to have a prior claim seems to fly in the face of normal equitable principles designed to prevent a conflict of interest: cf *Holder* v *Holder* [1968] Ch 353, CA. Nevertheless, the application of the rule to executors is well-established: *Re Stewart* [1908] 2 Ch 251. Umlaut will therefore be permitted to bring evidence outside the will that Acute intended to give him the shares. Since such evidence derives from the intended donee, however, it will need to be treated with caution: cf cases involving secret trusts: *Re Rees* [1950] Ch 204, CA, and *Re Tyler* [1967] 1 WLR 1269.

If, therefore, the intended trust in favour of Grave was not perfected in 1996, Umlaut may be able to satisfy the court that he is entitled to the shares under the rule in *Strong* v *Bird* in priority to both Cedilla and Grave.

QUESTION 4

Three months ago, Lear, a keen rambler, caught a chill after spending a stormy winter's night wandering lost on the moors. He was taken to hospital suffering from pneumonia. When his eldest daughter, Goneril, visited him, he handed her the key to a deed box which was in his study at home. Lear told Goneril that he did not expect to live much longer and that, if anything were to happen to him, Goneril was to have the contents of the box.

Shortly after, when Lear's middle daughter, Regan, was by his bedside, Lear handed to her the Land Certificate relating to his country cottage in Gloucestershire, which he owned in fee simple. He advised Regan that, if he did not pull through, Regan was to have the cottage.

Last month, during a visit by his youngest daughter, Cordelia, Lear wrote a cheque for £10,000 in her favour. He informed her that this was to be her share of his property on his death.

Last week Lear, who remained seriously ill in hospital, deliberately took an overdose of sleeping pills, from which he died.

Goneril has now opened the deed box, and finds that it contains the keys and vehicle registration document to Lear's car, and a bank pass book relating to Lear's deposit account with the Serpent's Tooth Bank plc. It is discovered that, a couple of weeks before his death, Lear had leased the country cottage to Edmund for a term of 21 years. In his will, Lear gave all his property to charity.

Advise Lear's daughters.

Commentary

Those with little or no Latin should note that *donatio* is a noun meaning gift, so one can refer either to a '*donatio mortis causa*', or to a gift '*mortis causa*'. The plural is *donationes mortis causa*. Succour may be sought from remarks of Lord Simon of Glaisdale in *Brumby* v *Milner* [1976] 1 WLR 1096, a tax case, where his Lordship deprecated the unnecessary use by lawyers of Latin terms. In the present case, however, the English equivalent is slightly more of a mouthful, and the Latin reminds us of the Roman Law origins of this principle, which finds its modern counterpart in the Civil Law.

Suggested Answer

Lear evidently intended the gifts to the daughters to take effect only in the event of his death. Such gifts would normally be testamentary in nature and valid only if made in accordance with the Wills Act 1837 (as amended). Such formalities are absent here. Nevertheless, Lear's daughters will be able to take the property concerned if they can establish a valid *donatio mortis causa* in respect of each item.

To constitute a gift *mortis causa*, three elements must be satisfied. These have been affirmed by the courts many times (e.g., in *Cain* v *Moon* [1896] 2 QB 283, and, most recently, in *Sen* v *Headley* [1991] Ch 425).

First, the gift must be intended to be conditional upon death, so that it is not perfect until death, before which time it can be revoked by the donor. The gift must also be intended to be automatically revoked in the event of the donor's survival. Such conditions will be readily inferred where the gift is made in contemplation of death, which appears to be the case here.

Secondly, the gift must be made in contemplation of death, which must be more than a contemplation that the donor, like all living things, must some day die. This requirement is met where the donor is suffering from a life-threatening illness (*Saulnier* v *Anderson* (1987) 43 DLR (4th) 19) and seems therefore to be met in the instant case. However, in *Re Dudman* [1925] 1 Ch 553, it was held that a *donatio mortis causa* made in contemplation of suicide (at that time a crime) was not valid. Suicide is no longer a crime (Suicide Act 1961) and the present position is unclear. Such a purported *donatio* might still be invalid today on the ground that the requisite contemplation of death imports an element of uncertainty as to whether and when death will ensue. Such uncertainty is absent if the donor has the intention of taking his own life. In the problem, however, at the time he made the *donationes mortis causa*, Lear may have contemplated death by pneumonia, not by suicide. In *Wilkes* v *Allington* [1931] 2 Ch 104, it was held that it does not matter if death occurs from a disease other than that contemplated. A *donatio* might therefore not be invalidated if death occurs by suicide not contemplated at the time the *donatio* was made: see *Mills* v *Shields* [1948] IR 367.

Thirdly, the donor must part with dominion over the subject-matter of the *donatio*. Delivery to the intended donee of the only key to a locked receptacle which contains the subject-matter suffices, even if the subject-matter could have been handed over: *Re Mustapha* (1891) 8 TLR 160. It has, however, been stated *obiter* that there is no sufficient parting with dominion if the donor retains a duplicate key: *Re Craven's Estate* [1937] Ch 423. The statement in the question that 'the key' was handed over to Goneril implies that it was the only key, in which case this requirement is satisfied. Moreover, it does not matter if the box itself contains another key which opens a further box: *Re Lillingston* [1952] 2 All ER 184.

On this principle, since the deed box contains the key to Lear's car, it would appear that (unless Lear retained a duplicate key) a valid *donatio* has been made of the car. Although the passing of dominion over a chattel is usually effected by physical delivery, delivery of the key both enables Goneril to take possession of the car and (together with the delivery of the vehicle registration document, which evidences Lear's ownership) effectively puts it out of Lear's power to deal with it.

Parting with dominion over a chose in action requires the donor to part with the essential evidence or *indicia* of title: *Birch* v *Treasury Solicitor* [1951] Ch 298. There, the Court of Appeal held (*inter alia*) that a *donatio mortis causa* of a chose in action represented by a deposit pass book to Barclay's Bank was effected by delivery to the donee of the pass book. In such instances, equity will perfect the imperfect gift by treating the deceased's personal representatives as trustees of the chose in action for the donee: *Duffield* v *Elwes* (1827) 1 Bli NS 497. This principle would therefore apply to Lear's deposit account with the Serpent's Tooth Bank plc.

Lear's country cottage is land and, until recently, it was doubted, on the basis of dicta in *Duffield* v *Elwes*, whether land could ever be the subject-matter of a *donatio mortis causa*. In *Sen* v *Headley*, however, the Court of Appeal held that it could. There was no difference in substance between the principle applicable to choses in action established in *Birch* v *Treasury Solicitor* and the parting with dominion over land by the delivery of the title deeds. Although the doctrine of *donationes mortis causa* is anomalous, it was preferable to avoid creating anomalies of anomalies. *Sen* v *Headley* concerned unregistered land, but the same principle would appear to apply to the delivery of the Land Certificate in registered land.

Although Lear has parted with dominion over the Land Certificate, whether he has parted with dominion over the cottage itself is less clear. He did after all subsequently lease it out. Such a situation was hypothesised in *Sen* v *Headley* by the Court of Appeal, which opined that a retention by the donor of a power to deal with the subject-matter did not invariably preclude a parting with dominion. It was a matter of fact in each case. Although the donor in *Sen* v *Headley* retained a key to the premises, the donee had her own set and was in *de facto* control. The problem does not state how many sets of keys there are, nor who has possession of them. If Regan has the only set of keys to the cottage, that might, in accordance with *Sen* v *Headley*, be a sufficient parting with dominion by Lear. Nevertheless, the legal principle is obscure. Mummery J at first instance could not see how the equitable interest of the donee, which arises only on the death of the donor, can be binding upon a tenant of a lease granted during the donor's lifetime. The Court of Appeal does not seem to provide a satisfactory answer to this.

It is well-established that delivery of the donor's own cheque to the intended donee cannot constitute a valid *donatio mortis causa*: *Re Beaumont* [1902] 1 Ch 889, *Re Leaper* [1916] 1 Ch 579. A cheque is merely a revocable order to a banker to pay a sum of money. The position may be otherwise if the cheque is presented and the donor's account credited during the donor's lifetime or before the bank has been informed of his death. Subject to these qualifications, Cordelia can derive no benefit from the cheque, which is mere waste paper.

5 Trusts, Powers and Discretionary and Protective Trusts

INTRODUCTION

A thorough understanding of the distinction between trusts and powers is essential. The different types of trusts — fixed and discretionary — have different rules determining their validity. There is also the distinction to be grasped between fiduciary and non-fiduciary powers.

An examination question may call for an analysis of the distinction between a discretionary trust and a power. These can look very similar, and they may be created for a similar purpose. A testator wishing to provide for the members of his family after his death could create a fixed trust under which each beneficiary has a fixed share. The testator may, however, prefer to give his trustees a discretion in the allocation of the beneficial interests, so that account can be taken of the changing needs and circumstances of the objects after the testator's death. The appropriate machinery for this is the discretionary trust.

It is important to distinguish individual and class rights. Under a discretionary trust, each individual object has, before distribution, specific rights in equity — personal rights which fall short of an equitable interest. Such personal rights are known as mere equities. As a class, however, the objects of a discretionary trust may have more extensive rights. If, the objects of a discretionary trust are all of full age and sound mind (*sui iuris*) and together form a closed class, they can compel the trustees to put an end to the trust and hand the trust assets over to them as they (the objects) direct. In other words, the equitable interest lies with the class as a whole. The objects of a discretionary trust of income do not have this right, however, if the trustees have a power to keep the income in the trust, i.e., a power to accumulate.

It is vital to be precise in your use of terminology. Confusion can easily arise because some terms are used by different judges or writers to mean different things; so, unless they define the sense in which they are using the terms, you will have to look to the context in order to determine what the meaning is. The term 'trust-power' is a dangerous one to use without any explanation of its meaning. A trust-power is a combination of a duty (a trust) and a power. For this reason, a discretionary trust is often called a trust-power, since it combines a duty to distribute with a power of selection. Unfortunately, the term trust-power can also be used to mean a fiduciary power, since this too combines a power and a trust obligation, i.e., a power to distribute and a duty to consider exercising it. In this chapter, the term trust-power is used to mean a discretionary trust.

Another problem is with the term 'mere power'. This expression is used in contradistinction to a trust-power (in the sense of a discretionary trust). It is, in other words, a power which the donee or fiduciary is not obliged to exercise. In this sense, the term 'mere power' embraces both fiduciary and non-fiduciary powers. By contrast, a 'bare power' (sometimes called a 'personal power') means a non-fiduciary power.

An individual object of a power (whether fiduciary or non-fiduciary) has a right (a mere equity) to prevent any appointment being made outside the defined class of objects. Only an object of a fiduciary power, however, has equitable rights (mere equities) in relation to the exercise of the power. These rights are broadly similar to those enjoyed by an object of a discretionary trust; but the crucial distinction, which was emphasised by Lord Wilberforce in *McPhail* v *Doulton* [1971] AC 424, is that trustees of a discretionary trust are under a greater duty to survey the class than donees of a fiduciary power. The right of an object to be considered is therefore correspondingly greater if the object is an object of a discretionary trust than if he is an object of a fiduciary power. The object of a non-fiduciary power, by contrast, has no right to be considered; and the donee of the power can appoint spitefully, or capriciously, or even go to sleep and forget about exercising the power at all.

Recent case law has tended to blur the differences between discretionary trusts and fiduciary powers. Thus *McPhail* v *Doulton* held that the test for certainty of objects of powers should be applied as the test for certainty of objects of discretionary trusts. Furthermore, a number of later cases involving pension funds, where the objects supply consideration in the form of contributions from their salaries, have extended the rights of the objects of powers. It is not yet clear, however, whether this latter development is applicable solely to pension fund trusts, or to all trusts under which the objects provide consideration in money or money's worth.

You should try to keep separate in your mind the rules relating to the validity of an instrument (whether as a fixed or discretionary trust or as a power) and the duties and powers of the trustee or donee in relation to the exercise of any power he has. A question concerned with the rights of the objects of a discretionary trust or power is not concerned with the validity of the instrument. Certainty of objects, administrative unworkability and capriciousness (where the definition of objects negatives any sensible intention on the part of the settlor) are concerned with matters of validity. Administrative unworkability invalidates a discretionary trust, but not, apparently, a power.

This chapter also includes a question relating to protective trusts, which are a two-stage combination of a fixed trust and a discretionary trust. Protective trusts in a family context are not as common today as they were in earlier times, so your course may not deal with them very extensively. Protective trusts are, however, of modern importance and relation to pension-fund trusts; see, e.g., *Re Scientific Investment Pension Plan Trusts* [1999] Ch 53. If protective trusts form part of your course, you will need to be familiar with the intricacies of the Trustee Act 1925, s. 33, as well as with the sometimes conflicting case law.

QUESTION 1

Adam, who has just died, made the following dispositions in his will:

(a) £50,000 to my trustees on trust to apply the net income of the fund in making, at their absolute discretion, grants to or for the benefit of any of the employees or former employees of Abel & Sons, their spouses or dependants, or any others having a moral claim on me.

(b) £5,000 to my trustees upon trust to be divided equally amongst my friends at the 'Paradise' public house, Edenton.

(c) £100,000 to be applied by my trustees as they see fit for the benefit of the middle classes of my home town, Edenton.

(d) The residue of my estate to my wife, Eve, absolutely, but I direct my trustees to allow such old friends of mine who wish to do so, to acquire any of my collection of stuffed reptiles at fifty per cent of market price.

Advise the trustees of the will as to the validity of these dispositions.

Commentary

There usually appears in examination papers a question on certainty of objects dealing with the ramifications of the House of Lords' decision in *McPhail* v *Doulton* [1971] AC 424 and its application by the Court of Appeal in *Re Baden's Deed Trusts (No. 2)* [1973] Ch 9. So, a careful preparation of the case law will repay the effort!

For a high mark, some discussion of the issues going beyond a simple application of the cases to the problem is desirable. Some further discussion of the issues of conceptual certainty, evidential certainty, ascertainability and administrative workability would be appropriate.

Suggested Answer

(a) A trust must be for ascertained or ascertainable beneficiaries: *Re Endacott* [1960] Ch 232, CA. The test to determine certainty of objects in a discretionary trust was decided by the House of Lords in *McPhail* v *Doulton* [1971] AC 424 ('can it be said with certainty that any given individual is or is not a member of the class?').

Since this decision, therefore, it is no longer necessary to prepare a complete list of objects of a discretionary trust as is still required in a fixed trust (*IRC* v *Broadway Cottages Trust* [1955] Ch 20, CA). In *McPhail* v *Doulton* (supra) the House of Lords adopted the test for certainty of objects of powers established in *Re Gulbenkian's Settlement Trust (No. 2)* [1975] AC 508, and the two tests are now the same.

It is necessary, therefore, to apply the test to the terms of Adam's will and ask: can it be said with certainty whether any individual is or is not an employee or former employee of Abel & Sons, or their spouse or dependant, or any other having a moral claim on Abel?

In *Re Baden's Deed Trusts (No. 2)* [1973] Ch 9, CA, the terms 'relatives' and 'dependants' were subjected to the test. It was considered that the terms were conceptually certain and, therefore, sufficient to satisfy the test although all three judges gave different reasons for finding 'relatives' certain.

The term 'spouses' is clearly certain as a concept and this part of the gift would be valid.

However, the gift also includes a category of 'any others having a moral claim on me'. It was said in *McPhail* v *Doulton* that such an expression is conceptually uncertain.

It is not clear whether this would cause the whole gift to fail for uncertainty or whether the courts could sever the offending part, thereby saving the valid parts (*Re Leek* [1969] 1 Ch 563, CA; *Re Gulbenkian's Settlements* [1968] Ch 126 at 138, CA).

(b)   The gift upon trust to be divided equally amongst my friends at the 'Paradise' is a fixed trust. The beneficiaries hold equitable interests under the trust in fixed shares. It is necessary to be able to draw up a list of all the beneficiaries in order for the division to be made. The older and stricter rule in *IRC* v *Broadway Cottages Trust* applies. The expression 'friends' is not a term that is sufficiently certain for such a complete list to be drawn up. The expression 'old friends' was held to be certain in *Re Gibbard's Will Trusts* [1967] 1 WLR 42 in relation to a power, but this case used the old test of whether it could be said of any one person that they were within the class (a test favoured by Lord Denning MR in his dissenting judgment in the Court of Appeal in *Re Gulbenkian*). This test was rejected by the House of Lords in *Re Gulbenkian* however, and so is not now good authority for this point. A gift to 'friends' was upheld in *Re Barlow's Will Trusts* [1979] 1 WLR 278, but this was a series of gifts with a condition precedent. The size of the gift to each recipient did not alter according to the numbers in the class, therefore it is not authority for certainty of the expression 'friends' in a fixed trust.

(c)   This gift constitutes a purported discretionary trust. It raises questions about certainty of objects and administrative workability.

First, the problem of certainty of objects is raised in respect of the definition of 'middle classes' (*McPhail* v *Doulton*). Again, it is necessary to decide whether such a concept is certain applying the test in *McPhail* v *Doulton*. Although it may be possible to say definitely whether some individuals are or are not members of the middle classes, there may be a number of people who cannot be classified in this way. There was a difference of approach amongst the judges in *Re Baden's Deed Trusts (No. 2)*.

Megaw LJ accepted that there may be a substantial number of persons about whom it could not be proved whether they are in or out. However, this may relate more to the question of evidential uncertainty. Conceptual certainty means that the class must be definable. Evidential certainty is the proof an applicant must supply to establish membership of the class. In the case of a gift to 'middle classes' it is difficult to define criteria for such a concept.

However, even if the gift is conceptually certain, then the question of administrative unworkability arises. In *McPhail* v *Doulton*, it was said that if the definition of 'objects is so hopelessly wide as not to form anything like a class', then the trust would be administratively unworkable. A discretionary trustee has duties to survey the class and this is impossible in a class of great width. This was the position in the case of *R* v *District Auditor, ex parte West Yorkshire Metropolitan County Council* (1986) 26 RVR 24, where a trust for the inhabitants of the county of West Yorkshire was held to be too wide and therefore void for administrative unworkability. If the trust could be construed as a power this rule would not apply: *Re Manisty's Settlement* [1974] Ch 17.

(d)   This gift must be distinguished from discretionary trusts. It is not a trust for a class but a number of individual gifts to any person who is able to prove to the trustees that he or she qualifies as 'an old friend'. Such a gift does not require conceptual certainty. The gift will be valid if only one person seeking to take can be identified as an 'old friend' (*Re Allen* [1953] Ch 810, CA). In *Re Barlow's Will Trusts*, the direction to sell a painting at a preferential price to 'any friends of mine who may wish to buy one' was held to be a valid gift. A friend was a social acquaintance of long standing and anyone who satisfied this condition precedent would take the gift.

On the basis of this authority, this final disposition is therefore valid.

QUESTION 2

In January 1980 Simon settled property on Tom and Tam 'on protective trusts' for Betty (who was then aged 20) until she should reach the age of 30 and, if no determining event had by then occurred, upon trust for Betty absolutely, if a determining event had occurred, then upon protective trusts for Betty until she should attain the age of 40, but, if no determining event had by then occurred, upon trust for her absolutely, and subject thereto, to hold the property in trust for Betty for life with remainder to her children, Romulus and Remus.

In December 1985 Betty asked the trustees to pay her £50,000 for the purpose of setting up a feline beauty parlour. Although such amount exceeded the income of the trust, Tom and Tam duly paid the money. In 1986, having taken legal advice that this constituted a breach of trust, they sought to remedy the breach by withholding a part of Betty's income from the following year. Betty's beauty parlour was not a success. In 1987 it went out of business and Betty went bankrupt. Tom and Tam continued to pay the fees at the local further education college where Betty was studying for a diploma in hairdressing and beauty.

In June 1997, Betty's husband petitioned for divorce on the ground of Betty's unreasonable behaviour. The divorce court awarded him custody of the children and ordered Betty to pay maintenance for the children, to be charged on Betty's interest under the settlement. Betty has refused to pay.

Advise Tom and Tam as to the following:

(a)   The legal effect of the aforementioned events on the settlement and the nature of the interests of Betty, Romulus and Remus under the settlement, from 1980 onwards.

(b)   Would your advice differ if Betty, as opposed to Simon, had been the settlor?

Commentary

The facts in the question make it appear long and confusing. However, if you have revised protective trusts, this is the question for you as it is discrete. A rough plan setting out the sequence of events is desirable.

Such a plan might look something like this:

```
1980    (Betty aged 20)
)
)   Determinable
)   interest for Betty
)
)           1985   advancement (terminating event?)
)           1986   impounding income (terminating event)
)           1987   bankruptcy (terminating event)
)
1990    (Betty aged 30)
)
)   Second determinable
)   interest for Betty
)
)           1997   court order (terminating event?)
)
2000    (Betty aged 40)
```

There is a number of points in the question, each supported by a case, so it is largely a matter of spotting them all. The more you spot, the higher the mark. A diagram of events might prevent you missing any.

The point on the matrimonial order raises two cases which are difficult to reconcile. Grasp the nettle and deal with the conflict, explaining which one is preferred and why. For further discussion on this point see (1963) 27 Conv NS517; F. R. Crane.

The reference to the note by R.E. Megarry in the *Law Quarterly Review* is not essential merely to pass, but demonstrates a breadth of reading which is essential for achieving a higher class.

Suggested Answer

(a) The wording of the disposition invokes s. 33, Trustee Act 1925, which initially creates a determinable interest for Betty, the principal beneficiary. Section 33(1)(i) defines very widely the events which will determine the interest of the principal beneficiary as 'any act or thing ... or event' which deprives her of the right to the whole or any part of the income.

The settlement does, in fact, create a series of protective trusts. The advantage of this is that, if a determining event occurs before Betty is 30, she gets a second chance before her interest is irrevocably reduced to a life interest. This application of the protective trust was recommended by R.E. Megarry as making the best possible use of the existing machinery ((1958) 74 LQR 184).

In December 1985 the trustees make an advance to Betty of £50,000 to set up a feline beauty parlour. Section 33(1) provides that '... an advance under any statutory or express power ...' is not a determining event. An advance may, therefore, be made if there is an express power in the settlement or, if the life tenant consents, under the provisions in the Trustee Act 1925, s. 32. This section confers upon the trustees power to pay capital for the advancement or benefit of any persons entitled, even if (like Betty), they are entitled merely contingently to the capital. An advancement properly made, therefore, does not constitute a determining event. Setting up a beneficiary in business is an appropriate reason for an advance.

If the advancement was not lawfully made under the terms of the trust however, then it would be of no avail for Betty to argue that she was still enjoying the benefit of the capital taken from the trust as she still had the feline beauty parlour. This argument was made on behalf of a principal beneficiary in *Re Smith's Will Trusts* (1981) 131 NLJ 292, but Megarry J held that in such circumstances, what the beneficiary is enjoying is the benefit of capital which has been taken out of the trust thereby depriving her of part of the income from the trust. However, whether the advance was lawfully made or not, the attempt by the trustees to impound Betty's income to make good the breach which they believed had occurred, is a determining event for the purposes of s. 33 (*Re Balfour's Settlement* [1938] Ch 928).

As soon as a determining event occurs (the advancement if unlawful in 1985, or impounding the income in 1986), then the principal beneficiary's interest ceases and the discretionary trust under s. 33(1)(ii) arises instead. This is a discretionary trust for Betty, her spouse and her children, Romulus and Remus, for the remainder of the ten year period of the protective trust, i.e., until 1990. Betty's bankruptcy in 1987 would also have been a determining event, but as the interest has already determined, it will be of no effect.

The trustees continue to pay Betty's college fees after the determining events. Once the determinable interest has come to an end, the discretionary trusts arise. The trustees are able to make payments at their absolute discretion to the principal beneficiary, his or her spouse and issue for their maintenance, support or other benefit. Betty, as the principal beneficiary, may, therefore, receive payments at the discretion of the trustees even though she has no proprietary interest in the trust. However, a difficulty arises where the principal beneficiary has been declared bankrupt. If she receives more than what is sufficient for her mere support, then the trustee in bankruptcy may impound any payments made to her. However, it would seem that where payments are made to a third party for services rendered to the principal beneficiary, the trustee in bankruptcy is unable to intercept such payments (*Re Coleman* (1888) 39 ChD 443).

In 1990, a second protective trust arises for a further ten year period until 2000.

In June 1997 a court order is made charging Betty's interest with a maintenance order. This order is available to the Family Division of the High Court under the Matrimonial Causes Act 1973. There are conflicting cases on whether this is an event which will determine her protective interest. In *Re Richardson's Will Trusts* [1958] Ch 504, it was held that such an order caused a forfeiture. However, in *General Accident Fire and Life Assurance Corporation Ltd* v *IRC* [1963] 1 WLR 1207, part of the income was ordered to be paid to an ex-wife and this did not cause a forfeiture. The object of the protective trust is to protect not only the principal beneficiary from financial disasters, but also his initial family who are beneficiaries under the discretionary trust, and Donovan LJ said that the section could give no protection against such a court order. *Re Richardson* was not referred to in the later case and commentators suggest that the *General Accident* case is to be preferred. In that event, the court order will not determine Betty's interest which would continue until 2000 when she would have obtained an absolute interest.

(**b**)   If Betty were the settlor instead of Simon, this would affect the advice about the bankruptcy which occurred in 1989. A settlor may protect another person from the consequences of their bankruptcy. However, settlors may not protect their own property from bankruptcy in this way. In *Re Burroughs-Fowler* [1916] 2 Ch 251, the settlor settled property in trust for himself until a specified event should occur, whereupon the income should be paid to his wife. One of the events was bankruptcy, which did occur. It was held that the trustee in bankruptcy was entitled to the income.

This applies only to bankruptcy, and not to other determining events. So, there would be no difference in the advice in respect of the other events. In 1987, when the bankruptcy occurs, Betty's interest has already determined as a result of the trustees' decision to withhold income (*Re Balfour's*

Settlement). As the discretionary trusts have already arisen, the bankruptcy can have no effect (*Re Detmold* (1889) 40 ChD 585).

QUESTION 3

> But it is difficult in borderline cases to draw a dividing line between discretionary trusts and powers.... The decision turns on the proper construction of the language of the instrument. The matter is made more difficult by reason of the fact that a discretionary trust may be 'exhaustive' or 'non-exhaustive'. (Hanbury and Martin, *Modern Equity*, 16th edn, London: Sweet & Maxwell, 2001, at pp. 63–64.)

Discuss.

Commentary

This essay question requires a discussion of the distinction between discretionary trusts and powers with reference to relevant literature; see, for example, (1974) 37 MLR 643, (Y. Grbich), *Farwell on Powers* (3rd edn, 1916) and *Halsbury's Laws of England* (4th edn, vol. 36, p. 529 (London: Butterworths). In particular, such reference must be made where an essay of this type is set as an assessed essay.

A straightforward explanation of the difference and the importance of the distinction between discretionary trusts and powers is required. The essay could be grouped under different headings to clarify the different aspects of the problem; for example, the different position of the trustees/donees, and the potential recipients.

Suggested Answer

At first sight a discretionary trust and a power may achieve the same purpose. A disposition is made which is available for a group of people but the selection of the recipients and the size of their shares is left to the decision of a third party. The purpose of such a disposition is not to benefit each member of the group equally regardless of their need, but instead, a power of selection is given to a trusted third party. That person is to make the selection according to criteria fixed by the settlor or at their absolute discretion. If the settlor wished each member of the group to benefit in any event, then this would have been achieved by creating a fixed trust in equal or other shares.

The person making the selection may be obliged to use up all the property or income in making a selection, as in an exhaustive trust, or there may be power to accumulate income and make no selection as in a non-exhaustive trust.

However, the basic difference that a trust imposes an obligation to distribute, whereas a power is merely an enabling provision, results in important differences in the duties of trustees of a discretionary trust and the donees of a power, and the position of the beneficiaries under each.

Duty of Trustees under Discretionary Trusts

A trustee is under a duty to perform the trust. If the trust is discretionary, the trustees are obliged to consider and exercise their discretion. If they fail to exercise their discretion the court can order them to do so. If the trust is exhaustive, they must make an appointment even though the decision as to the recipient and the size of the distribution is at the trustees' discretion. The court will intervene and make an appointment if the trustees fail to act, or if the trustees predecease the testator — the trust will not fail for want of a trustee. If no appointment is made the property will normally be divided equally between the beneficiaries on the basis that equality is equity, as in the case of *Burrough* v *Philcox* (1840) 5 My & Cr 72.

Duty of Donee of a Power

There is an initial distinction to be drawn between fiduciary powers and bare powers. A fiduciary power is a power of appointment granted to a trustee or to a person in a fiduciary position (*Re Mills* [1930] 1 Ch 654). Because such persons are in a fiduciary position, they cannot simply ignore the power. In *Re Hay's Settlement Trusts* [1982] 1 WLR 202, it was held that the donee of a fiduciary power must consider the exercise of the power and survey the potential beneficiaries from time to time. The court may intervene if the trustee exercises the power inappropriately.

However, even where there is a fiduciary power the donee is not required to exercise it. In *Re Gestetner's Settlement* [1953] Ch 672, a power given to trustees, to distribute amongst a huge and fluctuating class consisting of employees of a number of companies, was considered valid, even though it was impossible to consider all the potential objects. The test for certainty of powers, as established in *Re Gulbenkian's Settlement* [1970] AC 508, is, in fact, the same for certainty of objects in a discretionary trust. This was held to be the appropriate test in *Re Baden's Deed Trusts (No. 1)*, *McPhail* v *Doulton* [1971]

AC 424. The test is that it must be possible to say with certainty whether any given individual is or is not a member of the class.

A bare power does not impose on the donee any fiduciary duties. A donee of a bare power may exercise the power at will. If the power is not exercised, the court cannot compel the donee to exercise it or even to consider its exercise. If the donee predeceases the testator, then the power lapses. If no appointment is made under any power (whether fiduciary or not) the property will pass to the person entitled in default of its exercise, so that, if the donor of the power has not specified who is to take over in this event, the property may go back to the settlor or to the testator's estate under a resulting trust.

Position of Beneficiaries under a Discretionary Trust

The beneficiaries under a fixed trust own the property in equity, and, if of full age and sound mind, can call for the trust to be extinguished and the property distributed (*Saunders* v *Vautier* (1841) 10 LJ Ch 354). Under a discretionary trust, no individual beneficiary owns a particular part of the trust property until an appointment has been made (*Gartside* v *IRC* [1968] AC 553). However, as a group, all the potential beneficiaries own the trust property and, as in a fixed trust, if adult and of sound mind, they can call for the trust to be brought to an end.

Position of Objects of a Power

The objects of a power have no interest in the property. They cannot call for a distribution to be made. They only acquire an interest once a distribution is made in their favour. They have no right to seek the intervention of the court if no appointment is made. If no appointment is made, therefore, unless there is a gift over, the property will revert on resulting trust to the settlor or the settlor's estate. The only occasion on which the objects of a bare power can apply to court is to restrain the exercise of a power which is outside the terms of the instrument granting it, as this would be tantamount to a fraud on the power. Objects of a fiduciary power may additionally prevent or have set aside an appointment which is made capriciously, or where improper considerations are taken into account (*Klug* v *Klug* [1918] 2 Ch 67).

In some cases concerning pension funds however, the courts have taken the view that, as the beneficiaries are not volunteers, a fiduciary obligation attaches to the power and the courts do have a *locus standi* to act, even in the case of a fiduciary power, where there is nobody else to act because, for example, the company with the power has gone into liquidation (*Mettoy Pension Trustees Ltd* v *Evans* [1990] 1 WLR 1587). Moreover, it was said in *Imperial Group Pension Trust* v *Imperial Tobacco* [1991] 1 WLR 589 that if the company with a power to appoint under a pension fund does so, then it must do so bona fide and not in breach of its fiduciary duties to its employees.

Construction of Document to Distinguish between Power and Discretionary Trust

As indicated in the question, it may be extremely difficult to decide whether a power or a discretionary trust has been created. The language of the gift in a well drafted document should make it clear. Failing this, the court must decide whether the intention of the instrument is to impose an obligation to benefit the objects, or merely to enable them to be benefited.

First, an obligation cannot be deduced where the settlor provides a gift over in default of appointment. This implicitly acknowledges that no selection might be made and there is no power to force a selection. A power, therefore, has been created and not a discretionary trust (*Re Gestetner*). The reverse does not, unfortunately, always hold true. In *Re Weekes' Settlement* [1897] 1 Ch 289, it was held that there was no intention to create a trust for the objects of the power, even though there was no gift over, as the disposition did not impose any obligation.

In *Burrough* v *Philcox*, property was left by the testator to his two children for their lives. The survivor was given a power to leave the property in her will 'amongst my nephews and nieces or their children, either all to one of them, or to as many of them as my surviving child should think proper'. The court decided that this was effective to create a trust. As no selection was made, the court would intervene and make the gift in equal shares amongst the beneficiaries. Had the conclusion been that the gift was a mere power, then the court would have been powerless to intervene and the property would have resulted back to the settlor's estate. Lord Cottenham in *Burrough* v *Philcox* said that where there is a general intention in favour of a class with a particular intention to select particular individuals from that class then, if the selection fails, the class will benefit as a whole. The significant factor is an intention to benefit the objects of the gift if no selection is made.

So, the distinction is often hard to deduce in cases where the instrument is not clear. The distinction, nevertheless, is important in terms of the differing rights and duties of the trustees and donees and the potential objects of the trust or power.

6 Charitable Trusts

INTRODUCTION

In our experience the topic of charitable trusts is a favourite one for examiners and students alike. There are complexities in this area, however, and it can be difficult in borderline cases to decide whether a particular trust is charitable or not. Nevertheless, the law itself is probably more easily understood than in some other topics in equity and trusts. The examiners may devote an entire question to charitable trusts. On the other hand, a question on this area may be mixed with another topic. A favourite combination in practice involves a mixing with non-charitable purpose trusts.

QUESTION 1

Geoffrey, who died recently, left a will directing his executors and trustees to constitute his residuary estate a trust fund and to hold one third thereof upon trust for each of the following purposes:

(a) To provide sports equipment and prizes for snooker tournaments for university students.

(b) To assist the vicar and churchwardens of St. Peter's, Faversham, in parish work.

(c) To encourage the preservation of the world's rainforests.

Consider whether these dispositions are of a charitable nature.

Commentary

Since you are asked to advise as to the charitable nature of each disposition, it is unnecessary to consider whether any of them might be otherwise valid (e.g., as a trust of imperfect obligation). Had the question, however, demanded that you 'advise as to the validity' of the dispositions, a discussion of other means of upholding them would have been appropriate.

Do not waste time dealing with points which do not cause problems. There is no need, for instance, in part (b) of the present question, to write at length about whether the advancement of various esoteric beliefs might nevertheless be charitable.

If you are permitted to take statutes into the examination, you will not gain many marks for merely reciting what they contain. Reference to the Recreational Charities Act 1958 should, in such cases, refer to the relevant section and paragraphs, but quotations should be limited to the key words: e.g., in the answer to part (a) of the present question, to the issue of 'need'.

The answer does not conclude definitely whether any of the dispositions is charitable. This is because whether a particular purpose is charitable is a mixed question of law and fact. As a law student you are expected to know the law; but you cannot be decisive about matters of construction. For this reason, it is best merely to indicate what you consider the more likely construction and state the law relevant to it. You might, however, go on to consider the consequences which would flow from any other reasonable constructions.

An article on the relationship between politics and charity, which would be useful reading in preparation for an essay on that topic (a perennial favourite with examiners), is Forder 'Too Political to be Charitable?' [1984] Conv 263.

Suggested Answer

To be charitable, each of the dispositions must promote a charitable purpose, it must contain a public benefit, and the purpose must be wholly and exclusively charitable. It is necessary to consider each disposition separately.

(a)   The promotion of sport is not itself a charitable purpose: *Re Nottage* [1895] 2 Ch 649, CA. It may, however, be charitable if it can be regarded as a means of furthering a purpose which is charitable. Thus, the provision of squash courts in a school was held charitable in *Re Mariette* [1915] 2 Ch 284, because the judge regarded the playing of sport as an integral part of the boys' education, and the advancement of education is a charitable purpose within the second head of charity laid down by Lord Macnaghten in *Pemsel's Case* [1891] AC 531. This principle might apply to university students, most of whom are no more than a few years above school age. It is, however, a matter of construction whether, in each case, the purpose is merely the promotion of sport (and so not charitable, as in *IRC* v *City of Glasgow Police Athletic Association* [1953] AC 380) or a means of furthering a charitable purpose. In *IRC* v *McMullen* [1981] AC 1, the House of Lords held that a trust to provide facilities for pupils at schools and universities to play football was charitable as being for the advancement of education. In that case, however, the trust deed stated that this was a means of improving their minds. Since no such words are expressed here, the provision of sports equipment will be charitable under the second head of *Pemsel's Case* only if the court is willing to infer that the testator intended the avowed purpose to be merely a means to a charitable end.

The provision of prizes for snooker tournaments may be charitable if the game is itself educational and available only to young persons. In *Re Dupree's Deed Trusts* [1945] Ch 16, a trust for an annual chess tournament for boys and young men up to the age of 21 was held to be charitable, the court accepting the evidence of a school teacher that chess is educational. The judge did, however, regard it as near the borderline; and snooker, though a game of physical skill, must surely be considered less intellectual than chess. On that basis, the provision of prizes for snooker tournaments in the question would not be charitable for the advancement of education.

This is not, however, the end of the matter. Under the Recreational Charities Act 1958 it is charitable to provide facilities for recreation or other leisure time occupation in the interests of social welfare. The requirement of social welfare is satisfied if the facilities are provided to improve the conditions of life for the persons for whom they are primarily intended, and either such persons have need of such facilities (for the reasons there specified, including youth) or the facilities are to be open to the members or female members of the public at large. Although the majority of the Court of Appeal in *IRC* v *McMullen* took the view that the requirement of need imported some element of deprivation, the House of Lords in *Guild* v *IRC* [1992] 2 AC 310 held that this is not so. Assuming, therefore, that there is evidence of a need for such facilities and equipment at universities, both the purposes mentioned in (a) are likely to be held charitable. Unless both are held charitable, the trust will fail as not being wholly and exclusively charitable.

(b) As office-holders, the vicar and churchwardens promote a charitable purpose, regarding the advancement of religion, the third head of charity in *Pemsel's Case*. Therefore a gift to these persons described as such, without more, would be regarded as a good charitable gift for the advancement of religion. The problem here, however, is that a purpose is specified: namely, parish work. This means that the persons specified hold the property for such a purpose, and the charitable status of the gift depends upon whether a trust for parish work is wholly and exclusively charitable. In *Re Simson* [1946] Ch 299, a gift to a vicar 'for his work in the parish' was held charitable; whereas in *Farley* v *Westminster Bank Ltd* [1939] AC 430, HL, a gift to a vicar 'for parish work' was not. The difference was that in *Farley* the parish work was not limited to work which fell within the charitable scope of the vicar's office. It could, for example, include a civic reception for a footballer. It is, in each case, a matter of construction; but, unless the court can put a different construction on the present gift from that of the House of Lords in *Farley*, it will fail as not being wholly and exclusively charitable.

(c) The preservation of the environment is accepted as a charitable purpose within the fourth head of Lord Macnaghten's classification in *Pemsel's Case*. The public benefit means a benefit to the public in the United Kingdom; but scientific evidence has revealed the importance of the rain forests to the world's climate, and suggests that they contain as yet undiscovered species of plants which may assist in the development of cures for human diseases. The preservation of the animals in the forests may also tend to moral improvement of the human race: *Re Wedgwood* [1915] 1 Ch 113. Thus, subject to the possible qualification which follows, even though no rainforests are in the United Kingdom, this trust would appear to satisfy the public benefit requirement and, therefore, to be charitable.

The qualification is that a trust will be denied charitable status if its purpose is considered to be political. A trust which aims to change the law is political because the court has no means of judging whether a proposed change in the law is or is not for the benefit of the public in the United Kingdom: *McGovern* v *A-G* [1982] Ch 321. In the *McGovern* case it was thought that there was a risk that the aims of the trust established by Amnesty International might prejudice this country's relations with countries overseas. An additional reason for the denial of charitable status to political trusts is that the Attorney-General might be required to enforce trusts whose purposes are against the interests of the State: *Bowman* v *Secular Society Ltd* [1917] AC 406; *National Anti-Vivisection Society* v *IRC* [1948] AC 31, HL. It might therefore be argued that the purpose specified in the problem could be carried out by seeking to change the law of the UK or of other countries, and this would make it a political purpose and so vitiate charitable status. It is, perhaps, the word 'encourage' which causes anxiety on this point.

Nevertheless, given the scientific evidence mentioned above, the court might well consider that any potential political element is merely ancillary to the charitable purpose: *IRC* v *Temperance Council* (1926) 136 LT 27. If this is the case, the trust will still be wholly and exclusively charitable. Charities are, after all, permitted a limited amount of political activity, provided there is a reasonable expectation that such activity will further their stated purposes. They may, for instance, put forward a reasoned memorandum recommending changes in the law: see the Charity Commissioners' revised guidelines in their leaflet of 9 July 1995, 'Political Activities and Campaigning by Charities'. The borderline, indeed, between education and propaganda is sometimes narrow (see *Re Koeppler Will Trusts* [1986] Ch 423) and the courts will deny charitable status to political propaganda disguised as education (*Southwood* v *A-G*, unreported, 28 June 2000, CA). Only an unsympathetic judge, however, would be likely to deny charitable status to a trust for the purpose specified in the question.

QUESTION 2

To be charitable, a trust must promote a public benefit.

Discuss.

Commentary

In an essay question it is additionally important to have a structure in mind before you start writing, because such questions (unlike some problem questions) will not always suggest a structure to you. Examiners will be impressed by a well-structured and coherently argued essay. The basic structure to the following suggested answer is the distinction between the two senses in which public benefit is used. Note that, in the first sense, cases are drawn upon from those pertaining to the definition of charity. It is necessary to be selective, mentioning only those relevant to the answer. By preparing a preliminary structure, perhaps by way of a few rough notes, you will obtain a better idea of how much time (and therefore detail) you can afford to give to each aspect of the answer.

The question is short and therefore, perhaps, appealing. The danger with it is that the student may not spot everything which is asked. This is always a potential danger with very short questions. In our experience a large number of students will fail to deal with both aspects of public benefit, but not those who study this suggested answer!

Suggested Answer

This statement is generally correct. The concept of public benefit in the law of charity is used in two different senses.

First, it can mean that the purpose itself must be of public benefit. The absence of public benefit in this sense, when required, means that the trust cannot be for a charitable purpose. In the context of Lord Macnaghten's fourth head of charity in *Pemsel's Case* [1891] AC 531, 'other purposes beneficial to the community', this requirement is self-evident. Similarly, a trust cannot be charitable as being for the advancement of education (the second head) unless public benefit is established. Under both these heads, public benefit must be proved and it is not enough that the settlor himself believes that the purpose is beneficial to the public: *Re Pinion* [1965] Ch 85, CA (where the testator tried to foist upon the public as a museum a 'mass of junk'). In a borderline case, as in *Re Pinion* or *Re Dupree's Deed Trusts* [1945] Ch 16 (chess tournaments for young males in Portsmouth up to the age of 21), the court may derive assistance from expert evidence. If necessary, the court will weigh the benefits of the proposed purpose against any detriments: *National Anti-Vivisection Society* v *IRC* [1948] AC 31, where a moral benefit was outweighed by a tangible detriment.

In the case of the relief of poverty, this aspect of the public benefit requirement is satisfied if the persons to be relieved are needy, which imports the notion of 'going short': *Re De Carteret* [1933] Ch 103. The third head of *Pemsel's Case*, the advancement of religion, is in this respect, however, the most relaxed. The court assumes that the advancement of religion benefits the public and consequently the benefit does not have to be proven: *Re Watson* [1973] 1 WLR 1472, following *Thornton v Howe* (1862) 31 Beav 14; also *Re le Cren Clarke (sub nom Funnel v Stewart)* [1996] 1 WLR 288. Evidence that the purpose is immoral or against religion will, however, deny charitable status. This has not been established in respect of the religious sect known as the Moonies, which remains a charity in English law. One reason advanced by the courts for not admitting charitable status to trusts for political purposes is that it has no means of judging whether a change in the law is for the public benefit: *National Anti-Vivisection Society v IRC* and *McGovern v A-G* [1982] Ch 321.

Secondly, public benefit can mean that the community, or the section of the community, to benefit must be sufficient. Essentially this is a matter of degree. In one case an appeal for the widows, orphans and dependants of six fishermen drowned at sea was held charitable: *Cross v Lloyd-Greame* (1909) 102 LT 163. In the context of the fourth head of charity in *Pemsel*, the requirement of public benefit in this sense is particularly stringent. Thus, if the description of persons to benefit comprises a class within a class, the trust cannot be charitable: see *IRC v Baddeley* [1955] AC 572, HL. The Recreational Charities Act 1958, s. 1, provides that nothing in that Act is to derogate from the principle that for a trust to be charitable it must be for the public benefit: and see *Guild v IRC* [1992] 2 AC 310. On this basis it is arguable that the decision in *Baddeley* would still be the same today.

Furthermore, where the beneficiaries are defined by reference to a personal nexus, the trust cannot be charitable. This test was first established in the context of a blood relationship in *Re Compton* [1945] Ch 123, CA, and was applied by the House of Lords in *Oppenheim v Tobacco Securities Trust Co. Ltd* [1951] AC 297 to deny charitable status to a trust to educate the children of employees of a named company. Where however, the primary class to benefit does constitute a sufficient section of the community, a preference for a private class will not destroy the charitable nature of the trust, provided that the preference does not go to more than 75% of the trust income: *Re Koettgen's Will Trusts* [1954] Ch 252. This qualification does not, however, apply if the private class has a right in priority (*Caffoor v ITC* [1961] AC 584). Where no preference for a private class is specified in the trust, a de facto application by the trustees to a private class does not constitute an application for exclusively charitable purposes (*IRC* v *Educational Grants Association Ltd* [1967] Ch 993) and would appear to be a breach of trust.

There is one important exception to the personal nexus test, namely, it does not apply to trusts for the relief of poverty. Cases going back to the eighteenth century had held that a trust to relieve poor relations was charitable, and this principle had been extended for instance, in *Re Coulthurst* [1951] Ch 661, CA, to poor employees of a bank. In *Dingle* v *Turner* [1972] AC 601, the House of Lords affirmed that these earlier cases were not affected by the ruling in *Oppenheim*. In *Dingle* v *Turner*, Lord Cross opined that the *Oppenheim* test was established in order to prevent companies providing tax-free fringe benefits to their employees, and for this reason he thought that a trust to advance religion among the members of a company might be charitable, provided the benefits were purely spiritual. It should be noted, however, that the majority of their Lordships in that case expressly dissociated themselves from Lord Cross's view that, in determining charitable status, the courts ought to take tax benefits into account.

Even a trust for the relief of poverty cannot be charitable, however, if the persons to benefit, instead of being described merely by reference to a group (such as poor relations), are individually named: *Re Scarisbrick* [1944] Ch 229.

Although a trust for the advancement of religion is subject to the public benefit requirement in this second sense, such a requirement is generally applied less stringently. Thus, whereas in *Re Compton* (in the context of education) the court rejected the notion of indirect public benefit (viz, that the persons educated would mix with others in society), such a notion was admitted in the context of the advancement of religion in *Neville Estates Ltd* v *Madden* [1962] Ch 832. This was a trust to advance religion among members of the Catford Synagogue. Although this comprised only a small number of persons, the court held that the public benefit requirement was satisfied because such persons would mix with others in society and the benefit would thereby rub off. A similar approach is evident in *Re Hetherington, Gibbs* v *McDonnell* [1990] Ch 1, where a trust for the saying of masses for the soul of the testatrix was held charitable because the masses could be held in public.

There was no mixing with the public, however, in *Gilmour* v *Coats* [1949] AC 426, HL, where the purposes of a Carmelite convent were held not to be charitable. The nuns were a cloistered and purely contemplative order. Since they never mixed with society, the only public benefit could be that derived from spiritual edification or from intercessory prayer. The House of Lords held these benefits were not susceptible to judicial proof, and it was not sufficient that the Roman Catholic Church itself believed that these things benefited the public. *Gilmour* v *Coats* was distinguished from *Thornton* v *Howe* in *Re Watson* on the basis of the dissemination of the works in the earlier case. Nevertheless, the liberal approach adopted in recent cases involving the advancement of religion is not easy to reconcile with their Lordships' decision.

QUESTION 3

(a) Consider the legal differences between a charitable trust and a private trust.

AND

(b) By her will, Jemima (who died recently) left £100,000 'upon trust for charitable and deserving purposes'. Consider the validity of this disposition.

Commentary

Part (a) involves a broad range of knowledge. The skill here is not merely to show that you know what the differences are, but also to treat them in a balanced way. Given that this is only half of the question, you cannot be expected to go into great detail. The more fundamental differences are considered first, leaving the more technical ones (such as the numbers of trustees) until later. Taxation differences are also mentioned briefly at the end to indicate that the student is aware of them, but they are not elaborated upon since such differences do not relate to the substantive law of trusts. A possible variation of this question is to consider the advantages of charitable trusts over private trusts.

Part (b) illustrates the point that, where more than one construction can reasonably be placed upon a form of words, it is essential to consider all reasonable constructions.

Suggested Answer

(a) The primary legal difference is that a charitable trust aims to benefit society at large (or at least a sufficient section of it) whereas a private trust is designed to benefit specified persons or groups of persons, or (in a limited number of anomalous instances) for purposes which the law does not recognise as charitable. It is sometimes difficult to ascertain which has been created. This was illustrated by the uncertainty surrounding the legal status of the main fund raised following the Penlee Lifeboat Disaster. Since then, many public disaster funds (such as the main appeal fund following the Bradford City Fire Disaster) have been specifically drafted as private discretionary trusts in order to give the trustees greater flexibility in the application of the fund. The difficulty in distinguishing between a charitable or a private trust can be particularly acute in the context of a trust for the settlor's poor relations: *Re Segelman* [1996] Ch 171.

Whereas private trusts are enforced by the beneficiaries (the beneficiary principle: *Morice* v *Bishop of Durham* (1804) 10 Ves 522), charitable trusts are enforced by the Attorney-General on behalf of the Crown. This itself leads to another difference between the two sorts of trusts. Thus, whereas certainty of objects is an essential requirement for a private trust (*Re Astor's Settlement Trusts* [1952] Ch 534), it is not necessary for a charitable trust. Provided the purposes of a trust are wholly and exclusively charitable and the public benefit element is satisfied, the trust will not fail merely because the purposes are vague. Thus a trust for 'charitable purposes' is a good charitable trust. Similarly, in *Re Smith* [1932] 1 Ch 153, a gift 'unto my country England' was held to be charitable. Where the purposes of a trust are wholly and exclusively charitable but vague, the court or the Charity Commissioners will settle a scheme applying the property to specific purposes. If, however, the expressed purposes are so vague that the property could, consistently with the terms of the trust, be applied to non-charitable purposes, the trust cannot be charitable. Thus a trust for 'the general welfare and benefit' of children in a children's home was held not charitable because it could be applied in the provision of television sets for juvenile delinquents. Such a purpose could not be considered to be within the spirit of the preamble to the Statute of Elizabeth 1601: *Re Cole* [1958] Ch 877.

If the objects of a private trust fail, the property (in the absence of any express provision) will usually go on a resulting trust for the settlor or the settlor's estate. By contrast, if the objects of a charitable trust fail, the property can sometimes be saved for charity by the application of a cy-près scheme; if the failure occurs before the property has vested in trust for the charity, a general charitable intention must be shown by the settlor: *Re Wilson* [1913] 1 Ch 314. Cy-près is also applicable to charitable trusts in the instances specified in the Charities Act 1993, s. 13; and there is provision for the alteration of the objects of small charities in s. 74. Funds raised for charitable purposes which fail may be applicable cy-près under the Charities Act 1993, s. 14.

Whereas private trusts are subject to both rules against perpetuities (the rule against remoteness of vesting and the rule against perpetual trusts), charitable trusts are subject only to the rule against remoteness of vesting. Even this is subject to the qualification that a gift over from one charity to another may validly occur outside the perpetuity period: *Christ's Hospital* v *Grainger* (1849) 1 Mac & G 460.

Further distinctions arise in regard to the trustees themselves. In the case of a private trust, subject to a contrary provision in the trust instrument, the decisions of the trustees must be unanimous: *Re Mayo* [1943] Ch 302. By contrast, in the case of a charitable trust, except where statute provides otherwise (e.g., in the Charities Act 1993, ss. 74, 75), decisions need only be by a simple majority: *Re Whiteley* [1910] 1 Ch 608. Again, whereas the maximum number of trustees of a private trust of land is four, there is no such limit if the trust is charitable: Trustee Act 1925, ss. 36(6), 34(3)(a).

It might also be mentioned briefly that charitable trusts enjoy certain important fiscal exemptions and reliefs as compared with private trusts: these include limited exemptions from income tax, capital gains tax and inheritance tax. They also enjoy relief from business rates.

(b) To be charitable a trust must be wholly and exclusively charitable. Although a trust for charitable purposes alone satisfies this requirement, a trust for charitable and deserving purposes may not do so. This is because 'deserving purposes' are not necessarily charitable. Whether the disposition in the problem is charitable depends, therefore, upon whether the word 'and' is construed conjunctively or disjunctively. The former construction means that every purpose to which the property can lawfully be applied must be both charitable and deserving; such a trust will therefore be charitable. The latter construction means that the property could be applied to purposes which are either charitable or deserving (but not necessarily both); such a trust is not wholly and exclusively charitable. In *Re Sutton* (1885) 28 ChD 464, a trust for 'charitable and deserving objects' was construed conjunctively and so held charitable. A similar construction was applied to the words 'charitable and benevolent' in *Re Best* [1904] 2 Ch 354. By contrast, 'charitable or public purposes' were construed disjunctively in *Blair* v *Duncan* [1902] AC 37, as were the words 'charitable or benevolent' in *Chichester Diocesan Fund* v *Simpson* [1944] AC 341. Similarly, a trust for 'charitable institutions ... or any ... institutions operating for the public good' was held not charitable in *A-G of the Cayman Islands* v *Wahr-Hansen* [2001] 1 AC 75, PC.

These cases might suggest that 'and' tends to be construed conjunctively, whereas 'or' is usually construed disjunctively. Ultimately, however, it all turns on a construction of the particular gift in the context of the instrument as a whole. Thus in *A-G of the Bahamas* v *Royal Trust Co.* [1986] 1 WLR 1001, the Privy Council held that a gift for the 'education and welfare' of Bahamian children was to be construed disjunctively. The trust was therefore void because 'welfare' purposes were not wholly and exclusively charitable.

Thus, while Jemima's gift (because it uses the word 'and') appears to be prima facie charitable, whether this is so is essentially a matter of construction. If the gift is held not to be wholly and exclusively charitable, it will probably fail both for uncertainty of objects and for unenforceability: *Morice* v *Bishop of Durham* (1805) 10 Ves 522.

QUESTION 4

(a) Consider how the cy-près doctrine has been extended by statute.

AND

(b) By his will made in 1975, Tommy gave his entire estate to his executors and trustees upon trust to use the same to build a hostel for the working people of Walkley. Tommy died last year. The value of his estate is insufficient to enable the hostel to be built. Tommy's next-of-kin are claiming his estate.

Discuss.

Commentary

Part (a) asks you to consider, not to describe. If you have the statutes in the examination room with you, there should be no problem with mere description, and clearly some description of the scope of the provisions is needed. The examiners, however, will be looking for more than a recitation of the statutory provisions. Simply copying out the statutory provisions will not achieve many marks: it is definitely not to be recommended!

Part (b) demands that you consider the charitable status of the gift before going on to consider a possible application cy-près.

Suggested Answer

(a)   Section 13 of the Charities Act 1993 re-enacts a provision in the Charities Act 1960 which extended the scope of the cy-près doctrine beyond cases of failure and surplus. The section specifies five circumstances in which the original purposes of a charitable gift can be altered. Paragraphs (a) and (b) apply where the purposes have been fulfilled, or cannot be carried out, or where they provide a use for part only of the gift. Paragraph (e)(i) and (ii) apply where the purposes have, since being laid down, been adequately provided for by other means, or have ceased to be charitable in law. This last provision might, for instance, be applicable if the courts were to hold the purposes of gun clubs (which can be charities under the principle in *Re Stephens* (1892) 8 TLR 792) no longer charitable. Essentially, however, these paragraphs merely put pre-existing cy-près circumstances onto a statutory basis.

Paragraph (c), however, was an important extension of the doctrine. It enables property to be applied cy-près where it, and other property applicable for similar purposes, can be more effectively used in conjunction and made applicable to common purposes. Before the Charities Act 1960, in the absence of failure or a surplus, neither the court nor the Charity Commissioners had power to alter the purposes of charities. Thus, whilst a scheme might facilitate the administration of several trusts for broadly similar charitable purposes, such scheme could not make any alteration to the specific purposes of each charitable trust: *Re Faraker* [1912] 2 Ch 488. This would now be possible.

Under paragraph (d), cy-près is permissible where the original purposes were laid down by reference to an area which has since ceased to be a unit for some other purposes, or by reference to a class of persons or to an area which has since ceased to be suitable or practical. *Peggs* v *Lamb* [1994] Ch 172 concerned a charitable trust for the freemen of Huntingdon, whose numbers had seriously declined. The court applied paragraph (d) in order to extend the class of persons who could benefit to everyone living in that borough.

Paragraph (e)(iii) applies where the original purposes have ceased 'in any other way' to provide a suitable and effective method of using the property. It was used in *Varsani* v *Jesani* [1999] 2 Ch 219, CA, where there was a split over doctrinal matters amongst adherents of a charitable trust which had been set up to promote the faith of a particular Hindu sect. The Court of Appeal directed that the property be applied cy-près between the majority and minority groups.

All the paragraphs except (b) require reference to 'the spirit of the gift'. In *Re Lepton's Charity* [1972] Ch 276 it was stated that this means the basic intention underlying the gift. In that case the court used paragraphs (a)(ii) and (e)(iii) to authorise an increase, to allow for inflation, in the stipend payable to a minister out of the income of an eighteenth-century charitable trust. It should also be noted that s. 13(2) apparently preserves the need for a general charitable intention where that was required before the Act, i.e., in cases of initial failure only. A general charitable intention is not therefore needed in any other cy-près circumstances in s. 13.

The Charities Act 1985 (now repealed) gave small charities additional powers to modify their objects. The power has been re-enacted (and procedurally simplified) in the Charities Act 1993, s. 74. The section applies only to a small charity, which means one with a gross annual income not exceeding £5,000, and it does not apply to a charity which holds land for its particular purposes. Under s. 74(2)(c) the charity trustees may resolve to modify the trusts of the charity by replacing its purposes with other charitable purposes. This power applies only if the charity trustees are satisfied that the existing purposes have ceased to be conducive to a suitable and effective application of the charity's resources, and that the specified purposes are as similar to those existing purposes as is practical in the circumstances: s. 74(5). No such scheme can take effect, however, without the Charity Commissioners' consent.

(b) The specified purpose, a hostel for the working people, may be a charitable purpose. For a trust to be charitable its purpose must fall within the letter or the spirit of the preamble to the Statute of Elizabeth 1601. A simpler classification was the four-fold one of Lord Macnaghten in *Pemsel's Case* [1891] AC 531. The first head of charity listed by Lord Macnaghten was the relief of poverty. Poverty is not confined to destitution but includes simply going short. The trust may still be charitable for the relief of poverty if a poverty requirement can be inferred from the instrument — as occurred in *Re Cottam* [1955] 1 WLR 1299 — but not from extrinsic evidence alone: *Re Drummond* [1914] 2 Ch 90. In *Re Sanders' Will Trusts* [1954] Ch 265, a trust to provide dwellings for the working classes in Pembroke Dock was held not to be charitable: the judge did not consider the working classes were necessarily poor. By contrast, in *Re Niyazi's Will Trusts* [1978] 1 WLR 910, Megarry V-C held that a trust to build a working men's hostel in Cyprus was charitable: the case was near the borderline, but the two expressions together contained just enough indication that the purpose was to relieve poverty. On this basis, the present trust is likely to be held charitable.

If the trust is held to be charitable, the next issue is the insufficiency of the estate. This ranks as a failure of the purpose, which is a cy-près circumstance within the Charities Act 1993, s. 13. Since the trust fails *ab initio*, however, the court must be satisfied that the testator had a general charitable intention, i.e., an intention to benefit a wider purpose than that specified: *Biscoe* v *Jackson* (1887) 35 ChD 460. The issue is whether the testator intended the avowed purpose to be merely a means of effecting a wider purpose: see *Re Wilson* [1913] 1 Ch 314 and *Re Lysaght* [1966] 1 Ch 191. Whether a general charitable intention is present is ascertained by construing the words used in the context of the instrument as a whole and in the light of admissible extrinsic evidence: *Re Woodhams* [1981] 1 WLR 493. Generally, the more detailed the specified purpose, the more difficult it becomes to find the requisite intention: *Re Good's Will Trusts* [1950] 2 All ER 653. On the other hand, the fact that a gift is one of residue (or of the testator's entire estate) may indicate a general charitable intention, since no specified amount is provided: cf *Re Goldschmidt* [1957] 1 WLR 524.

If a general charitable intention is found, the property will be applied cy-près; if not, it will pass to Tommy's next-of-kin.

QUESTION 5

(a)   By his will made in 1990, Boris, who died last month, gave one third of his residuary estate to each of the following institutions: the Rotherham Rabbit Sanctuary; the Dronfield Donkey Home; and the Broomhill Animal Hospital.

The Rotherham Rabbit Sanctuary was an incorporated charity, which closed last week. In accordance with a provision in its constitution, its members have decided to apply its assets to another charity, the South Yorkshire Rabbit Fund. The Dronfield Donkey Home was an unincorporated charitable association which ceased to exist a year before Boris's death because of lack of funds. No institution called the Broomhill Animal Hospital has ever existed.

Advise Boris's executors how they should deal with Boris's residuary estate.

AND

(b)   Last year, the residents of the village of Eastwick decided to raise funds to build a cottage hospital. Money was raised for this purpose by means of street collections and the sale of raffle tickets. The appeal fund trustees also received a large number of cheques for various amounts. Unfortunately, the total sums raised proved insufficient to enable the hospital to be built.

Advise the trustees how they should deal with the funds raised.

Commentary

The candidate should note that in part **(a)**, the question states that the first two named institutions were charities. There are therefore no marks to be obtained from discussing whether the institutions with these names are charitable.

For essays on the statutory predecessor to the Charities Act 1993, s. 14, the student is referred to the valuable article by Wilson, [1983] Conv 40. There is also a general discussion of the impact of the original section in Luxton, *Charity Fund-raising and the Public Interest*, Avebury, 1990, pp. 136–49. Other sources of fund-raising which a question such as this might require you to deal with are membership subscriptions and deeds of covenant. The student should note carefully the amendments which were made when the original section was re-enacted in the Charities Act 1993.

Suggested Answer

(a) A gift to an incorporated charity, such as the Rotherham Rabbit Sanctuary, will be construed as a gift to the particular institution beneficially, unless (which does not appear to be the case here) the words of the will indicate otherwise: *Re Vernon's Will Trusts* [1972] Ch 300n, applied *Re ARMS (Multiple Sclerosis Research) Ltd* [1997] 1 WLR 877. Therefore, as the Sanctuary was in existence at Boris's death, the gift to it would have vested on his death, and will be applied in the same way as its existing assets: *Re Slevin* [1891] 2 Ch 230. In *Re Slevin* itself, the court held that the legacy passed, with the charity's other assets, to the Crown, but this might be explained on the basis that the members of the charity had not made provision for the application of its assets to another similar charitable institution before its dissolution. In the problem, therefore, this share of Boris's residuary estate will pass to the South Yorkshire Rabbit Fund.

As the Dronfield Donkey Home ceased to exist before Boris's death, it might appear that the gift would lapse, in the same way that a gift by will to an individual generally lapses if the legatee predeceases the testator. The Home was, however, an unincorporated charitable association, and it has been held that a gift to such an institution is treated as being made upon trust for its purposes: *Re Vernon's Will Trusts*. If, therefore, those purposes are still capable of being carried out, the gift will be applied to them. The failure of the particular institution, the Home, is regarded as a mere failure of the particular machinery by which those purposes were to be carried into effect, not a failure of the purposes themselves. A scheme will therefore be needed; but as the purposes are the same, this is not a cy-près scheme, so no general charitable intention need be sought.

If the purposes of the Dronfield Donkey Home can no longer be carried out after its closure, however, there will be a failure of the purposes of the gift. As the institution closed before Boris's death, the failure will be failure *ab initio*. This share of residue can therefore be applied cy-près only if a general charitable intention can be found on Boris's part. A general charitable intention means an intention to benefit charity in a broader way than merely benefiting the particular named institution: *Re Finger's Will Trusts* [1972] Ch 286. Where (as here) a specific institution has been named, the finding of a general charitable intention might be difficult (*Re Rymer* [1895] 1 Ch 19; *Re Spence* [1979] Ch 483); but it is not impossible (*Re Finger's Will Trusts*). It is a matter of construction of Boris's will whether a general charitable intention can be found. The fact that the gift is one of residue is slight evidence that a general charitable intention might be present: *Re Goldschmidt* [1957] 1 WLR 524. The fact that a gift is one of several to charity in the same will might also suggest a general charitable intention (*Re Satterthwaite's Will Trusts* [1966] 1 WLR 277); but whether this principle can be applied here depends upon whether the gift to the Broomhill Animal Hospital is charitable (which is considered below). If no general charitable intention can be found, this second share of residue will go (in the absence of any gift over) on resulting trust for Boris's next-of-kin.

As no such institution by the name of the Broomhill Animal Hospital has ever existed, the court will first need to determine if Boris has merely misdescribed an existing institution which does exist: *Bunting* v *Marriott* (1854) 19 Beav 163. If he has, that share of residue will simply pass to that institution (regardless of whether it is a charity or not). In the absence of mere misdescription, the gift will fail *ab initio* unless it can be applied cy-près. The cy-près doctrine is, however, available only to charitable gifts, and it is unclear whether Boris had a charitable institution in mind, or a non-charitable institution, such as an anti-vivisection society. In *Re Jenkins's Will Trusts* [1966] Ch 249, it was held that a gift to a non-existent anti-vivisection society was clearly not a charitable gift and so not applicable cy-près.

In the problem, however, the name of the legatee does not necessarily suggest a non-charitable body, and is consistent with a charitable institution. In *Re Satterthwaite's Will Trusts*, the court considered that the fact that the gift to a non-existent animal hospital was one of several made to charity in the will, indicated both that a charitable institution was intended and that the testator had a general charitable intention. In that case, therefore, the court applied the gift to the non-existent institution cy-près. If the court were able to take the same approach to the gift to the Broomhill Animal Hospital, it too would be applicable cy-près. It has also been pointed out that if a gift is made to a non-existent charitable institution, it is easier to find a general charitable intention than if the gift is made to an institution which formerly existed but has closed down: *Re Harwood* [1936] Ch 285. If the gift is found not to be to a charitable institution, or not to be made with a general charitable intention, this share of residue will pass (in the absence of a gift over) to Boris's next-of-kin.

(b) The provision of a cottage hospital is clearly a charitable purpose: the relief of the 'impotent' is expressly mentioned in the preamble to the Statute of Elizabeth 1601, and it falls within the fourth head of charity as classified by Lord Macnaghten in *Pemsel's Case* [1891] AC 531, namely, other purposes beneficial to the community (see *Re Resch* [1969] 1 AC 514).

The insufficiency of the funds raised means that the charitable purpose has failed *ab initio*. In such circumstances, equity itself does not permit an application cy-près unless the donors had a general charitable intention. Donors putting money in collecting boxes, however, might be presumed to be giving for a specific purpose and not with a general charitable intention. Thus, in *Re Gillingham Bus Disaster Fund* [1959] Ch 62, CA, anonymous contributions to a non-charitable fund were ordered to be held for such contributors on a resulting trust.

To avoid a similar outcome with failed charitable collections, the Charities Act 1993, s. 14 (which re-enacts with amendments provisions originally contained in the Charities Act 1960) provides that, in certain circumstances, funds given to charity are applicable cy-près, i.e., to other charitable purposes similar to those for which the funds were raised. Section 14(1) can apply only where (*inter alia*) the property belongs to donors who gave for specific charitable purposes which fail. It has been argued that the section has little impact on anonymous contributions, since these never belong to the donors: Wilson, [1983] Conv 40. First, anonymous contributions may be treated as abandoned and so pass as *bona vacantia* to the Crown, which results in an application cy-près: see dicta in *Re Ulverston* [1956] Ch 622. Secondly, they may be treated as having been given out and out: see dicta of Denning LJ in *Re Hillier* [1954] 1 WLR 700. Out and out gifts might be considered to be made with the widest possible general charitable intention: see Sheridan and Delany, *The Cy-près Doctrine*, London: Sweet & Maxwell, 1959.

If, however, s. 14 applies, some donations made by cheque may be applicable cy-près under s. 14(1): first, where, after prescribed advertisements and inquiries, a donor cannot be identified or found; and, secondly, where a donor has executed a disclaimer in the prescribed form: s. 14(1). Some of remaining donors by cheque may have given such small amounts that it would be unreasonable to incur expense in returning their money. This is dealt with by s. 14(4), which enables the court to treat property as belonging to unidentifiable donors where it would be unreasonable either:

(i)   having regard to the amounts likely to be returned to the donors, to incur the expense of returning it; or

(ii)   having regard to the nature, circumstances and amount of the gifts, and the lapse of time since they were made, for the donors to expect them to be returned.

A donor who cannot be identified, but whose donation is applied cy-près other than by virtue of s. 14(3) or (4), must claim within six months of the making of the scheme. The charity trustees are permitted to deduct properly incurred expenses from any repayment: s. 14(5). This sub-section might deal, for instance, with a large donation made by a donor who cannot be identified or found.

The street collections and the money raised by raffles will be dealt with by s. 14(3). Thus the proceeds of cash collections made by means of collecting boxes and (*inter alia*) of any lottery (after allowing for prizes) are deemed (without advertisement or inquiry) to belong to unidentifiable donors. Such money will therefore be applicable cy-près.

7 Trusts of Imperfect Obligation

INTRODUCTION

This is a brief topic upon which it is possible to find discrete questions, but it may also be incorporated into questions on other topics such as certainties or charities. For an example of this, see Chapter 6, question 3 (a) the answer to which requires at least a mention of the 'beneficiary principle'. It is an important topic in that it deals with one of the fundamental principles of trusts. Comparatively recently, the courts have devised convenient interpretations of the rules to save dispositions which might otherwise fail as purpose trusts. These cases (referred to in the suggested answers) are important and a familiarity with them is essential to a study of this subject.

QUESTION 1

Daniel, who died recently, made the following dispositions in his will:

(a) £50,000 to the Seaview District Council for the erection and maintenance of a statue on the promenade in memory of my late wife.

(b) £5,000 for the care of my cat Tortoiseshell and any kittens she may have.

(c) £20,000 for the fostering of cordial relations and understanding between countries.

(d) The residue of my estate to the Cranford Cricket Club for the purpose of building a new pavilion and changing rooms.

The Cranford Cricket Club is a non-charitable unincorporated association.

Advise Daniel's executors as to the validity of these dispositions.

Commentary

This is a typical problem question on this area of the law, where the examiner chooses from the cases examples of trusts which may or may not fail for certainty of objects or perpetuity. Although it is a fairly compact area of law, you need to know the cases on it and the reasoning applied in them to answer the question well.

It is possible that such a question might also include a charitable disposition. For example, in part (a), if the disposition had been for the erection and maintenance of a shelter on the promenade, it might have been valid as a charitable disposition under the fourth head of charity (trusts for other purposes beneficial to the community).

To obtain good marks on such a question, you would probably have to demonstrate not merely a knowledge of any authorities which may be relevant to the precise terms of the gifts, but also a broader understanding of the underlying principles, for example, a knowledge of the cases on monuments in part (a) and of Cross J's analysis of gifts to unincorporated associations in part (d).

This area of the law being fairly self-contained should, however, be an area on which well-prepared students should be able to acquit themselves well.

Suggested Answer

(a) To be valid, a trust must comply with the requirement for certainty of objects, that is, there must be ascertainable persons able to enforce the trust. In *Morice v Bishop of Durham* (1805) 10 Ves 522 a trust for 'such objects of benevolence and liberality as the Bishop of Durham in his own discretion shall most approve of' was held to be void. Grant MR said that such 'an uncontrollable power of disposition would be ownership and not trust'.

To be valid a trust must also comply with the rule against perpetual trusts, unless it is a charitable trust.

The gift in this clause is essentially a trust for a purpose and there are no particular objects that are able to enforce it. It cannot be brought within any of the four heads of charity in *Pemsel's Case* [1891] AC 531 and is therefore a non-charitable purpose trust. It is not dissimilar to the disposition in *Re Endacott* [1960] Ch 232, where a testator left his residuary estate to the North Tawton parish council 'for the purpose of providing some useful memorial to myself'. The gift could not take effect as an outright gift to the parish council as the purpose attached to it created a trust. It was not charitable, and was too wide and uncertain to fall within the anomalous cases 'when Homer has nodded' (per Harman LJ), namely, the maintenance of tombs. A valid trust within this category should probably have some funerary association and should not be excessive in amount (*Re Endacott*). £50,000 might well be regarded as excessive.

The courts have made a concession for such trusts for the maintenance of tombs and monuments and of individual animals (such trusts having been described by Roxburgh J in *Re Astor's Settlement Trusts* [1952] Ch 534 at p. 547 as 'concessions to human weakness or sentiment'), but only as regards lack of objects and not perpetuity, so that a trust for the erection and maintenance of a monument limited to 21 years might be valid. The gift here is for the maintenance of the statue as well as its erection, and therefore will be void additionally as infringing the perpetuity rule.

If the statue could be regarded as a monument then a donation for its erection, but not its maintenance, might be valid under this exception to the general rule (*Mussett v Bingle* (1876) WN 171).

(b)   Although a trust for the care of animals generally (*Re Wedgwood* [1915] 1 Ch 113) and the care of cats in particular (*Re Moss* [1949] 1 All ER 495) can be a charitable trust, a trust for the care of individual animals is not. Nevertheless, a trust for the care of individual animals can be valid as a private trust, this being another anomalous exception to the rule requiring certainty of objects. Again, however, any such trust must not infringe the rule against perpetuities.

Although there are cases such as *Re Haines, The Times*, 7 November 1952 and *Re Dean* (1889) 41 ChD 552, where the judges appear to have taken judicial notice of the fact that the particular animals concerned would be unlikely to live beyond the perpetuity period (a cat in *Re Haines* and horses and hounds in *Re Dean*), it would seem that such judicial indulgence is misguided. The rule against perpetual trusts, which was expressly preserved by the Perpetuities and Accumulations Act 1964, s. 15(4), must be applied at the time the trust is created and it must be possible to say at that time that the trust will not continue for longer than the perpetuity period, which in the present case is 21 years. Moreover, the rule against perpetuities has never recognised animal lives as lives in being for the purposes of calculating the perpetuity period (*Re Kelly* [1932] IR 255).

One must therefore conclude that the disposition to Tortoiseshell and her kittens is void, although had it been limited to 21 years or 'for so long as the law allows' then it could have been valid for 21 years. It could also have been limited to the life or lives in being of a person or persons living plus 21 years as in *Re Howard, The Times*, 30 October 1908, where the lifetime of the survivor of two specified servants was used to measure the perpetuity period for the maintenance of a parrot.

(c)   This disposition would again be a purpose trust without objects able to enforce it and would therefore fail unless it could be brought under one of the heads of charitable trusts. However, a disposition with laudable objects is not necessarily charitable and it is unlikely that this one would be. Although similar objects were held to be charitable within the head of education in *Re Koeppler's Will Trusts* [1986] Ch 423, the disposition there was to 'Wilton Hall', a recognised series of lectures which the testator had organised during his lifetime. This is much more vague however in its application.

In *Re Astor's Settlement Trusts* a trust for (*inter alia*) the maintenance of good understanding between nations and the preservation of the independence and integrity of the newspapers was considered too vague and uncertain as to its application for the court to administer and was void.

(d) A gift to a non-charitable unincorporated association may also fail for lack of certainty of objects and for perpetuity.

There have been cases where the courts have interpreted gifts to associations as being gifts to the current members beneficially as in *Re Clarke* (1901) 2 Ch 110, where a gift to the 'Corps. of Commissionaires' was held to be a valid gift to the members beneficially for the time being.

In *Re Lipinski's Will Trusts* [1976] Ch 235 however, Oliver J followed the principle of *Re Denley's Trust Deed* [1968] 1 Ch 373 by finding that although a trust for the erection of buildings for the Hull Judeans (Maccabi) Association was expressed as a purpose trust, it was in fact for the benefit of ascertainable individuals, namely, the members of the club, and he therefore held the trust to be valid. It was argued that because the testator had made the gift in memory of his late wife, this tended to a perpetuity and precluded the association members for the time being from enjoying the gift beneficially: this argument was rejected by Oliver J. Applying the principle of *Re Lipinski's Will Trusts* to this disposition therefore, it might well not fail for certainty of objects.

The further requirement of compliance with the rule against perpetuities must also be satisfied as regards a disposition to an unincorporated association. Gifts to members of an unincorporated association were considered in detail by Cross J in *Neville Estates Ltd* v *Madden* [1962] Ch 832. He identified two categories of gifts to unincorporated associations which would not infringe the perpetuity rule, namely, where the gift is to the members themselves as joint tenants beneficially, or to the members as members of the association, but there is nothing in the rules of the association to preclude the members from deciding, if they so choose, to divide the gift up between themselves. In both these cases the possibility of immediate division of the gift makes it inoffensive to the rule against perpetuities. Cross J's third category however is where there is some factor, such as the rules of the association (see *Re Grant's Will Trusts* [1980] 1 WLR 360), or the nature of the gift (see *Leahy* v *A-G (NSW)* [1959] AC 457), which precludes any immediate division of it between the members of the association for the time being. Such gifts will be void. This analysis by Cross J was adopted by Brightman J in *Re Recher* [1972] 1 Ch 526 where he was prepared to accept as valid a gift to the members of an association on a contractual basis according to the terms of the association's rules, which did not preclude the members from dividing up the gift between themselves if they so decided.

Assuming that there is nothing in the rules of the Cranford Cricket Club which would preclude the members for the time being from dividing the gift between themselves if they decided to do so, the gift would not fail for perpetuity and could therefore be a valid trust.

QUESTION 2

> There can be no trust over the exercise of which this court will not assume control ... (Grant MR in *Morice* v *Bishop of Durham* (1804) 10 Ves 522).

Keeton and Sheridan, *The Law of Trusts*, 10th edn, London: Professional Books Ltd, 1974, wrote:

> Modern cases regard (Grant MR) as saying that a trust must have definite human or corporate objects or be charitable. Construing his judgment in this sense has impeded the development of purpose trusts.

Explain the rationale for Grant MR's dictum and discuss the solutions which the courts have found to some of the problems raised by the rule.

Commentary

This is a fairly typical essay question on trusts of imperfect obligation which requires you to demonstrate an understanding of the rationale for such a rule. You should also be aware of the criticisms of the rule and the ways in which the courts have mitigated the harshness of it in some of the more recent cases.

Suggested Answer

One of the three requirements for certainty for a trust is certainty of objects. The reason expressed for this by Grant MR was that there must be a person or persons able to enforce the obligations of the trust against the trustees, as otherwise property would be left in their hands entirely without obligation attaching to it. This would abnegate the essential nature of a trust of division of legal and equitable ownership and would be equivalent to unfettered ownership.

Trusts for charitable purposes are enforced by the Attorney-General so that this problem does not arise. However, trusts for non-charitable purposes clearly do present a problem in this respect.

A further objection to enforcing a non-charitable purpose trust is the difficulty of interpreting and applying the purpose. This was illustrated in *Re Astor's*

Settlement Trusts [1952] Ch 534. The court must be able to control and administer a trust itself if necessary. Any uncertainty or ambiguity as to the purpose to be carried out will make this impossible and is a further reason for the invalidity of such trusts.

A further problem with non-charitable purpose trusts is the unlimited scope of purposes which the courts might be called upon to recognise as valid. Although many non-charitable purpose trusts might be useful and beneficial to some persons, other such purported trusts may benefit nobody. The case of *Brown* v *Burdett* (1882) 21 ChD 667, where a house was left in trust to be shut up for 20 years, illustrates the undesirable purposes for which eccentric testators might create trusts. Such capricious trusts will not be recognised. However, any decision on the desirability or otherwise of any particular purpose necessarily involves a difficult value judgment. From a practical point of view, Roxburgh J said in *Re Astor's Settlement Trusts* 'it is not possible to contemplate with equanimity the creation of large funds devoted to non-charitable purposes which no court and no department of State can control, or in the case of maladministration, reform'.

Non-charitable purpose trusts must also comply with the perpetuity rule. An application of this rule invalidates any non-charitable purpose trust which might subsist for more than a life or lives in being plus 21 years, or if no lives are specified, then for more than 21 years. Purpose trusts infringe this rule if they provide for the tying up of capital for more than the permitted period. If all the capital can be spent at once, this problem does not arise: *Re Lipinski's Will Trusts* [1976] Ch 235.

Nevertheless, it must be conceded that many purpose trusts may be valuable and for the law automatically to deny validity to them is harsh. There are certain exceptions to the rule therefore which have always been recognised, and more recently the courts have been prepared to interpret purpose trusts more generously where possible to recognise 'indirect' objects and so validate them.

The clearly recognised anomalous exceptions are trusts for the maintenance of tombs and monuments and of individual animals. All such trusts must, however, comply with the perpetuity rule.

A gift to an unincorporated association may necessarily involve problems as to both certainty of objects and perpetuity, as the association is a fluctuating body of people which may include future members, and may have purposes which are perpetual. This problem was addressed by Cross J in *Neville Estates Ltd* v

Madden [1962] Ch 832, who was able to find that a disposition to the members for the time being beneficially (either as joint tenants or tenants in common) is unobjectionable. They themselves are the object of the gift and so they may, if they wish, divide the gift between themselves at any time. Such a disposition is also unobjectionable on the point of perpetuity.

A second possibility is that the gift is one to the members as members of the association, in which case they take beneficially, but subject to the contractual rules of the association. Provided that there is nothing in the rules to prevent the members from agreeing to change them if necessary in order to take the gift beneficially, then the gift will again be unobjectionable on grounds of certainty of objects or perpetuity. If however, there is something in the nature or terms of the gift, or the rules of the association, which precludes the members from taking beneficially, then the gift will be for the purposes of the association and will offend the certainty of objects rule and possibly also the perpetuity rule. In *Re Grant's Will Trusts* [1980] 1 WLR 260 the rules of the local Chertsey and Walton Constituency Labour Party were subject to the rules of the National Labour Party and could not be altered by the local party. The members could not alter the rules to make the gift one which they had control over and it therefore failed.

In *Re Recher's Will Trusts* [1972] Ch 526 Brightman J found that a gift to an anti-vivisection society would have been valid as within Cross J's second category, although it might have surprised the testatrix to know that this was the legal position! (In this case, a gift to an amalgamated association which was incorporated after the testatrix's death was void, as it contemplated a different contractual situation from that subsisting at death.)

In *Re Denley's Trust Deed* [1968] 1 Ch 373 land was left on trust for use as a recreation ground for the employees of a company. Goff J upheld the trust as he was able to find that the employees were the *de facto* beneficiaries, even though the trust was expressed as a purpose trust, and so had *locus standi* to enforce the trust. This was followed in *Re Lipinski's Will Trusts* where a trust 'solely' for the erection and improvement of new buildings for the Hull Judeans (Maccabi) Association was held to be valid on two separate grounds, one of them being that the members of the association could be treated as the *de facto* objects of the trust. The other ground was on the contract-holding construction described in *Re Recher's Will Trusts*. Oliver J held in *Re Lipinski* that the expressed purpose of the gift being 'in memory of my late wife' did not imply an intention to create a permanent endowment but was merely a tribute to the testator's wife and therefore did not necessarily tend to a perpetuity.

Clearly legal recognition afforded only to trusts with objects able to enforce them is open to criticism on the grounds of harshness and inflexibility and creates difficulties with endowments for unincorporated associations. Whilst any general abrogation of the rule would be undesirable, the modifications made by the courts where there are discernible 'indirect' objects are to be welcomed.

8 Implied and Resulting Trusts

INTRODUCTION

Apart from difficulties of classification, this topic should not cause great intellectual difficulties. This area, which takes well to problem questions, may well be mixed with another — there is often a combination with constructive trusts.

QUESTION 1

Distinguish a resulting trust from an implied trust and a constructive trust.

Commentary

This question raises difficult, but absorbing, issues. Students deeply interested should read Birks, P., *An Introduction to the Law of Restitution*, Oxford University Press, 1985, which places many different areas of law, including the law of trusts and the rules relating to tracing, in a restitutionary framework.

Suggested Answer

The Law of Property Act 1925, s. 53(2) excludes from the scope of s. 53(1) the creation or operation of 'resulting, implied or constructive trusts'. This might suggest that these are different examples within a single classification; but this is not so. These are, in fact, examples drawn from different methods of classification, and the terms are not therefore necessarily mutually exclusive.

The term 'resulting trust', is ambiguous. As Professor Birks has indicated, it appears to be used in two distinct senses: Birks, *An Introduction to the Law of Restitution*, pp. 57-64. First, it is used merely descriptively, i.e., to denote a trust under which a transferor or settlor retains a beneficial interest. Birks calls such a trust 'resulting in pattern'. In this sense, a beneficial interest, retained by a settlor under even an express trust, can be described as resulting: e.g., where S transfers property to T in trust for B for life, remainder for S himself. Secondly, the term is used to denote, additionally, that the settlor's interest under such a trust arises only by implication — which therefore makes it a particular species of implied (or presumed) trust. Birks calls such a trust 'resulting in origin'.

An implied trust is a trust which arises from the presumed intention of the transferor. Thus if A transfers property into the name of B, who is in law a stranger, there is an equitable presumption (except, perhaps, in the case of land) that B holds the legal title in trust for A: *Re Vinogradoff* [1935] WN 68. The presumption (which can easily be rebutted by evidence of a contrary intention) is therefore one of resulting trust. Where an implied trust leaves the beneficial interest with the settlor, it is also (in both senses) a resulting trust.

Because of this closeness of identity, resulting trusts have sometimes been treated as synonymous with implied trusts. This, however, disregards the fact that some trusts classifiable as implied (e.g., those arising under mutual wills) are not resulting. It is equally wrong to treat resulting trusts solely as a sub-species of implied trust because, as Megarry J lucidly explained at first instance in *Re Vandervell's Trusts (No. 2)* [1974] Ch 269, not all resulting trusts are implied. Megarry J there distinguished between 'presumed resulting trusts', which arise from the implied intention of the transferor, and 'automatic resulting trusts', which do not depend upon intentions or presumptions, but are an automatic consequence of the transferor's failure to dispose of what is vested in him. An automatic resulting trust therefore arises where, for instance, S transfers property to T upon trust for B for life, but does not state what is to happen to the property on B's death. In this instance, the resulting trust arises, not from S's implied intention, but merely from S's failure to dispose of the entire beneficial interest in the property transferred to T.

The distinction between the two types of resulting trust emerged in the litigation involving the Vandervell family. In *Vandervell v IRC* [1967] 2 AC 291, the House of Lords held that Mr Vandervell was liable to pay tax on dividends declared on shares which he had transferred to a charity. One reason was that he had failed to dispose of his interest in a resulting trust of an option to repurchase the shares. The retention of an interest under a resulting trust was probably the last thing Mr Vandervell intended, since it deprived the scheme of the very tax advantages which it was designed to secure. As Megarry J pointed out in *Re Vandervell's Trusts (No. 2)*, however, Mr Vandervell's interest under a resulting trust was automatic, and not based upon his presumed intention.

A different view was taken in *Davis v Richards & Wallington Industries Ltd* [1990] 1 WLR 1551, where Scott J inferred from the circumstances that the members of a pension scheme should not be taken to have intended to retain any interest in a surplus by way of resulting trust. Similarly, in *Westdeutsche Landesbank Girocentrale v Islington LBC* [1996] AC 669, at p. 708, Lord Browne-Wilkinson doubted that there was such a thing as an automatic resulting trust; in his view, all resulting trusts are based on intention. More recently, however, Lord Millett, giving the advice of the Privy Council in *Air Jamaica Ltd v Charlton* [1999] 1 WLR 1399, at p. 1412, whilst expressing the view that a resulting trust gives effect to intention, said that that a resulting trust can arise even when the transferor positively wishes to part with the beneficial interest, and he expressed the view that, on this point, *Davis v Richards & Wallington Industries Ltd* was wrongly decided. Lord Millett's observations effectively support the automatic resulting trust, since, in the light of his comments, it is difficult to see how evidence of intention could ever rebut a resulting trust of this sort: see Harpum [2000] Conv 170, at p. 178.

It has been said that both resulting and constructive trusts arise by operation of law, although only the former give effect to intention: *Air Jamaica Ltd* v *Charlton*, at p. 1412 (Lord Millett). Indeed, a constructive trust frequently arises regardless of intention. In English law, a constructive trust is not founded on a single principle, but it might be broadly stated that it is a trust imposed by equity in specific circumstances to promote justice and good conscience. In some circumstances these objectives might involve the imposition of a constructive trust in order to ensure that effect is given to the intention of a settlor (as under the rule in *Re Rose* [1952] Ch 499) or of parties to an agreement. Examples within the latter category are the trusts which arise under mutual wills, or the common intention constructive trust in relation to a family home (as illustrated in *Grant* v *Edwards* [1986] Ch 638). Since these sorts of constructive trust are based upon the intention of the parties, they might also be classified as implied trusts. Such constructive trusts are also closely akin to the doctrine of proprietary estoppel: *Yaxley* v *Gotts* [2000] Ch 162, CA.

A resulting trust is always a substantive trust, and therefore arises from the moment the defendant has the property in his hands. A constructive trust, by contrast, although generally treated as a substantive institution, does sometimes have remedial overtones (as in the case of the trust which arises under mutual wills). In the *Westdeutsche Landesbank* case, Lord Browne-Wilkinson opined that there might be merit in developing the concept of a remedial constructive trust in English law as part of the broader development of the law of restitution. The advantage of a remedial constructive trust (which is recognised in the USA) would be that it would arise only when imposed by the court instead of when the property was acquired by the defendant, and so would not interfere unjustly with the property rights of third parties.

An area in which the distinction between a resulting and a constructive trust has not always been made clear is in the determination of beneficial interests in a family home where the parties have failed to specify what their interests should be. The original source of the confusion is to be found in dicta of Lord Diplock in *Gissing* v *Gissing* [1971] AC 886, HL. In various cases in the Court of Appeal, Lord Denning MR attempted to develop the concept of a new model constructive trust of a remedial nature. This approach was subsequently rejected in *Burns* v *Burns* [1984] Ch 317, CA, and in *Lloyds Bank plc* v *Rosset* [1991] AC 107, HL.

Some recent cases have, however, renewed the confusion between resulting and constructive trusts in relation to the family home. Under a resulting trust the size of the claimant's share is determined by the amount of his or her contribution: *Re Densham* [1975] 1 WLR 1519. By contrast, under a common intention constructive trust the size of the share depends upon the agreement of the parties. In *Midland Bank plc* v *Cooke* [1995] 4 All ER 562, however, the Court of Appeal held that a wife who had contributed less than 7% of the purchase price was nevertheless entitled to a half share in the matrimonial home. The fact that she had contributed financially indicated that she was to have a beneficial interest; and the court inferred from the circumstances that the parties intended her to have an interest, even though there was no evidence that they had ever discussed this matter. Furthermore, in calculating the size of that interest, the court considered that it could have regard to the parties' overall conduct, whether such conduct related to the acquisition of a beneficial interest or not. The decision seems to revive the confusion between resulting and constructive trusts which it was thought that *Lloyds Bank plc* v *Rosset* had finally expunged. Similar criticisms can also be made of *Drake* v *Whipp* [1996] 1 FLR 826, CA.

QUESTION 2

In 1993, Rook bought shares which he transferred into the name of his nephew, Pawn, then aged 17. Pawn, however, delivered the share certificate to Rook, and always paid the dividends he received in respect of the shares into Rook's own bank account.

In 1995 Rook voluntarily, and without any expression of intention, conveyed his freehold land known as 'Castle' into Pawn's name.

Last year Rook handed Pawn a cheque in the sum of £5,000 which he had made out in Pawn's favour. At the same time Rook declared: 'This is to enable you to pay your creditors.' In fact Pawn's debts at the time amounted only to £3,000. Having paid off his creditors, Pawn gave the balance of £2,000 to his girlfriend, Queenie.

Rook died recently. In his will he gave all his property to Knight.

Advise Knight whether he has any claim to the shares, to 'Castle', or to the money received by Queenie.

Commentary

Only candidates who think that the expression '*in loco parentis*' means that your father is a train driver should experience difficulty with this question. Note that, as all the issues depend upon matters of construction and evidence, no definite conclusions are reached upon the facts.

Suggested Answer

As the sole beneficiary under Rook's will, Knight will have a claim to these items of property if he can establish that Rook retained a beneficial interest in them by way of a resulting trust. Let us deal with each item in turn.

The Shares

In certain cases, where a person puts his property into the name of another, it is presumed (in the absence of evidence to the contrary) that he intended the legal title to carry with it the beneficial interest. This is known as the presumption of advancement. It arises in three instances: transfers from husband to wife; transfers from a father to his legitimate child; and transfers from a person *in loco parentis* to his quasi-child. Transfers which do not fall within these three categories are known as transfers to strangers. Here the presumption is reversed, i.e., there is a presumption of resulting trust. It is presumed that the transferor did not intend the legal title to carry with it the beneficial interest. These presumptions are weak and are easily rebutted by evidence of the transferor's intention. Even evidence of a close relationship between the parties may be sufficient: *Fowkes* v *Pascoe* (1875) 10 Ch App 343; contrast *Re Vinogradoff* [1935] WN 68.

There is nothing in the question to indicate that, at the time he transferred the shares into the name of his nephew, Pawn, Rook stood *in loco parentis* to Pawn. In the absence of contrary evidence, therefore, the presumption is that Pawn holds the shares on a resulting trust for Rook. It is necessary to consider the impact upon this presumption of Pawn's acts subsequent to the transfer. The payment of the dividends to Rook is somewhat equivocal: it could indicate that Pawn considers himself merely a trustee for Rook, who (under a resulting trust) would have the entire equitable interest under the trust and thus (*inter alia*) a right to the dividends received. On the other hand, the payment to Rook of the dividends could be characterised as merely a series of independent gifts to Rook, of property which is now Pawn's both at law and in equity: see the judgment of Lord Denning MR in *Re Vandervell's Trusts (No. 2)* [1974] Ch 269, CA.

Pawn's delivery of the share certificate to Rook per se is evidence of a resulting trust, since it effectively puts it out of Pawn's power to deal with the shares.

Unless this can be explained on some other basis — that the certificate was returned, for instance, to Rook for safe-keeping — it points away from Pawn having the beneficial interest in the shares. However, were Rook found to be *in loco parentis* to Pawn in 1993, the mere delivery to Rook of the share certificate might not be sufficient to rebut the presumption of advancement: see *Scawin* v *Scawin* (1841) 1 Y & CCC 65. Some additional evidence may be needed: in *Warren* v *Gurney* [1944] 2 All ER 472, CA, this was supplied by a contemporaneous declaration by the father that no gift was intended. In the present case, the additional factor may be the gift of the dividends. Such evidence is not as cogent, however, as that in *Re Gooch* (1890) 62 LT 384. There, a father bought shares in a company in the name of his son, but the latter always paid the dividends to his father and even handed him the share certificate. Additionally, it was shown that the shares were transferred to the son in order that he could qualify as a director of the company. The presumption of advancement was rebutted.

'Castle'

Although the normal presumption upon a transfer to a stranger is one of resulting trust, this presumption may not apply in the case of a transfer of land. This is because the Law of Property Act 1925, s. 60(3), states: 'In a voluntary conveyance a resulting trust for the grantor shall not be implied merely by reason that the property is not expressed to be conveyed for the use of benefit of the grantee.' Section 60(3) could be interpreted to mean that in a voluntary conveyance of land there is always a presumption that the equitable interest passes to the grantee even if the conveyance does not state that it is for his use or benefit. Another interpretation, however, is that s. 60(3) is merely intended to ensure that, with the repeal of the Statute of Uses 1535, a beneficial interest can pass post-1925 if intended to pass even where the words 'use or benefit' are not contained in the conveyance. In *Hodgson* v *Marks* [1971] Ch 892, the court found evidence of the transferor's intention and therefore found it unnecessary to consider the effect of s. 60(3), which Russell LJ considered to be debatable, as did Lord Browne-Wilkinson in *Tinsley* v *Milligan* [1994] 1 AC 340.

In the absence of evidence of Rook's intention, Knight's claim depends upon the court's preferring the latter interpretation.

The Money Received by Queenie

In order to determine whether Knight has a claim to the surplus, it is necessary to construe Rook's intention when he handed Pawn the cheque.

First, if certainty of intention can be found, his words might be interpreted as creating a trust in favour of Pawn's creditors. If this is so, the normal principle is that once the trust has been performed, the surplus is held on a resulting trust for the settlor — in this case, Rook. Other outcomes are, however, possible, depending upon a construction of Rook's intention. Thus, it might be found that he intended that, once the trust had been performed, any surplus should belong to the trustee (Pawn) beneficially: *Re Foord* [1922] 2 Ch 519. This might be presumed if Rook stands *in loco parentis* to Rook. Yet again, it might be found, as in *Smith* v *Cooke* [1891] AC 297, that Rook intended that the beneficiaries (in this case the creditors) should take any surplus.

Secondly, Rook's words could be held to indicate a gift of the money subject to an equitable charge in favour of the creditors. Upon this construction, it is presumed that the recipient of the fund (in this case Pawn) takes the beneficial interest in it subject only to the payment of the creditors.

Thirdly, the matter could be construed as a contract, whereby Rook pays Pawn £5,000 in consideration for Pawn's paying off his own creditors. On this basis, Pawn has performed his part of the agreement. Strictly, there is no surplus because no debts are charged upon the £5,000, but, in effect, the remaining £2,000 is Pawn's own.

Fourthly, it might be possible to treat Rook as making Pawn a conditional gift of £5,000, i.e., a gift subject to a condition that Pawn pays his own creditors.

In each of these last three constructions, neither Rook nor Knight, as the beneficiary under Rook's will, has any claim to the money paid to Queenie. Knight will therefore have a claim to trace the money into the hands of Queenie only if the first construction is adopted with a resulting trust of the surplus.

QUESTION 3

Three years ago, a bowling club was set up in Plymouth as an unincorporated non-charitable association. Under the rules of the club, members were required to pay an annual subscription of £20, which entitled them to play bowls at the club throughout the year, to use its tea-room and other facilities, and to be considered for inclusion in the team for matches with other clubs. Non-members could also play bowls at the club, subject to the payment of £2 per game. Additional funds to support the club were raised through street collections in Plymouth.

The opening of a massive new sports complex in Plymouth has caused interest in the bowling club to decline, and the club's committee has now decided to disband the club. At present, some £20,000 remains in the club's 'Common Fund', into which all payments and donations had been placed.

Advise the club's committee how they should deal with this fund.

Commentary

This is the sort of question frequently found in examinations. Sometimes it will involve a members' club, sometimes more outward-looking types of association. Make sure you deal with the allocation of each part of the fund. Note that the question-setters have been kind, and have expressly told you that the club is a non-charitable unincorporated association. Do not look this gift horse in the mouth. For additional discussion in essays, the student will find valuable analyses by Rickett, (1980) 39 CLJ 88, and by Green, (1980) 43 MLR 626.

Suggested Answer

A number of different legal approaches has been applied to resolve the issue of entitlement to the surplus funds of an unincorporated association upon its dissolution.

One approach is to treat the contributors to the fund as entitled to the surplus by way of a resulting trust. Such a trust arises because the court will presume, in the absence of an expression of intention on the part of the contributors, that they did not intend to part with their contributions out and out. This principle was applied in *Re Hobourn Air Raid Distress Fund* [1946] Ch 194, where factory employees raised a fund to provide for those amongst them who suffered in air raids. The Court of Appeal held that the surplus was held on a resulting trust for the contributors in proportion to the amount each had paid in.

This approach can cause administrative problems, however, where there are many contributors and where the fund has existed for a long time. In such circumstances, two alternative outcomes are possible without abandoning the concept of the resulting trust.

First, it might be presumed that each contributor initially retained an interest in his contribution under a resulting trust until his contribution is spent. On this basis, withdrawals from the fund could be treated as being made according to the rule in *Clayton's Case* (1816) 1 Mer 572, i.e., first in, first out. This would clearly favour later contributors over earlier ones. No reported decision, however, has applied *Clayton's Case* in this context.

Secondly, in *Re Printers* [1899] 2 Ch 184, upon dissolution of a trade union, the surplus of the funds (which had been raised by weekly contributions from members) was held by way of resulting trust for existing members only, rateably according to their contributions. As was pointed out in *Re St Andrews Allotment Association* [1969] 1 WLR 229, however, it is difficult to see how the existing members could take by way of resulting trust a surplus partly derived from the contributions of past members.

An alternative approach is to treat the matter, not as one of trust, but as one of contract. Thus in *Cunnack v Edwards* [1896] 2 Ch 679, a surplus remained in a friendly society's funds after the death of the last widow annuitant. The Court of Appeal held that the members had contributed on the basis of contract, i.e., each payment was made in consideration for the payment of an annuity to the subscriber's widow. Each member had therefore enjoyed their full contractual entitlement from the fund. Thus the surplus went *bona vacantia* to the Crown. This contractual approach was also used in *Re West Sussex Constabulary's Widows, Children and Benevolent (1930) Fund Trusts* [1971] Ch 1, to deal with parts of the surplus remaining on the dissolution of a police benevolent fund. Goff J held that members' contributions, together with funds raised by way of entertainments and raffles, had all been given on a contractual basis, and should therefore go *bona vacantia* to the Crown. There, in contrast to *Re Gillingham Bus Disaster Fund* [1958] Ch 300, the judge said that anonymous contributors must be taken to have given out and out, so that this part of the surplus also went to the Crown. That part which represented the contributions of identifiable donors, however, was held for such donors on a resulting trust.

A different line of reasoning, however, emerges from a more recent line of authorities. Thus in *Re Recher's Will Trusts* [1972] Ch 526, Brightman J considered that the property of an unincorporated association was held for the members beneficially for the time being subject to the contract which exists between them, i.e., the association's rules. On this basis, unless the rules provide otherwise, the assets are held for the members at the date of dissolution equally, not on any principle of resulting trust, but simply because it is their property.

Problems with the contract-holding approach remain to be addressed: how, for instance, interests can be acquired and lost by new and old members respectively without written assignments complying with the Law of Property

Act 1925, s. 53(1)(c). Nevertheless, for the time being at least, this approach has found favour with the courts, e.g., in *Re Sick and Funeral Society of St. John's Sunday School, Golcar* [1973] Ch 51, *Re GKN Bolts & Nuts Ltd (Automotive Division) Birmingham Works Sports and Social Club* [1982] 1 WLR 774, and it could also explain *Re St Andrews Allotment Association*. The contract-holding approach was applied to a friendly society in *Re Bucks Constabulary Friendly Society (No. 2)* [1979] 1 WLR 936. Walton J considered that the judge in *Re West Sussex* was wrong to rely on *Cunnack v Edwards*. In Walton J's view, *Cunnack v Edwards* turned on the friendly society statutes then in force which forbade distribution of surplus to the members.

In the context of outward-looking associations and those which benefit members' widows and orphans, the authorities are therefore in some disarray. Furthermore, pension funds may be a special case, where contractual principles are not necessarily incompatible with a resulting trust: *Davis v Richards & Wallington Industries Ltd* [1990] 1 WLR 1511. In the context of members' clubs, however, such as the bowling club in the problem, where the benefits are confined to the members alone, there is now a fair body of opinion favouring the contract-holding approach of *Re Recher*. Thus, subject to a contrary indication in the bowling club's rules, that part of the surplus representing members' subscriptions belongs to the members at the date of dissolution.

The members' club cases, however, have not substantially had to deal with outside contributions. Assuming the criticisms of *Re West Sussex* made in *Re Bucks* are sound, the receipts from non-members for use of the green are paid under a contract and therefore form part of the general assets of the club. The contributions from street collections will probably be treated as absolute gifts, whether or not for the reasons stated in *Re West Sussex*. Greater difficulties might arise in the case of donations from identifiable donors. Dicta in *Re Bucks* suggest that even these would belong to the present members.

In conclusion then, in the absence of anything to the contrary in the club's rules, it is probable that the whole 'Common Fund' belongs equally to those who were members at the date of dissolution.

9   Constructive Trusts

INTRODUCTION

This subject lends itself to both problem and essay questions. The knowledge gained from studying the topic may also make a useful contribution to general questions on equity such as 'Is equity as long as the Chancellor's foot?' or 'Is equity past the age of child-bearing?'

Whilst some of the concepts — such as unconscionable behaviour, unjust enrichment and fiduciary duties — are straightforward, others — such as mutual wills and a stranger's liability for breach of trust — are complex and involve difficult cases. This is particularly true of the liability of an agent or a receiver in complicated fraud cases. The plots (and the length) of some of these would compare favourably with many novels!

Questions 4 and 5 in this chapter are on secret trusts, which most textbooks now treat as express trusts. Question 5 requires a consideration of the categorisation of secret trusts, which, for reasons pointed out, could be crucial to a beneficiary.

Constructive trusts cover some of the 'high growth' areas of equity. For example, the 'new model constructive trust' of property owned by cohabitees has been developed by the courts over the last 30 years or so. There has, more recently, been a number of cases dealing with the liability of agents and receivers who deal with 'trust' property. The principles relating to cohabitees now appear to be more settled, as are the circumstances under which an agent may incur liability as a constructive trustee; but the position of someone who receives property as a result of a breach of trust or fiduciary duty is still not finally settled. This is an area where you should be on the look-out for new cases which further refine the principles for the application of a constructive trust.

Because it is a developing area, articles are frequently published on it in journals such as the *Law Quarterly Review* or the *Conveyancer*, and for any assessed essay you would need to refer to these. Reference has been made to some articles in the answers. The articles may be helpful too in shedding light on particularly difficult subjects, or in discussion of recent cases. There is a full and clear discussion of the subject in *Parker & Mellows: The Modern Law of Trusts*, 7th edn, by A. J. Oakley, London: Sweet & Maxwell, 1998.

Equity and Trusts courses vary as to the emphasis they give to constructive trusts, although all courses will include it in the syllabus to some extent. You must therefore be guided by your lecturer as to the emphasis which you should give the subject in preparing for your examination. There is of course no point in reading in depth a topic which your lecturer has barely mentioned — it will almost certainly not be examined in depth.

The general advice for all examinations holds good for this subject. Think hard about the question before you start to write. If you have a two-part question, allocate your time roughly equally between the two parts, unless the examination paper indicates, or common sense suggests, that one part is worth more marks than the other.

QUESTION 1

English law provides no clear and all-embracing definition of a constructive trust. Its boundaries have been left perhaps deliberately vague ... (Edmund Davies LJ in *Carl Zeiss Stiftung* v *Herbert Smith & Co. (a firm) (No. 2)* [1969] 2 Ch 276).

Discuss with reference to decided cases.

Commentary

This is a very general essay question on the nature of constructive trusts — the sort of question for which you might achieve a pass if you had not actually revised constructive trusts too specifically but had a general overall knowledge of the subject. However, to do well on it, you would need to have a good knowledge of the cases and the recent developments.

The material in this essay answer might well be adapted to similar essays on constructive trusts, such as a discussion of Lord Denning's statement in *Hussey* v *Palmer* [1972] 1 WLR 1286, CA, that 'a constructive trust is one imposed by equity whenever justice and good conscience require it'. However, do always remember that no matter how similar two essay questions may be, you should always slant your answer to the particular question asked.

Suggested Answer

A constructive trust is one imposed by the court on a person in whom the legal title to property is vested. It has the effect of divesting such person of the whole, or part, of the equitable beneficial interest which they then hold as trustee for someone else.

The underlying rationale for the imposition of most constructive trusts is the unjust enrichment of the legal owner, which would result if they were allowed to retain the whole of the beneficial interest, and a constructive trust usually involves some fraudulent or unconscionable behaviour on the part of the legal owner. This is the application of a very general equitable principle and it is hardly surprising that the circumstances in which the courts have been prepared to impose a constructive trust are wide and varied. Moreover, it is an ever evolving area of equity where the courts are constantly re-defining and reviewing the principles on which a constructive trust will be imposed in new cases, often applying the maxims of equity to do so.

Oakley, in his book *Constructive Trusts*, 2nd edn, 1987 (updated in chapter 10 of Parker and Mellows, *The Modern Law of Trusts*, A.J. Oakley, London: Sweet & Maxwell, 1998), identifies three well-established categories of constructive trusts. These are where someone obtains an advantage from fraudulent or unconscionable behaviour, where a fiduciary derives a profit from the fiduciary relationship and where there is a disposition of property in breach of trust. Other, less certain classifications he suggests are secret trusts (now usually treated as express trusts) and mutual wills, and trusts arising on the incomplete transfer of a legal title and on a specifically enforceable contract for sale.

The application of such a wide equitable jurisdiction as the constructive trust has inevitably led to different approaches by the judges. Lord Denning was always a judge with a strongly developed sense of justice, and he said in *Hussey* v *Palmer* [1972] 1 WLR 1286, CA, that a constructive trust 'is a trust imposed by law whenever justice and good conscience require it. It is a liberal process, founded on large principles of equity, to be applied in cases where the defendant cannot conscientiously keep the property for himself alone, but ought to allow another to have the property or a share of it'. This suggests very much that a constructive trust is really another equitable remedy, as it is in American law, but A.J. Oakley argues that it should not be so regarded and that it is institutional in nature, as it imposes heavy duties of accountability on the trustee and affects property rights. The view that the constructive trust should be constrained in its application is put by Bagnall J in *Cowcher* v *Cowcher* [1972] 1 WLR 425, where he says that it should only be imposed on 'sure and settled principles' as otherwise 'no lawyer could safely advise on his client's title and every quarrel would lead to a law suit'. However, Lord Denning's more liberal approach has received further support from the speech of Lord Browne-Wilkinson in *Westdeutsche Landesbank Girocentrale* v *Islington LBC* [1996] AC 669, at 716 where he said:

> The court might by way of remedy impose a constructive trust on a defendant who knowingly retains the property of which the plaintiff has been deprived. Since the remedy can be tailored to the circumstances of the particular case, innocent third parties would not be prejudiced and restitutionary defences, such as change of position, are capable of being given effect.

The reality is probably somewhere between the two views, in that the courts do apply settled principles but the principles themselves are frequently reviewed and modified or extended.

A good illustration of the development of constructive trusts in the context of a desire to effect justice on the one hand and a desire to keep within well defined boundaries on the other hand are the cases involving co-ownership of property where the legal title is vested in one co-owner only. In *Gissing* v *Gissing* [1971] AC 886, the House of Lords laid down the requirements for a party whose name was not on the legal title to property to acquire a beneficial interest. These were that there should be an agreement between the two co-owners, or a common intention, that the co-owner whose name is not on the title should have a beneficial share and that that co-owner should act upon this to his detriment with regard to the property. However, some subsequent cases, such as *Cooke* v *Head* [1972] 1 WLR 518, CA, and Lord Denning MR in *Eves* v *Eves* [1975] 1 WLR 1338, CA, adopted a more liberal view in order to achieve justice in the instant case. This approach was however, disapproved by the Court of Appeal in *Burns* v *Burns* [1984] Ch 317, which returned to the principles laid down by the House of Lords in *Gissing* v *Gissing*. The principles received confirmation and some refinement by Lord Bridge in *Lloyds Bank Ltd* v *Rosset* [1991] AC 107, but in *Midland Bank* v *Cooke* [1995] 4 All ER 562, the Court of Appeal resiled from Lord Bridge's definitive requirements for inferring a common intention, and was prepared to consider 'the whole course of dealing between the parties relevant to their ownership and occupation of the property' (per Waite LJ).

Constructive trusts have been used in widely differing situations to give effect to the maxim of equity, applied in *Rochefoucauld* v *Bousted* [1897] 1 Ch 196, that 'Equity will not allow a statute to be used as an instrument of fraud'. Evidence of secret trusts is admissible in contravention of the Wills Act 1837, as to refuse to admit evidence of the trust could result in the perpetration of a fraud on the intended beneficiary or the testator. In *Bannister* v *Bannister* [1948] 2 All ER 133, CA, evidence was accepted of an oral agreement between the plaintiff and the defendant that the defendant should be allowed to occupy the cottage which she had sold to the plaintiff at below the market price. This did not comply with the Law of Property Act 1925, s. 40 (then the relevant statutory provision governing the formality requirements for a contract for the disposition of land), but to disallow evidence of the oral agreement meant the plaintiff would otherwise have obtained an unfair advantage by fraud. More recently, in *Lyus* v *Prowsa Developments Ltd* [1982] 1 WLR 1044, the court accepted that a purchaser who took property expressly subject to the right of another was bound by that right even if it was not registered under the Land Registration Act 1925, as it could have been.

The courts have shown themselves ready to apply a constructive trust to the profits derived by a fiduciary from his fiduciary relationship in a number of differing circumstances, and in *Boardman* v *Phipps* [1967] 2 AC 46 the House of Lords decided (Lord Upjohn dissenting) that a profit made as a result of information acquired from the fiduciary relationship was within the principle. In *Reading* v *A-G* [1951] AC 507, HL, the concept of fiduciary relationship was extended to that of an army officer and the Crown. The principle means that a trustee may not profit from his position and the courts have applied this to widely differing circumstances. For example, in *Keech* v *Sandford* (1726) Sel Cas Ch 61, a trustee in whose name a lease was renewed was held to be a constructive trustee of it for the trust, and in *Re Macadam* [1946] Ch 73, a trustee who was able to use his position as trustee to appoint himself as director of a company was held to be a constructive trustee for the trust of his director's fees.

One of the constructive trusts which has seen the most litigation in recent years, however, is the trust imposed where a person knowingly receives or deals with trust property in breach of trust. This type of constructive trust was recognised by Lord Selborne in *Barnes* v *Addy* (1874) 9 Ch App 244, but the definition of its requirements has been judicially considered in a number of more recent cases, often involving fraud. An attempt was made by Peter Gibson J in *Baden Delvaux & Lecuit* v *Société Générale* [1983] BCLC 325 to define the types of knowledge which would make an agent accountable as a constructive trustee. Whilst some decisions regarded constructive notice as sufficient (*Selangor United Rubber Estates Ltd* v *Cradock (Bankrupt) (No. 3)* [1968] 1 WLR 1555), others did not, and required evidence of 'a want of probity' in failing to enquire further (*Cowan de Groot Properties Ltd* v *Eagle Trust plc* [1992] 4 All ER 700). This latter approach would seem to be more in line with the general principles of constructive trusts that the defendant's conscience must be affected; and as regards agents dealing with property, the Privy Council case of *Royal Brunei Airlines San Bhd* v *Tan* [1995] 2 AC 378, has now settled that, in cases of assistance, dishonesty is required to make an agent liable. It is arguable that the constructive trust imposed upon an agent is not a true constructive trust in the sense that such an agent is not holding the property himself on trust. The court simply declares the agent a constructive trustee in order to impose a personal liability to account upon him. David Hayton has described this as 'a fiction which provides a useful remedy where no remedy is available in contract and tort'.

It is still not clear what is necessary to impose a constructive trust in cases of 'recipient liability', which Lord Nicholls said in *Royal Brunei Airlines* is 'restitution based'.

It is clear from the widely differing situations in which a constructive trust has been applied that it is a versatile and flexible weapon of equity, capable of apparently unlimited adaptability to changing social and commercial circumstances. It justifies the statement by Lord Denning MR in *Eves* v *Eves* that 'Equity is not past the age of childbearing'. However, its adaptability necessarily requires that its boundaries should not be too rigidly defined.

QUESTION 2

Angela was the Council tenant of a house when Bertram, a married man, went to live with her there 10 years ago. A year later, the Council offered to sell the house to Angela at a discounted price, being 40% less than the market price, and Angela discussed this with Bertram. They agreed that the house should be conveyed into Angela's name alone as she was the tenant with the right to buy and Bertram was involved in divorce proceedings and property claims from his wife. Of the £30,000 discounted price, £5,000 was contributed by Bertram and the remaining £25,000 was raised by a mortgage in Angela's name which was guaranteed by Bertram.

Angela and Bertram contributed equally to the mortgage repayments until Angela had a baby about a year later, after which Bertram paid them. Angela and Bertram decided to modernise the kitchen and the bathroom, and Bertram, being a qualified carpenter, made all the fitments and did most of the work. Three years ago, they decided to build an extension and Angela took a further mortgage with the Quicklend Bank plc for £30,000 to pay for this. Repayments on this mortgage were also made by Bertram.

Six months ago Bertram left Angela and is now claiming a share of the house. Angela has defaulted on the mortgage instalments to the Quicklend Bank plc who are claiming possession.

Advise Bertram and the Quicklend Bank plc.

Commentary

This is the type of question which could arise in land law, family law or trusts, although each might have a particular slant. There has been much litigation surrounding the area of constructive trusts, but the principles are now fairly well settled. A resulting trust may also arise in these cohabitee situations, and you should also be prepared to consider this.

It is also an area which has developed since its early recognition in *Gissing* v *Gissing* [1971] AC 886, where Lord Diplock said (at p. 905) 'A resulting, implied or constructive trust — and it is unnecessary for present purposes to distinguish between these three classes of trust ...'. Hayton (in his article referred to below) puts forward some sound reasons for distinguishing a resulting trust from a constructive trust. The distinction has now received judicial approval in the judgment of Peter Gibson LJ in the case of *Drake* v *Whipp* [1996] 1 FLR 826. In any answer to this type of question on a trusts paper, you should make the same distinction.

It may be possible to calculate a party's interest under a resulting trust when the property is first bought, as a proportion of the total purchase price. The imposition of a constructive trust may increase that share, but examiners are not likely to expect you to attempt complicated calculations to ascertain an exact amount! All you can be expected to do is to know the circumstances which have been taken into account in increasing a party's share under a constructive trust.

The parties in this question are not married, but you should of course remember that in the case of married couples there is legislation governing the distribution of matrimonial property, notably the Matrimonial Proceedings and Property Act 1970, s. 37 and (on divorce) the Matrimonial Causes Act 1973, but you would not be expected to deal with these in any depth in a trusts examination. Lord Denning MR has said that s. 37 is merely declaratory of the existing law as to constructive trusts, but there could be a different result in that the section applies 'subject to any agreement to the contrary'. For a presumed agreement to share beneficial ownership equally readily attributed to a married couple, see *Midland Bank plc* v *Cooke* [1995] 4 All ER 562.

Suggested Answer

If the original purchase price of £30,000 represented a discount of 40%, then the market price was £50,000 and £20,000 was allowed to Angela as a Council tenant exercising her right to buy. Of the original purchase price, therefore, £20,000 may be regarded as having been contributed by Angela, £5,000 by Bertram and £25,000 by a mortgage to which they originally contributed equally but latterly Bertram has paid. In *Springette* v *Defoe* (1992) 65 P & CR 1, CA, the discount on the market price on a sale to a council tenant was credited to the tenant who was entitled to it under the legislation.

Where a person contributes to the purchase price of property and there is no evidence of an intention of gift and no circumstances from which a presumption of advancement arises, there will be a resulting trust for that person of a proportionate part of the equitable interest according to their contribution. There would therefore be a resulting trust for Bertram of one tenth of the equitable interest and some part of the one half for which they both contributed to the mortgage.

A person whose name is not on the title deeds may also acquire an equitable interest in property under a constructive trust if they comply with the requirements laid down in *Gissing* v *Gissing* [1971] AC 886, HL. There must be evidence of an agreement (express or inferred) or a common intention that that person is to have a beneficial interest in the property at the time of its acquisition. In *Drake* v *Whipp* [1996] 1 FLR 826, there was undisputed evidence of a common intention that the parties were to share beneficially. Additionally, the equitable owner must have acted on this understanding to their detriment. In *Lloyds Bank Ltd* v *Rosset* [1991] AC 107, HL, Lord Bridge expressed the view that the detriment could be some material alteration in a party's position in the case of an express agreement, but that in the case of an inferred agreement some direct contributions to the purchase price of the property, either initially or by way of contribution to the mortgage instalments, would be necessary.

It is possible to infer such a common intention from what was said when the property was purchased, and a party who has impliedly agreed to this may be estopped from denying it later. In *Eves* v *Eves* [1975] 1 WLR 1338, CA, the man said that the woman's name could not be included on the legal title because she was under age, and in *Grant* v *Edwards* [1986] Ch 638 it could not be included because it would prejudice any settlement in the woman's divorce proceedings. In both cases, the reasons given for omitting the woman's name implied that her name would otherwise have been included on the legal title, and it was possible to draw an inference from this that she was intended to have a share of the beneficial interest in the property.

The parties' agreement in this case as to why Bertram's name should be left off the legal title might similarly lead to the inference of a common intention that he should have a share of the beneficial interest. His initial contribution of £5,000 and his guarantee of the mortgage (as in *Falconer* v *Falconer* [1970] 1 WLR 1333, CA) would also assist in reaching this conclusion. The Court of Appeal in *Midland Bank* v *Cooke* [1995] 4 All ER 562, adopted a more liberal approach than Lord Bridge in *Rosset* as to circumstances which might give rise to an inference of common intention, and indicated that the court may consider all the dealings between the parties with regard to the property.

Assuming there is sufficient evidence of a common intention, Bertram would then have to show that he subsequently acted to his detriment in reliance upon this. He has contributed substantially to the mortgage repayments and carried out improvements to the property, and these might both be regarded as sufficient conduct to his detriment to enable him to acquire an interest under a constructive trust, thereby increasing his original equitable interest under a resulting trust.

The extension appears to have been a joint venture, in that the mortgage to finance it was in Angela's name but Bertram has made the repayments. In *Hussey* v *Palmer* [1972] 1 WLR 1286, CA, a mother-in-law's payment for an extension to her son-in-law's house was held to give rise to a constructive trust in her favour. Similarly here, Bertram could again have an increased share of the equitable interest in the increased value of the property under a constructive trust.

In determining the extent of Bertram's interest under a constructive trust, the court should not try to calculate this arithmetically (as with a resulting trust), but should adopt 'a broad brush approach' (per Peter Gibson LJ in *Drake* v *Whipp*, supra).

The Quicklend Bank plc have made a further loan to Angela and it is necessary to consider whether they are bound by any equitable interest in the property which Bertram has. In his article 'Equitable rights of cohabitees' [1990] Conv 370, D.J. Hayton suggests that, as regards third parties, an interest acquired under a resulting trust is more likely to be binding than one acquired under a constructive trust. An interest under a resulting trust is acquired for money or money's worth at the time when the property is purchased, whereas an interest under a constructive trust may have an element of voluntary settlement, and in any event will not be acquired until the party has acted to his detriment, which will necessarily be subsequent to the purchase. In *Re Densham* [1975] 1 WLR 1519, the original contribution of half the deposit on a house which the wife made towards the purchase price was held to give her a one ninth share in the equitable interest under a resulting trust which was good subsequently against the husband's trustee in bankruptcy, but any increased share which she might have acquired under a constructive trust was void under bankruptcy law as there was an element of voluntary settlement in it which a trustee in bankruptcy can set aside.

On this basis, it would appear that the mortgage with Quicklend Bank plc will be subject to Bertram's initial interest under the resulting trust. A mortgagee will not have the advantage of a trustee in bankruptcy of being able to set aside a voluntary disposition, however, and it would appear that the mortgage with Quicklend Bank plc will be subject to Bertram's initial interest under a resulting trust, and probably also subject to any increased interest which Bertram may have acquired under a constructive trust. This was the decision in *Midland Bank* v *Cooke*, and this would seem to be consistent with the general principles of property law where third parties are deemed to have notice of the possible proprietary rights of occupiers in unregistered land (*Kingsnorth Finance Co. Ltd* v *Tizard* [1986] 1 WLR 783), and an occupier's proprietary rights are an overriding interest in land with registered title (*Williams & Glyn's Bank Ltd* v *Boland* [1981] AC 487).

QUESTION 3

Five years ago Olga, a spinster, married Clive, a widower with three children. They agreed to make wills in identical terms leaving their property to each other and then to Clive's two daughters, Amy and Bea. Wills in accordance with this agreement were executed by both of them shortly after they married. Clive had quarrelled with his son Nigel and did not want him to benefit from his estate.

About three years ago Clive became seriously and terminally ill. Amy was a nurse and Clive told her that if she would take unpaid leave to go and live with him to look after him, as Olga was not strong enough, he and Olga would ensure that his house 'Greensleeves' would be left to her. Amy took unpaid leave and nursed her father for nine months before he died. While living at the house, she paid for the modernisation of the kitchen and bathroom.

Some three months before he died Clive and Olga executed identical codicils to their wills, both signed on the same day, varying the ultimate disposition of 'Greensleeves' so that Amy should receive it from the survivor of them and the remainder of their property should ultimately be divided between Amy and Bea.

After Clive died, Olga gave away considerable property which had belonged to Clive to charity. She also won £500,000 on the football pools. Nigel, who lived near to Olga, visited her regularly and did small jobs for her. Olga died recently and a will was found among her papers, dated a few days before she died, revoking all previous wills and testamentary dispositions and leaving all her property 'to my wonderful stepson Nigel'.

Advise Amy and Bea.

Commentary

This question raises some of the unresolved difficulties relating to mutual wills. You should be aware of these problems and also of the necessary requirements to establish mutual wills. Apart from this, however, the question is fairly straightforward.

The facts of the question disclose two possible causes of action available to one of the parties (Amy) whom you are asked to advise. If you come to the conclusion that Amy is likely to succeed on one ground, you should of course nevertheless go on to consider the other ground also. REAL cases are often pleaded in the alternative!

Suggested Answer

The enforceability of mutual wills depends upon an agreement between the parties making them. The agreement is that they will both make wills in substantially the same form, leaving property in accordance with the agreement, and they agree not to revoke the wills. It will be an unenforceable agreement until such time as the first of the parties dies, as it will not be supported by consideration until then. However, when the first party dies, the consideration is the benefit which the survivor receives under their will, and the agreement then becomes binding on the conscience of the survivor, who has received a benefit.

It is often difficult to find sufficient evidence of the agreement to establish that the parties did intend to make mutual wills. The fact that the wills are identical is some evidence but is not in itself sufficient (*Re Oldham* [1925] Ch 75) as there should also be an agreement not to revoke the wills. In the case of *Re Goodchild* [1996] 1 WLR 694, the Court of Appeal held that identical wills made by a husband and wife on the same date were not mutually binding as the necessary contractual obligation not to revoke the wills was lacking. However, in *Re Cleaver* [1981] 1 WLR 939, where two sets of wills were made by a husband and wife in identical form and a further will by the surviving wife consistent with her second identical will, this was held to be sufficient evidence of an agreement. The identical wills made here, together with identical codicils giving effect to identical changes, would probably be sufficient evidence to establish the necessary agreement as in *Re Cleaver*.

It is probable therefore that Amy and Bea will be able to challenge Olga's will leaving all her property to Nigel, and require her estate to be administered according to the terms of her will and codicil made shortly before Clive died. The decision in *Goodchild* suggests that even if there is no legally binding obligation not to revoke a will, the moral obligation ensuing on the death of the first testator to die binds that person's property in the hands of the second testator, who is therefore under an obligation to deal with it as agreed.

There are a number of vexed questions with regard to the property which is subject to any trust created by mutual wills and there do not seem to be any very satisfactory answers.

Does any trust arising attach only to the property which the survivor receives from the other party to the agreement, or does it attach to all the survivor's property on death? If the latter, then the £500,000 which Olga won on the football pools would also be subject to any trust arising. As the survivor entered into an agreement to leave all their own property to the same third party too, this would seem to be a tenable argument. In *Re Dale* [1994] Ch 31, it was held that the trust attached to all the property held by the survivor at the date of the survivor's death. In *Re Hagger* [1930] 2 Ch 190, also a first instance decision, it was considered that the trust should at least attach to all the property held by the survivor at the date of the first death. In *Re Green* [1951] Ch 148, it was held that the trust attached only to the property received under the will of the first party to die, but this intention was clear from the terms of the will.

Does the trust arising prevent the survivor from disposing of any property they receive under the will of the first to die? If so, it would effectively be only a life interest in that property which the survivor has. In the Australian case of *Birmingham* v *Renfrew* (1937) 57 CLR 666, Dixon J said that the survivor could enjoy the property as if an absolute owner, subject to restrictions on his rights of alienability, but that on his death this 'floating obligation' crystallised and attached to the property. If this is correct, presumably an action could have been brought during Olga's lifetime to prevent her from disposing of any very large sums of money. This point did not arise and was not considered in *Re Dale*.

Additionally, Amy may have grounds to claim the house under the equitable doctrine of estoppel. This could apply to the circumstances of the question in two ways. First, it could apply to make the oral agreement between Clive and Amy enforceable notwithstanding the absence of the requisite formality for a contract for the disposition of land. Secondly, Amy's acting to her detriment in reliance upon a promise made by her father could found a claim in proprietary estoppel.

An oral agreement for the disposition of land will be void as it does not comply with s. 2 of the Law of Property (Miscellaneous Provisions) Act 1989, which requires any such agreement to be in writing and signed by both parties. Before 1989, such an agreement had to comply with the formality requirements of s. 40 of the Law of Property Act 1925, but equity would enforce a purely oral agreement if there was a sufficient act of part performance by the party seeking to enforce it, and in *Wakeham* v *Mackenzie* [1968] 1 WLR 1175 a housekeeper was able to enforce an oral agreement to leave the house to her in return for work she had done. Section 40 was repealed by the 1989 Act and the Law Commission envisaged that the equitable doctrine of part performance would be replaced by estoppel. In *Yaxley* v *Gotts* [2000] Ch 162, an oral agreement that a builder who converted a building into flats should have one of the flats in return for his work was held to be binding not only on the person with whom he agreed, but also on his son who knew of the agreement and adopted it. The Court of Appeal applied estoppel, although Robert Walker LJ felt that the situation could also give rise to the imposition of a constructive trust. The agreement between Amy and Clive, whereby she gave up work to go and look after him, might therefore be enforceable against Olga and her estate.

Amy has also acted to her detriment by spending money on the house in modernising the kitchen and the bathroom. The doctrine of esetoppel is much wider in its scope than the replacement of the doctrine of part performance and may be used to enforce a promise upon which the promisee has acted to their detriment.

The promisor is then estopped from going back on their promise and an equity attaches to the property to which it relates, not only in the hands of the promisor himself but also in the hands of a volunteer acquiring the property from him. Thus in *Inwards* v *Baker* [1965] 2 QB 29, CA, a son who was persuaded by his father to build a bungalow on a plot of land belonging to the father was able to remain there after the father died and the land passed to his mistress. In *Pascoe* v *Turner* [1979] 1 WLR 431, a man who told a cohabitee with whom he lived that his house and contents all belonged to her, and was aware that she was spending her frugal savings on repairing and redecorating the house after he had left, was estopped from denying this and was obliged to convey the fee simple in the property to her.

Moreover, estoppel is not restricted by the fundamental premise of testamentary freedom (*Gillett* v *Holt* [2000] 2 All ER 289). The acquiescence relied upon to found a claim of proprietary estoppel should relate to the property. Amy has acted to her detriment in modernising the property and, if this was in reliance upon her father's promise, this may well be sufficient. Both Olga and Nigel are volunteers, so that Amy's claim to the house, which is necessarily equitable and not registrable under the Land Charges Act 1972 (per Denning LJ in *Ives (ER) Investment Ltd* v *High* [1967] 2 QB 379), might succeed on this ground also.

QUESTION 4

By his will Peter bequeathed 50 casks of brandy to Smee absolutely. Shortly after the will was made, Peter handed Smee a sealed envelope marked 'Not to be opened until after my death'. He asked Smee to hold the brandy on the terms contained therein, and Smee agreed. The sealed instructions state that Smee can drink as much of the brandy as he likes during his life, but that he must, by his will, bequeath whatever is left to Peter's mistress Tinkerbell.

Peter and Tinkerbell were in a flying accident last month. Tinkerbell was killed instantly and Peter died the next day. Tinkerbell had witnessed Peter's will. Smee says he intends to sell the brandy and spend the proceeds on a world cruise. Advise Tinkerbell's executors.

Commentary

This is a particularly difficult problem question which you might want to avoid even if you have revised secret trusts and mutual wills very well! If you fail to appreciate all its different aspects, however, you should nevertheless be able to pick up some marks fairly easily for knowing some of the points involved, such as what happens if the secret beneficiary witnesses the will or predeceases the testator.

Definitely a question to think hard about, though, before you set pen to paper!

Suggested Answer

As the brandy is bequeathed to Smee absolutely with no indication on the face of the will that it is to be held by him on trust, this purports to create a fully secret trust.

For a fully secret trust to be valid, it must be accepted by the trustee at any time before the death of the testator. Provided that the trust itself has been accepted, it is probably sufficient if the exact terms are contained in a sealed envelope which is not to be opened until after the testator's death (Lord Wright MR obiter in *Re Keen* [1937] Ch 236, CA). Although *Re Keen* was concerned with a half secret trust, there would seem to be no reason why the principle should not be applicable also to a fully secret trust. It is possible that in the case of a half secret trust, communication has to be by handing over the sealed envelope before the execution of the will (*Re Bateman's Will Trusts* [1970] 1 WLR 1463), but in the case of a fully secret trust, it could be handed over at any time before death.

Assuming that these circumstances create a valid secret trust for Tinkerbell, it will not matter that Tinkerbell, who was a beneficiary under the trust, witnessed Peter's will: *Re Young* [1951] Ch 344, where it was held that a beneficiary under a half secret trust who had witnessed the will was nevertheless able to take under it. The reason is that the beneficiary took under the secret trust and not under the will, so that the Wills Act 1837, s. 15 (which invalidates a gift to the witness) did not apply. There would seem to be no reason why this principle should not apply also to a fully secret trust.

It is more questionable, however, whether Tinkerbell's predeceasing Peter will render the trust void. In *Re Gardner (No. 2)* [1923] 2 Ch 230, where the secret beneficiary predeceased the testatrix, Romer J held that there was a valid trust for her estate, but this decision has been criticised. Normally a gift to a beneficiary who predeceases the testator will lapse. Even if the doctrine of lapse is avoided by construing the secret trust as one which arises at the moment it is accepted by the secret trustee during the lifetime of the testator, it cannot be fully constituted until his death, and it must be fully constituted to be valid. Nevertheless, if the decision in *Re Gardner (No. 2)* is applied, Tinkerbell's estate would be able to benefit.

A more serious problem in construing Peter's arrangement as a secret trust is that of certainty of subject-matter. In *Sprange* v *Barnard* (1789) 2 Bro CC 585, where a testatrix left property to her husband for his sole use and at his death 'the remaining part of what is left' was to be divided between a brother and sister, the trust failed for uncertainty of subject-matter. So a secret trust of whatever brandy Smee does not drink may well similarly fail for uncertainty of subject-matter.

However, it might be possible to argue that the arrangement resembles the type of agreement necessary for mutual wills. Smee agrees to hold the brandy on the terms contained in the envelope and he is thereby (although he does not realise it) agreeing to dispose of it in a certain way by his will. In *Ottaway* v *Norman* [1972] Ch 698, a similar sort of arrangement was successfully enforced by the secret beneficiary, but the case was pleaded as a secret trust and not as mutual wills, and as such was only valid as regards that property which was certain, namely a bungalow. However, mutual wills may be valid even if they involve just the type of uncertainty of subject-matter as here (see Dixon J in an Australian case *Birmingham* v *Renfrew* (1937) 57 CLR 666, as to the nature of enjoyment and obligation under such an arrangement, namely, rights of virtually full ownership during the survivor's lifetime and an obligation as regards the property which crystallises on his death).

The usual type of agreement for mutual wills is that the parties to it agree to benefit each other and then an agreed third party, but there would seem to be no reason why one party who accepts a benefit should not do so on terms which require him to confer a benefit on a third party, as indeed was the case in *Ottaway* v *Norman*. In *Re Dale* [1994] Ch 31, it was not even considered necessary for the survivor to receive a personal benefit. It would be necessary however to establish a clear agreement, and it would be arguable that it could not be a binding agreement if Smee did not know the full terms of what he was agreeing to.

Therefore it is just possible, although unlikely, that an action by Tinkerbell's executors might succeed if pleaded as a mutual will.

QUESTION 5

(a)   '... the whole basis of secret trusts ... is that they operate outside the will' (Megarry V-C in *Re Snowden (deceased)* [1979] Ch 528).

Discuss.

(b)   Meg, a wealthy but eccentric elderly spinster wished to leave a large sum of money to the Battersea Dogs' Home but did not want her family to know. She therefore asked her old friend James if he and his son Sam would hold £50,000 which she intended to leave to them in her will in trust for the Home. James agreed. Meg made a will the following week leaving £50,000 to James and Sam. James did not tell Sam of Meg's wishes and Meg also forgot to mention anything about it to Sam. Subsequently, Meg decided to increase the legacy to £100,000 and executed a codicil to this effect. She told neither James nor Sam about the codicil, however.

Advise Meg's executors as to what extent the secret trust is effective. Would your answer differ if the legacy had been left to James and Sam 'as tenants in common for purposes I have made known to them'?

Commentary

The two parts of this question make it a fairly lengthy one. You should not be deterred by this as it means that there are a lot of points for you to pick up. However, it does mean that your answer to the essay part must be fairly concise and you must avoid going into too much detail on it at the expense of the time required to answer the problem part.

Part (a) of the Question may also lend itself to a discursive essay which could be set perhaps as assessed coursework. In that case, you would obviously need to do some more in-depth reading of the judgments in *Blackwell* v *Blackwell* [1929] AC 318 and the cases such as *Re Young* [1951] Ch 344 which throw up a conflict between the rules of probate and the principles of equity. You will also find articles written on the subject in *The Conveyancer* and other legal periodicals (two by Bryn Perrins: 'Can you keep half a secret?' (1972) 88 LQR 225, and 'Secret Trusts: the key to au dehors' (1985) Conv 248, and a more recent one by Patricia Critchley (1999) 115 LQR 631, 'Instruments of fraud, testamentary dispositions, and the doctrine of secret trusts'). As pointed out in the answer to this question, the classification of secret trusts could be highly significant if the secret trust were one of land because of s. 53, LPA 1925.

Suggested Answer

(a)   Equity's enforcement of secret trusts necessarily involves accepting evidence of a testator's intentions which were not embodied in his will and which do not therefore comply with the Wills Act 1837, s. 9.

To be valid, a secret trust must be accepted by the secret trustee, although the time of acceptance varies according to whether the trust is a fully secret trust or a half-secret trust. To allow the secret trustee to renege on this agreement would amount to a fraud on the beneficiaries of the trust and on the testator, in that he would not have left property to the secret trustee if the latter had not agreed to the trust. Such rationale may also explain equity's intervention in half-secret trusts, under which the trustee himself cannot derive any benefit as legatee or devisee. Fraud on the beneficiary was the rationale accepted for secret trusts in *McCormick* v *Grogan* (1869) LR 4 HL 82, but this applied only to fully secret trusts. In *Blackwell* v *Blackwell* [1929] AC 318, however, Viscount Sumner took the view that a secret trust is created and becomes binding as a result of the communication of it by the testator to the secret trustee and his acceptance of it during the testator's lifetime, and that the trust which consequently arises is therefore governed by the law relating to trusts and is outside the scope of the Wills Act 1837.

Although this is a better explanation for the operation of secret trusts, it is not entirely satisfactory because the secret trust depends upon the proving of the will for its constitution. This dependence has thrown up some unhappy conflicts in cases where strict adherence to the Wills Act 1837 would have invalidated a secret trust, but the courts have nevertheless been prepared to recognise its existence.

It is debatable, for example, to what extent a secret trust will be enforceable if the secret trustee predeceases the testator or disclaims the gift under the will, and this may vary according to whether the secret trust is fully secret or half-secret. In the case of a half-secret trust the principle that equity will not allow a trust to fail for want of a trustee would probably apply to save the trust. However, Cozens-Hardy LJ in *Re Maddock* [1902] 2 Ch 220, CA, expressed the opinion that a fully secret trust would fail if the secret trustee renounced or disclaimed the gift or died in the lifetime of the testator.

In *Re Gardner (No. 2)* [1923] 2 Ch 230, the beneficiary under a half-secret trust had predeceased the testatrix. This should have resulted in the gift to her lapsing, but Romer LJ held that it went to her personal representatives. Note, however, that this decision has been criticised. In *Re Young* [1951] Ch 344, one of the beneficiaries of a half-secret trust witnessed the testator's will which would have invalidated any gift to him in the will itself. The court held that the legacy was nevertheless valid because the beneficiary took under the trust and not under the will. Many of the decisions therefore illustrate the courts' willingness to modify the strict requirements of the Wills Act 1837 where necessary to give effect to a secret trust. This suggests that the tendency is indeed to regard secret trusts as being governed by the law relating to trusts, deriving from the agreement between the testator and the trustee. This would mean that they are more properly classified as express trusts rather than constructive trusts (A. J. Oakley's opinion — see question 1). This is not an entirely academic question when it is recalled that s. 53(1)(b) applies to the creation of an express trust of land. A constructive trust of land is exempt by s. 53(2).

(b) In *Re Stead* [1900] 1 Ch 237, Farwell J had to consider the situation where a fully secret trust was communicated to one joint tenant trustee but not the other. He stated the rules applicable in a technical way, distinguishing between secret trustees who were joint tenants and secret trustees who were tenants in common. In the case of tenants in common, an acceptance of the secret trust by one only will never bind his co-trustee, as tenants in common take a distinct and separate share in property left to them. In the case of joint tenants, however, communication to one of them before the will is made binds all of them, but communication after the will binds only those to whom communication is made.

In his article 'Can you keep half a secret?' (1972) 88 LQR 225, Bryn Perrins suggests that the distinction between joint tenants and tenants in common arises from a misinterpretation of early cases, notably *Huguenin* v *Baseley* (1807) 14 Ves 273, in which the rationale for deciding whether a co-trustee, with whom there was no communication, was bound or not, was whether the testator was induced by the promise of the secret trustee to make (or to leave unrevoked) the gift to him in the will. As the relationship between joint tenants is closer than that between tenants in common, a testator is more likely to assume that a joint tenant will readily accept an obligation imposed on a fellow joint tenant and this could therefore induce the gift to them jointly in the will. Thus communication to one of them before the will is made should bind both of them. It is probably more difficult, however, to prove that a gift previously made was left unrevoked by a subsequent promise, so that even a joint tenant trustee where communication is after the will would not generally be bound. A gift to tenants in common gives each of them a distinct and separate share and it is clearly inappropriate to expect that communication to one of them should bind the others whether before or after the execution of the will.

Applying these rules to the question, the secret trustees are joint tenants as there are no words of severance used in the gift. Communication was made to one of them before the will was made and, following the 'inducement' rationale behind the technical statement of the rules in *Re Stead*, the communication will bind both of them. Both James and Sam are bound by the secret trust for £50,000.

However, the subsequent codicil has to be communicated to the secret trustee and accepted in the same way or it will not bind the trustees: *Re Colin Cooper* [1939] Ch 811. Meg's failure to inform either James or Sam will mean that neither of them is bound by the trust as regards the increased legacy and the trust will not affect the further £50,000 which they will take beneficially as joint tenants.

If the legacy had been left to James and Sam as tenants in common, then only James would have been bound by the secret trust of the first gift of £50,000 in Meg's will, as tenants in common are presumed to take distinct and separate shares and a communication to one will never bind another. James therefore holds £25,000 in trust for the Home. As it is clear from the face of the will that there is a trust, however, Sam will not be able to take beneficially and will hold his share for the residuary legatee. As far as the codicil is concerned, neither of them is bound, and each of them will hold the additional sum given by the codicil on trust for the residuary legatee.

QUESTION 6

Alf is a trustee of the Beta Trust which has a 30% shareholding in Gamma Ltd, a pharmaceutical company developing a new drug to stimulate memory, primarily for students taking examinations. In his position as trustee, Alf learned that tests on the drug were indicative of a successful outcome, and he therefore purchased a 25% shareholding in the company himself. He was subsequently elected as a director of the company and has received considerable sums in director's fees.

Shortly after Alf became a director, the company's lease on its factory premises expired and its landlord wanted to sell the reversion for £100,000. The company could not afford this, so Alf and the company's solicitor, Delta, put up £50,000 each and purchased the reversion themselves jointly. They then granted a new lease to the company at a lower rent than under the previous lease.

The company were also interested in a new drug for improving concentration which had been patented. It was agreed between Alf and Delta that Alf would negotiate to buy the patent and, if successful, would receive for his efforts one per cent of the purchase price. He negotiated a purchase for £20,000.

Alf began to have doubts about the company's future and decided to sell his shareholding and retire from the directorship. Having retired as a trustee from the Beta Trust six months previously, he sold his shares in Gamma Ltd to the trust for £5,000 below the market value.

The new drugs which the company were developing have recently failed pharmaceutical tests and the company's shares are now almost worthless.

Alf and Delta have received an offer of £150,000 for the freehold of the factory premises and would like to sell it.

Discuss Alf's liability as a fiduciary in the various circumstances.

Commentary

This is a fairly lengthy question involving different fiduciary relationships and different breaches of fiduciary duties. It is the type of question which you should therefore spend some time thinking through, jotting down different points and any relevant cases before embarking on the answer. The risk is, if you do not do this, that you will get to the end and find that there are some points or cases which you have omitted. The question is wide in its scope and requires a fair knowledge of the subject to produce a reasonable answer.

Suggested Answer

Equity has consistently demonstrated a harsh attitude to the rule that a fiduciary may not benefit from his position. The rule has been applied even where there is no conflict of interest between the fiduciary and the principal and no evidence of an actual consequent injury to the principal. Indeed, in the House of Lords case of *Boardman* v *Phipps* [1967] 2 AC 46, the trust, as well as the fiduciary, benefited from the fiduciary's activities, but the strict accountability rule was nevertheless applied. Even in these circumstances, a fiduciary will still be accountable for a profit derived from his fiduciary relationship. The only modification of this strict approach is the Privy Council case of *Queensland Mines* v *Hudson* (1978) 18 ALR 1, which appears to be a decision on the particular merits of the case.

Moreover, a fiduciary relationship is broadly defined and is not restricted to trustee and beneficiary. A director is in a fiduciary position to his company, an agent to his principal, and an employee may also be in a fiduciary relationship to his employer (*Agip (Africa) Ltd* v *Jackson* [1991] Ch 547, CA) although this depends on the nature of the work and the terms of the employment contract (*Nottingham University* v *Fischel* [2000] IRLR 471). In *Reading* v *A-G* [1951] AC 507 it was held that an army officer was in a fiduciary position to the Crown.

A trustee who uses his position to appoint himself as a director of a company is prima facie accountable to the trust for any remuneration he receives as a director: *Re Macadam* [1946] Ch 73. In order to be able to keep his director's fees, Alf would have to show that his appointment as a director would have been made even if the votes attaching to the trust's shares had been used against him (per Harman J in *Re Gee* [1948] Ch 284). So if Alf can show that he would still have been elected as a director, notwithstanding that the voting rights of the Beta Trust's shares had been used to vote against him, then he will be able to keep his director's fees. Otherwise, he will be prima facie accountable to the Trust for them. He would also be able to retain his director's fees if authorised in the trust instrument: *Re Llewellin* [1949] Ch 225.

If the trust property includes a lease, a trustee to whom the lease is renewed (*Keech* v *Sandford* (1726) Sel Cas Ch 61), or who purchases a reversion on the lease (*Protheroe* v *Protheroe* [1968] 1 WLR 519, CA), will become a constructive trustee of the lease or reversion for the beneficiaries. In *Protheroe*, a husband and wife were co-owners of a leasehold interest in their matrimonial home. They separated and the husband subsequently purchased the reversion on the lease. It was held that this became trust property in which his wife also had an interest. As a director of Gamma Ltd, Alf is in a fiduciary position to the company and would therefore hold one-half of the reversion on the lease as a constructive trustee for the company. He would similarly be accountable for one-half of any profit made on its sale. It is irrelevant that the company itself could not have purchased the reversion, or that the company itself benefited from the transaction. In *Regal (Hastings) Ltd* v *Gulliver* [1942] 1 All ER 378, HL, directors purchased shares, which the company could not afford to purchase, in order to enable the company to take a lease of a cinema, and subsequently to sell it with other property owned by the company at a profit. They were nevertheless held accountable for their profits as they had acquired their shares through their fiduciary position. Delta, as the company's solicitor, would also be in a fiduciary position and similarly accountable.

In *Guinness plc* v *Saunders* [1990] 2 AC 663 a director who received an unauthorised fee of 0.2% of the value of a takeover bid was held by the House of Lords to be a constructive trustee of this for the company. Neither was he able to claim payment for his services on a *quantum meruit* as he had created a conflict of interest between himself (in whose interest it was to pay a high price) and the company. Assuming that Delta was not authorised to award director's remuneration, the agreement between Delta and Alf would not be binding on the company, and any commission would be a profit derived from Alf's fiduciary position as a director. He would therefore not be able to claim any such commission. As in *Guinness plc* v *Saunders*, any such agreement would also create a conflict of interest between Alf and the company in that Alf has an interest in purchasing for a high price and the company in purchasing for a low price. He would similarly not have any claim for work undertaken in this connection on a *quantum meruit*.

The case of *Boardman* v *Phipps* [1967] 2 AC 46, HL, indicates that a trustee or fiduciary who uses information obtained as a result of his fiduciary position to make a profit will be a constructive trustee of that profit for the trust. If Alf's knowledge were the reason for his acquisition of his 25% shareholding and this resulted in profits, he might be accountable for these. If it could be shown that Alf had serious doubts about the company's future when he sold the shares to the Trust, this would amount to a breach of his fiduciary duty and he might be made liable for the subsequent loss to the Trust.

The rule in *ex parte Lacey* (1802) 6 Ves 625, which is strictly applied, precludes a trustee from purchasing trust property, and this applies even after a trustee has retired: *Wright* v *Morgan* [1926] AC 788. A trustee's liability does not necessarily cease on his retirement: he or his estate will remain liable for breaches of trust committed during his trusteeship. The rule in *ex parte Lacey* applies to any dealing between the trustee in his personal capacity and in his capacity as trustee. In *Bentley* v *Craven* (1853) 18 Beav 75, it was held that an agent employed to purchase sugar for a company could not sell to the company sugar he had purchased himself, even at the market price, unless his interest was declared and accepted by the company. In that case, Romilly MR said (obiter) that the same principle would apply to other fiduciary relationships, including a dealing by a trustee with a trust. The transaction necessarily puts the agent in a position of conflict with his principal as to price. Unless there is a full disclosure as to the agent's interest, which is accepted by the principal, the principal may either repudiate the transaction or claim any profit which the agent makes on it. It is quite possible here, therefore, that the Trust could repudiate the sale to them and claim back the purchase price. It is irrelevant that it was an advantageous sale to the Trust at the time when it was made.

QUESTION 7

The issue on this appeal concerns only the accessory liability principle. Different considerations apply to the two heads of liability. Recipient liability is restitution-based, accessory liability is not. (Lord Nicholls in *Royal Brunei Airlines Sdn Bhd* v *Tan* [1995] 2 AC 378, HL).

Explain and discuss the basis of liability of a third party who deals with, or receives, property in breach of a fiduciary obligation.

Commentary

As indicated in the introduction to this chapter, this is one of the most complicated areas of law. The Privy Council case of *Royal Brunei Airlines Sdn Bhd* v *Tan* [1995] 2 AC 378, has clarified the basis of liability upon which an agent may be made liable as a constructive trustee, but further cases are needed to settle the basis of liability for a recipient, which is moving towards restitution and a strict liability. The cases themselves have often been complex fraud cases, making it difficult to apply notions of 'knowledge' or 'unconscionability'. A knowledge of the principles of and the cases on tracing, which is related to this subject, should assist.

Suggested Answer

The classic statement as to the liability of an agent who deals with trust property (or property which is subject to a fiduciary obligation) inconsistently with the interests of the trust or the obligation is that of Lord Selborne in *Barnes* v *Addy* (1874) 9 Ch App 244, where he said: '... strangers are not to be made constructive trustees merely because they act as the agents of trustees in transactions within their legal powers ... unless those agents receive and become chargeable with some part of the trust property or unless they assist with knowledge in a dishonest and fraudulent design on the part of the trustees'. This recognises that the demands of commercial expediency will usually preclude an agent from making exhaustive enquiries as to the propriety of a transaction in which he is instructed and affords to an agent a necessary measure of protection. Lord Selborne went on to say that, without such protection, no agent could safely undertake business on behalf of someone else.

The problem which has beset the courts is the degree of knowledge required by the agent to fix him with liability as a constructive trustee for receiving or dealing with 'trust' property. In some of the cases, the judges have said that the same degree of knowledge is necessary for both heads of liability (see Megarry V-C in *Re Montagu's Settlements* [1987] Ch 264 (but this was only obiter), Knox J in *Cowan de Groot Properties Ltd* v *Eagle Trust plc* [1992] 4 All ER 700, and Millett J in *Agip (Africa) Ltd* v *Jackson* [1990] Ch 265, where he opined that there could be little sense in requiring dishonesty and actual knowledge to make a receiver liable whilst negligence or constructive knowledge would suffice for an agent's liability).

Before the decision in *Royal Brunei Airlines Sdn Bhd* v *Tan* [1995] 2 AC 378, a number of complicated fraud cases came before the courts where agents (often banks) had assisted in the disposal of monies in breach of a fiduciary obligation. In some of these cases, the courts had found that constructive knowledge of a fraudulent design was sufficient to fix a bank with liability (*Selangor United Rubber Estates* v *Cradock (Bankrupt) (No. 3)* [1968] 1 WLR 1555; *Karak Rubber Co. Ltd* v *Burden (No. 2)* [1972] 1 WLR 602). This was contrary to the earlier decision in *Williams-Ashman* v *Price and Williams* [1942] 1 Ch 219, which adhered strictly to the protection afforded to an agent by *Barnes* v *Addy* and did not impose liability even for negligence (although nowadays this would of course be actionable in tort). Constructive knowledge has now been firmly rejected, however, as the basis for an agent's liability by Lord Nicholls in *Royal Brunei Airlines*. Although the Privy Council case is not of course a binding precedent for the English courts, the decision has been welcomed for its clarification of the basis for what Lord Nicholls has called accessory liability, which is dishonesty judged objectively but taking account of the agent's business experience. Unfortunately, there is no clear guidance as yet as to the basis for imposing a constructive trust in cases of recipient liability.

Many of the earlier cases used a five-fold classification of knowledge, agreed by counsel and accepted by Peter Gibson J in *Baden Delvaux & Lecuit* v *Société Générale* [1983] BCLC 325 to determine whether a defendant had sufficient knowledge to have been acting dishonestly. *Baden* (like many of the cases in this area) involved a large international fraud, whereby a bank was instructed to transfer a large sum of money (being part of the proceeds of a fraud) to Panama. The bank was uneasy about the instruction, but the only notice it had received that the monies belonged to the plaintiff was a letter from the plaintiff's accountant; and as against that, the direction to transfer the money was in accordance with a court order (which was in fact erroneous) made in the Bahamas. In an action against the bank for disposing of the money and thereby assisting in a breach of a fiduciary obligation, Peter Gibson J accepted counsel's categorisation of the types of knowledge which could make the bank liable. These were:

(a)   actual knowledge;

(b)   wilfully shutting one's eyes to the obvious ('Nelsonian' knowledge);

(c)   wilfully and recklessly failing to make the enquiries which a reasonable and honest man would make (called by David Hayton 'naughty' knowledge);

(d)   knowledge of circumstances which would indicate the facts to an honest and reasonable man;

(e)   knowledge of circumstances which would put an honest and reasonable man on enquiry.

The judge decided that, in the circumstances, the bank did not have sufficient notice.

In most of the cases where the degree of knowledge has fallen to be considered, the judges have accepted the first three categories as a trigger for liability but not the last two, which are akin to constructive notice. Megarry J in *Re Montagu* criticised the importation into commercial areas of a doctrine evolved in property law to determine whether a purchaser of land is to be bound by equitable interests affecting the land. This criticism has received approval (see Lord Browne-Wilkinson in *Westdeutsche Landesbank Girocentrale* v *Islington LBC* [1996] AC 669) and indeed makes sense. A purchaser of land has all the time in the world to make enquiries and to investigate a title, but a person involved in a commercial transaction is expected to respond to his client's instructions with speed and efficiency. Millett J in *Agip* felt that the heads of knowledge were only helpful in assisting to identify dishonesty or 'a want of probity', and Knox J in *Cowan de Groot* again referred to 'a want of probity' as the requirement for liability for both knowing assistance and knowing receipt. He also pointed out, however, that even where an agent makes the appropriate enquiries as to the nature of a transaction, he may well not discover the truth, as fraudsters are not generally people who readily disclose their activities! In *Baden*, the bank was suspicious, but its suspicions were allayed by reassurances from its clients and the erroneous court order. The circumstances of the cases differ so enormously that they are not easily susceptible to the application of a given formula.

Happily, the appeal to the Privy Council in the *Royal Brunei Airlines* case has now settled the requirement to make an agent liable as a constructive trustee as dishonesty, which Lord Nicholls said was synonymous with 'want of probity'. Moreover, dishonesty should be judged from an objective viewpoint, and will be what Knox J in *Cowan de Groot* described as 'commercially unacceptable conduct in the particular context involved'. The court must also take account, however, of the agent's experience and personal attributes and his reasons for acting as he did. Lord Nicholls said that 'knowing' assistance was not an apt test for accessory liability, and that the scale of knowledge accepted by Peter Gibson J in *Baden* was best forgotten.

The *Royal Brunei Airlines* case dealt, of course, only with accessory liability, so that there is no clear indication as to what is required to make a recipient liable as a constructive trustee. However, there have been successful actions at common law to recover property to which a claimant has a legal title. In *Jones (FC) & Sons (Trustee)* v *Jones* [1997] Ch 159, a trustee in bankruptcy was able to recover the bankrupt's money and a profit made from it by investment after the bankruptcy order. In *Lipkin Gorman* v *Karpnale* [1991] AC 548, a firm of solicitors was able to recover money received by the Playboy Club that had been misappropriated by a former partner in their firm. These actions are, as Lord Nicholls indicated, basically actions for restitution. Their success depends upon the claimant being able to show that the defendant has received his property (or other property exchanged for it by applying the process of tracing). In *Lipkin Gorman*, the House of Lords said that the right of recovery against an innocent recipient should be subject to a defence of 'change of position', and the Playboy Club in that case were only required to divulge their winnings derived from the misappropriation subject to any monies they had paid out on successful bets. The action is essentially a personal claim at common law to recover the value of the legal owner's property. An equitable proprietary claim can of course be brought by a person with an equitable title, and *Re Diplock* [1948] Ch 465 (discussed in Chapter 12) is an example of this. Such an action will be good against an innocent volunteer and everyone except equity's darling (a bona fide purchaser for value without notice); but in common with all equitable remedies, it is discretionary and will not be granted if it would cause undue hardship. This was in fact the ground on which the proprietary claims against some of the charities in *Re Diplock* failed. This has been criticised as being unduly generous to the innocent volunteer at the expense of the equitable owner, and in *Boscawan v Bajwa* [1996] 1 WLR 328, Millett LJ indicated a preference for the partial defence of 'change of position' to equitable tracing to the all-or-nothing defence of an inequitable result. He suggested that this should be left to develop on a case-by-case basis. He also allowed a claim by subrogation, which had previously been rejected in *Re Diplock*.

As the law currently stands, it seems that, at least in commercial transactions, the personal liability of a defendant who receives property in breach of trust or in breach of fiduciary duty depends upon his being a constructive trustee, and he will be a constructive trustee only if his conscience is affected (Lord Browne-Wilkinson in the *Westdeutsche Landesbank* case). The defendant's liability in such circumstances is therefore based on fault, not restitution, as Lord Nicholls stated in the quotation set out in the question. The defendant may be enriched in such circumstances, but his enrichment will be treated as legal and justifiable unless it can be established that there was a want of probity on his part. The onus is therefore on the claimant to establish such want of probity.

Different principles may apply in non-commercial transactions. This was the position in *Re Diplock*, where the mere fact that the charities were innocent volunteers did not save them from being personally liable to account for the property they had received. Their liability was absolute, not fault-based. In *Re Diplock*, Lord Simonds indicated that, for historical reasons, such action *in personam*, whilst available to persons entitled in equity to property wrongfully distributed under a will, might not be available to claimants where property has been wrongfully distributed under an *inter vivos* trust. Such distinction seems to be unjustifiable in principle; and if the action *in personam* in *Re Diplock* were made available in all cases of distribution of property in breach of fiduciary duty, the potential liability of an innocent recipient of such property would turn on whether the receipt occurred in the course of a commercial, or a property, transaction.

Writing extra-judicially, Lord Nicholls has suggested that 'Restitutionary liability, applicable regardless of fault but subject to a defence of change of position, would be a better-tailored response to the underlying mischief of misapplied property than personal liability which is exclusively fault-based.' However, in *BCCI Ltd* v *Akindele* [2000] 4 All ER 221, at p. 236, Nourse LJ expressed doubt whether such an approach would be preferable in many commercial transactions, and he thought that, in a case such as that before him, where directors had misapplied a company's funds, it might be commercially unworkable.

As far as recipient liability is concerned, therefore, the law is currently far from clear. It may be in a process of transition towards a restitution-based liability independent of fault, with change of position as a defence. As yet, however, that position has not been reached, and the doubts expressed in the *Akindele* case indicate that such a development is by no means assured.

QUESTION 8

(a) Wynken and Nod are the two partners in a firm of solicitors, Blynken & Co. Wynken acts for the Fishnet Trust. Wynken, on the instructions of Sleepy, the sole trustee of the Trust, paid out £30,000 to one of the beneficiaries believing her to be entitled to this sum, although had he looked at the trust deed in his office safe he would have realised that she was not.

Consider the liability to the beneficiaries of the Fishnet Trust of (i) Wynken and (ii) Nod.

Would your answers differ if it were found that Sleepy's appointment as trustee had not been properly effected?

(b) Spark was employed as an agent by Watts Ltd to sell the company's electrical goods.

He called on Flex and agreed to sell to him a consignment of refrigerators for £70,000, which was £10,000 below the market price. Flex was aware of this but was told by Spark that they were an end of range consignment.

Spark also said that he wanted an immediate payment by cheque rather than payment by the usual invoice system. Flex therefore gave Spark a cheque for £70,000 payable to Watts Ltd, and the refrigerators were delivered to Flex. Spark had opened another bank account in the name of Watts Ltd, two months earlier, and he paid the cheque into it. There were no other transactions on the company's account. Spark then transferred the money in this account to a personal account of his in Luxembourg.

Spark has now disappeared.

Advise Watts Ltd.

Commentary

This question requires the application of the principles of law outlined in the suggested answer to Question 7 to given circumstances. Although the circumstances for imposing a constructive trust on an accessory to a breach of a fiduciary duty have been clarified in *Royal Brunei Airlines Sdn Bhd* v *Tan* [1995] 2 AC 378, the case did not concern a person who receives property in breach of such a duty. The law is therefore still uncertain in this area, and because liability will depend upon a detailed analysis of the facts, you cannot be expected to reach any definite conclusions. What you can be expected to do however is to show that you recognise the points of law which the questions raise and to demonstrate a knowledge of the principles applied in the different cases. This is a difficult area and the same observation may be made as regards Question 7 — it is not a topic for the faint hearted!

Suggested Answer

(a)(i) Wynken is an agent who has assisted in a breach of trust. Whilst it is possible that he may be liable in damages for negligence, he will not incur accessory liability under a constructive trust unless he has acted dishonestly (*Royal Brunei Airlines Sdn Bhd* v *Tan* [1995] 2 AC 378) and this does not appear to be the case.

In *Barnes* v *Addy* (1874) 9 Ch App 244, a solicitor who drew up a deed appointing, against his better judgment, the husband of a beneficiary to be the sole trustee of a trust was held not to be liable for the trustee's subsequent default. Lord Selborne LC was at pains to stress that an agent should not be liable for breach of trust unless he has knowledge of the trustee's fraudulent or dishonest design or unless he receives and becomes chargeable with some part of the trust fund. The principle is therefore that an agent should be safe if he acts honestly in carrying out the instructions of his principal.

In *Williams-Ashman* v *Price and Williams* [1942] 1 Ch 219, a firm of solicitors, on a trustee's instructions, paid out money to someone who was not a beneficiary. They were held not liable to account for the loss, even though they could have ascertained the true position from a trust deed in their possession at any time. More recently, in *Re Montagu's Settlement Trusts* [1987] 1 Ch 264, Megarry V-C found that there was no liability even for wrongful (and beneficial) receipt of trust property provided that it was innocent and the result, as in that case, of 'an honest muddle'.

The earlier cases (*Selangor United Rubber Estates* v *Cradock* [1968] 1 WLR 1555 and *Karak Rubber Co. Ltd* v *Burden (No. 2)* [1972] 1 WLR 602) where constructive notice, which it might be said that Wynken had, are now no longer good law.

(ii) If Wynken were liable as a constructive trustee then his partner Nod might be vicariously liable, under s. 10 of the Partnership Act 1980, if Wynken was acting 'in the ordinary course of business'. In *Dubai Aluminium Co. Ltd* v *Salaam* [2000] 3 WLR 910 the Court of Appeal said that what was 'in the ordinary course of business' for any particular partnership must be a matter of fact in each case. They said that the 'wrongful act or omission' referred to in s. 10 was wider than common law torts and would cover accessory liability in equity. They distinguished the *Brunei* case, however, where an innocent person was dealing with a dishonest agent, from the situation in *Dubai* where the persons dealing with the partner were themselves dishonest and could not possibly have thought that the partner, who was also implicated, was therefore acting in the ordinary course of business. Nod's liability might therefore depend upon whether Sleepy could genuinely have believed that Wynken was acting in the ordinary course of business.

If the trustee's appointment had not been properly effected then Wynken could not have been acting as an agent. In *Blyth* v *Fladgate* [1891] 1 Ch 327, Smith, a partner in a firm of solicitors, continued to deal with trust funds after the death of the sole trustee. He was held liable for the resulting losses and his co-partners were also held liable as intermeddlers. Similarly, in the problem, Wynken may have realised that he was effectively acting as a principal and be liable.

In *Mara* v *Browne* [1896] 1 Ch 199, it was suggested (obiter) in the Court of Appeal that the protection of *Barnes* v *Addy* should still be available to an agent who does not realise that his principal has not been properly appointed. If, therefore, Wynken did not realise that the trustee was not validly appointed, he may escape liability.

In *Re Bell's Indenture*, Vinelott J indicated that the liability of an agent's co-partners depends upon whether the agent was acting for a properly appointed trustee. Another explanation for the earlier cases is, however, possible. Thus in *Blyth* v *Fladgate* the funds, before being invested by Smith, had already been received by the firm in the course of the firm's business. Each partner was therefore liable, under principles of partnership law, for their subsequent misapplication. In *Mara* v *Browne*, by contrast, the solicitor, Browne, paid the trust monies into his own private bank account: there was, therefore, never any receipt by the firm. On this basis, if the trust fund had been received by the firm (perhaps by being paid into the firm's client account) then if Wynken is liable, so is Nod: see Luxton [1981] Conv 310. It should be noted that in *Agip (Africa) Ltd* v *Jackson* [1991] Ch 547, Fox LJ, albeit without any analysis of the earlier cases, assumed that a co-partner of an agent who became liable as a constructive trustee was also liable.

(b) Spark, as an agent of Watts Ltd, stood in a fiduciary relationship to the company, and he clearly breached that duty by the opening of the account in his principal's name and using it to make off with the proceeds of the cheque paid to him by Flex.

There are two claims which Watts Ltd might possibly have against Flex. The first would be a proprietary claim to recover the refrigerators from Flex. Watts Ltd would not be able to trace at law, since their agent would have had authority to pass the legal title in the refrigerators to a purchaser. They would, however, satisfy the first two requirements to trace in equity: namely, a fiduciary relationship (with Spark) and traceable property (the refrigerators). Flex might nevertheless have the defence of bona fide purchaser for value without notice, which is a complete defence to a tracing claim in equity. Flex has provided consideration for the purchase, since it has paid for the refrigerators by cheque. The central issue would therefore be whether it had notice, which in equity includes actual, constructive and imputed notice. If the circumstances surrounding the transaction, for instance, should have put Flex on inquiry that a fraud was being perpetrated by Spark, Watts Ltd would be able to trace the refrigerators into Flex's hands. The company would then be able to obtain an order in equity for their specific return. If, however, Flex could establish the bona fide purchaser defence, he would have a complete defence to a tracing claim.

If Flex did have notice, however, the refrigerators would be traceable into his hands. Flex might have a change of position defence, if he has since disposed of the refrigerators, but such a defence would be available only if Flex was an honest recipient. It is possible that he could have constructive notice without being dishonest, e.g., if he was simply duped by Spark. On the facts of the problem, there are circumstances which might indicate that Flex was put on notice, or himself lacked probity. It is a matter of evidence, and it might be considered that Flex was offered a satisfactory explanation why the purchase price was less than might be expected. Furthermore, Flex did write a cheque in favour of the agent's principal, Watts Ltd, not to the agent himself. On the facts, then, Flex may have a complete defence to a tracing claim.

The second possible claim which Watts Ltd might have against Flex is a personal claim to make him account as a constructive trustee for the normal sale price of the refrigerators (£80,000). Flex will be liable as a constructive trustee only if it can be established that he was a dishonest accessory to the fraud, or received the refrigerators with knowledge of the fraud. In *Royal Brunei Airlines* v *Tan* [1995] AC 378, the Privy Council held that, for accessory liability, dishonesty is a necessary ingredient. Liability as a constructive trustee on this head merely on the ground of negligence (which had been held sufficient in some earlier cases, notably *Selangor United Rubber Estates* v *Cradock (No. 3)* [1968] 1 WLR 1555) would therefore no longer seem to be good law. In the case of knowing receipt, it was also recently held that a claim against a recipient of property in breach of a fiduciary duty will lie only if it would be 'unconscionable' for him to keep the property: *BCCI Ltd* v *Akindele* [2000] 4 All ER 221, CA.

For each type of liability as a constructive trustee, therefore, dishonesty (or want of probity) on the part of Flex is required. The onus of proof of dishonesty would be on Watts Ltd. Purchasing property at an undervalue is not necessarily evidence of want of probity: *Cowan de Groot Properties Ltd* v *Eagle Trust plc* [1992] 4 All ER 700.

If Flex could establish the defence of bona fide purchaser to the first claim set out above, he would, of course, also have a defence to an action to make him liable as constructive trustee.

10   Administration of Trusts

INTRODUCTION

Administration of trusts involves a study of a number of discrete, but related, topics. You may well find that different topics within administration of trust form separate halves of a single question. Trustee investment, for instance, might form part (a) of a question in which part (b) is variation of trusts. You are therefore advised to revise all aspects of administration of trusts which appear on your course.

QUESTION 1

(a)   Ann, Bob, and Cindy are the trustees of a private trust set up under the will of a testator who died earlier this year; the beneficiaries are members of the testator's family. The assets of the trust comprise shares in the testator's family business, Fruitrite Ltd, which engages in market-gardening. Ann is a solicitor, Bob is an accountant, and Cindy was a friend of the testator and has considerable experience of market-gardening.

The trust instrument contains no provision for remuneration of the trustees. Advise the trustees whether they are entitled to claim remuneration for acting as trustees.

(b)   Trevor is the sole trustee of an exhaustive discretionary trust of income, the objects of which are the nephews and nieces of Sally. Sally has two nephews, Benjy and Damian, and one niece, Caroline. Six months ago Trevor lent Benjy the sum of £20,000 out of his (Trevor's) own money. Caroline and Damian have now learned that Trevor has decided to pay the entire income of the trust for the present year, some £15,000, to Benjy. Caroline and Damian claim that Trevor exercised his discretion under the trust in Benjy's favour only in order that Benjy would be in sufficient funds to repay that loan. Caroline and Damian wish to have the proposed exercise of the discretion prevented, and further wish to compel Trevor to distribute the income for the present year among all three objects equally.

Advise Caroline and Damian.

Commentary

Part (a) of the question involves an area affected by the Trustee Act 2000, with which the examiners will expect you to be familiar. The answer deals mostly with the exceptions to the basic rule, but the student should always remember to state what the basic principle is before coming to the exceptions. Part (b) concerns review of trustees' decisions. Unless the examination paper indicates otherwise, you might reasonably assume that, where a question is in separate parts, such as this one, each part carries equal marks. The candidate should therefore try to allocate roughly an equal amount of time to tackling each part.

Suggested Answer

(a)   The general rule is that a trustee is not entitled to claim remuneration for carrying out his office: *Robinson* v *Pett* (1734) 2 P Wms 249. This general rule admits of a number of exceptions. A trustee is entitled to charge if the trust instrument so provides, but as the trust instrument in the problem does not contain a charging clause, this exception need not be considered further.

An important exception to the general rule was recently introduced in the Trustee Act 2000. If the requirements of that Act are met, a trustee of a private trust who acts in a professional capacity may be entitled to receive reasonable remuneration out of the trust funds for any services that he provides to the trust. The requirements are that the trustee is not a sole trustee, that each other trustee has agreed in writing that he may be remunerated (Trustee Act 2000, s. 29(2)) and that no provision for remuneration is made by the trust instrument (s. 29(5)(a)). A trustee acts in a professional capacity if he acts in the course of a profession or business which includes the provision of services in connection with the management or administration of trusts generally (or any particular aspect of such management or administration) or a particular kind of trust (s. 28(5)). A trustee is entitled to remuneration under the statutory provision even if the services in question could be provided by a lay trustee (s. 29(4)).

In the problem, there appear to be two trustees who might be able to take advantage of such statutory provision of remuneration. These are Ann and Bob, each of whom is likely to be able to satisfy the requirement that they act in a professional capacity. If each of them is to be entitled to remuneration, each will need the agreement in writing of the other two trustees. If such agreement is obtained, Ann and Bob will be able to charge for all work that they perform as trustees, not merely work undertaken in their professional capacities.

Cindy, however, will be unable to take advantage of the statutory provision for remuneration. Although it might be advantageous to the trust to have as one of its trustees a person, such as Cindy, who has expertise in the business in which the trust's shares are invested, she does not act in a professional capacity for the purposes of the Trustee Act 2000. If, therefore, Cindy wishes to claim remuneration for acting as a trustee, she will need to come under one of the other exceptions to the general rule.

Any beneficiary who consents in advance to Cindy's receiving remuneration will be estopped from bringing any claim against her to make her account for any remuneration she does receive; but Cindy could still be made to account for remuneration at the behest of those beneficiaries who did not so agree. Cindy could therefore safely receive remuneration only if she has the consent of all the beneficiaries, and only if such beneficiaries are all *sui iuris* and together form a closed class. The problem does not itself indicate whether the beneficiaries meet these requirements, but even if they do, they might not all agree.

The final avenue open to Cindy would be to seek the consent of the court to approving prospective remuneration. That the court has jurisdiction to award future remuneration was confirmed in *Re Duke of Norfolk's Settlement Trusts* [1982] Ch 61. The criterion for such award is the overall benefit of the trust; but it is clear that the power will be exercised only in exceptional circumstances, where the trustee's skill and experience are of particular value to the trust. In the *Norfolk* case, the Court of Appeal did make an award of future remuneration beyond that permitted in the trust instrument, but that was in circumstances where it became apparent that the work that would need to be undertaken as trustee considerably exceeded that which might have been apparent at the time the trustee accepted office. Unless Cindy could make out a comparable case, it is unlikely that the court would make an award of future remuneration in her favour.

(b) If Trevor has exercised the discretion vested in him in order to ensure that he is repaid the debt Benjy owes him, this is an improper exercise of the discretion. It is improper because the power of selection must be exercised in good faith and for its proper purpose: the trustee must consider the objects' interests, not his own. If Caroline and Damian can prove that the exercise was so motivated, they can apply to the court to have the improper appointment set aside, and Trevor will be personally liable to them for any loss resulting from the breach of trust: *Molyneux* v *Fletcher* [1898] 1 QB 648.

The problem for Caroline and Damian, however, is essentially one of proof. A trustee is not obliged to give reasons for the exercise of his discretions: *Re Beloved Wilkes' Charity* (1851) 3 Mac & G 440 and *Re Londonderry's Settlement* [1965] Ch 918, CA. If, however, a trustee does give reasons, and these are improper, the objects can have the exercise set aside: *Klug* v *Klug* [1918] 2 Ch 67.

A beneficiary or object has a prima facie right to inspect trust documents: *O'Rourke* v *Darbishire* [1920] AC 581, HL. This right, however, does not extend to documents which detail the trustees' reasons for selecting amongst the objects of a discretionary trust. This principle derives from *Re Londonderry*, where one of the objects of a fiduciary power objected to the small amount of capital allocated to her by the trustees. She asked to see copies of the minutes of trustees' meetings and other correspondence in the hope that these would reveal the basis for the trustees' allocation. The Court of Appeal stated that disclosure of such confidential information could cause infinite trouble in the family out of all proportion to any resulting benefit. Moreover, if the trustees knew that they could be required to make such disclosure, it might interfere with the proper exercise of the discretion.

The Court of Appeal in *Re Londonderry* thought that the position would be entirely different were a case made of *mala fides*. The problem for the objects, however, is that such evidence of *mala fides* may be difficult to obtain without recourse to such documents. Thus, in the absence of a statement by Trevor revealing bad faith, Caroline and Damian may find it difficult to prove that the exercise was improper. It has, however, been suggested that beneficiaries could circumvent this problem by their instituting litigation alleging an improper exercise of the trustees' discretion, and then obtaining disclosure of documents in the proceedings: Megarry (1965) 81 LQR 196.

Even if Caroline and Damian succeed in having the exercise set aside, they cannot themselves compel Trevor positively to exercise his discretion as they direct. All three objects together, assuming they are all *sui iuris* and form a closed class, could compel the distribution of the income to them under an extension of the rule in *Saunders* v *Vautier* (1841) 4 Beav 115. Caroline and Damian, however, are only two of the three objects of the discretionary trust of income.

It is unclear, however, whether the court would itself be able (or willing) to exercise the trustee's dispositive discretion under a discretionary trust. In *Klug* v *Klug* itself, the court did order the advancement to be made; but it may be that it was merely giving effect to the wishes of the remaining trustee whose decision was not tainted by improper considerations. In *McPhail* v *Doulton* [1971] AC 424, the House of Lords stated that the court would, if called upon to do so, execute a discretionary trust in the manner best calculated to give effect to the settlor's intentions; and, ultimately, where a proper basis for distribution appears, this could be by itself directing the trustees so to distribute. In so holding, it revived the authority of eighteenth-century cases where the court had itself executed a discretionary trust: *Warburton* v *Warburton* (1702) 4 Bro PC 1, and *Richardson* v *Chapman* (1760) 7 Bro PC 318. This jurisdiction will be exercised only in the last resort: cf. *Mettoy Pension Trustees* v *Evans* [1990] 1 WLR 1587, where the court exercised the same jurisdiction to execute a fiduciary power. In practice, therefore, where a trustee persistently fails properly to exercise his discretion to appoint amongst the objects, the latter might be better advised to seek such trustee's removal and replacement: *Re Gestetner Settlement* [1953] Ch 672 admits of such possibility.

QUESTION 2

Six months ago, Topaz, a trustee, wished to sell some jewellery which belonged to the trust. He asked Jade, a jeweller whom he knew to have been fined for smuggling stones into the country a few years earlier, to carry out a valuation. Jade valued the jewellery at £100,000. In reliance upon this, Topaz instructed Jade to sell the jewellery for that amount to Sapphire, which he did. A month later, Sapphire sold the jewellery at an auction for five times that amount.

Three months after the sale, Jade had still not accounted to Topaz for the proceeds. Topaz then began to press Jade for payment, but was met with evasive replies. Last week, Topaz learned that Jade lost the entire £100,000 proceeds whilst gambling, and is now insolvent.

(a) Advise the beneficiaries of the trust as to their rights against Topaz.

(b) How would your advice differ if the trust had contained a clause excluding the trustee from all liability other than for 'wilful default'?

Commentary

The need to answer only what is asked and no more is vividly illustrated in part (a) of this question. You should deal with the rights against Topaz only. It earns no marks whatever to consider any rights the beneficiaries may have against any other parties mentioned. Differently worded, it could easily have become a question on tracing and third party receivers or dealers — but it is not. If you know your stuff, your answer should be a little gem.

The powers of a trustee to delegate have been considerably extended by the Trustee Act 2000; the examiners will expect you to be fully acquainted with the new law. It should be noted that the appointment of an 'agent' under the statutory provision is not restricted to the appointment of an agent in the contractual sense, i.e., for entering into agreements with third parties. Thus, although a person appointed to value property is not a contractual agent, the Trustee Act 1925, s. 22(3), expressly permits trustees to have the trust property valued 'by duly qualified agents'. It seems likely that the term 'agent' is used in a similarly wide sense in the Trustee Act 2000. A trustee is, for example, under a duty to keep proper accounts (*Pearse* v *Green* (1819) 1 Jac & W 135, 140). Such a duty comprises a 'delegable function' (s. 39(1)) of a trustee of a private trust, so it seems that an accountant might be appointed to maintain the trust accounts as an agent under s. 11.

Part (b) concerns the validity of trustee exclusion clauses. These are quite common in trust instruments nowadays, and it seems generally to be accepted that the Unfair Contract Terms Act 1977 does not apply to trustee exclusion clauses: Goodhart, 'Trust Law for the Twenty-First Century (1996) 10 *Trust Law International* No. 2, 38. Since the Court of Appeal in *Armitage* v *Nurse* [1998] Ch 241 upheld the validity of a very wide exclusion clause, however, such clauses have been a matter of concern, being the subject of a Consultation Paper, *Trustee Exemption Clauses*, produced by the Trust Law Committee in 1998.

During the passage of the Trustee Bill 2000 through the House of Lords, some of their Lordships expressed concern that professional persons acting for a settlor in drawing up a trust instrument are effectively free to insert an exclusion clause protecting them from liability, whilst at the same time charging for their professional services to the trust. The Lord Chancellor agreed that the matter needed to be looked into and referred it to the Law Commission. It is therefore possible that, after the Law Commission has reported, there may be further trust legislation to restrict the validity of such clauses. For an analysis of the validity of trustee exclusion clauses at present, see Luxton, 'Trustee Exclusion Clauses: Lost in the Heather?' in *Modern Studies in Property Law: Volume 1: Property 2000*, ed. Elizabeth Cooke, Oxford: Hart Publishing, 2001, chap. 3, at pp. 59–75.

Suggested Answer

(a) The sum of at least £100,000 has been lost to the trust as a result of Jade's gambling. It may be that a further £400,000 has been lost through a sale to Sapphire at a considerable undervalue. The beneficiaries have a personal right of action against Topaz to require him to make good this loss if they can establish that Topaz has committed a breach of trust.

In the absence of any provision in the trust instrument, trustees may authorise any person to exercise any delegable function as their agent; and the appointment of an agent to value and to sell trust assets is a delegable function (Trustee Act 2000, s. 11(1), (2)). More specifically, trustees may have trust property valued by duly qualified agents (Trustee Act 1925, s. 22(3)). Topaz may nevertheless be liable to the beneficiaries on various grounds.

First, it could be argued that the appointment of Jade as an agent was wrongful in itself. In appointing a person to act as agent, a trustee is under the statutory duty of care set out in the Trustee Act 2000, s. 1(1) and Sch. 1, para. 3(1)(a). In appointing an agent, Topaz must therefore exercise such care and skill as is reasonable in the circumstances, having regard in particular to any special knowledge or experience he holds himself out as having, or, if he acts as a trustee in the course of a business or profession, to any special knowledge or experience that it is reasonable to expect such a person to have. A trustee will not be liable for any act or default of the agent unless he has failed to comply with that duty of care (Trustee Act 2000, s. 23(1)). In its Report which led to the Trustee Act 2000, the Law Commission took the view that the statutory duty of care codified the liability of a trustee in equity: *Trustees' Powers and Duties*, Law Com No. 260, 1999, para. 3.24. Assuming that this is correct, the principles laid down in the case law before the Trustee Act 2000 continue to apply. The cases establish that a trustee is to be judged by the test of the prudent man of business acting in his own affairs: *Speight* v *Gaunt* (1883) 9 App Cas 1. A prudent man of business would employ an agent only in his proper field (*Fry* v *Tapson* (1884) 28 Ch D 268); and in appointing a jeweller to value and sell jewellery, Topaz has probably satisfied this requirement. A prudent man of business, however, would probably not appoint as his agent to value and sell jewellery belonging to the trust a person whom he knows to have been convicted of a crime involving dishonesty. It is therefore likely that the choice of Jade as agent was itself a breach of trust, so that Topaz is personally liable for the loss to the trust.

Secondly, whilst the Trustee Act 2000 permits a trustee (subject to specified exceptions) to delegate discretions as well as duties, on the facts of the problem Topaz initially asked Jade merely to value the jewellery. The decision to instruct Jade to sell would therefore have needed to be made on the basis of that valuation. If Topaz simply accepted Jade's valuation without himself considering it, this would itself be a breach of trust.

Thirdly, a trustee may not appoint an agent to exercise any 'asset management function' as his agent, except by an agreement which is in, or is evidenced in, writing and on terms that the agent will comply with a policy statement which the trustee has prepared (Trustee Act 2000, s. 15(1), (2)). An asset management function includes the acquisition of property which is to be subject to the trust (s. 15(5)(b)). If Jade was appointed to deal with the sale of the jewellery on the basis that the proceeds of sale would be paid to him, his appointment involved the exercise of an asset management function. Topaz will therefore be liable if his appointment of Jade did not meet the requirements of s. 15.

Fourthly, when a trustee has appointed an agent, he must keep under review the arrangements under which the agent acts, and must consider if there is a need to exercise any power of intervention (which includes giving the agent directions, and revoking the appointment) (Trustee Act 2000, ss. 21, 22). The trustee is therefore effectively under a duty to supervise the agent after appointment, in respect of which he is again subject to the statutory duty of care (s. 2 and Sch. 1, para. 3(1)(e)). It might therefore be argued that Topaz was in breach of his duty as trustee to protect the trust assets, in that he left a large sum of money (the sale proceeds) in Jade's hands for an undue length of time. Three months is surely longer than a prudent man of business would allow. It is likely that Topaz's inaction amounts to a breach of trust.

(b)   An exclusion of liability for wilful default first appeared in trust instruments in the eighteenth century; but the exclusion of liability was put on a statutory footing in various Trustee Acts of the nineteenth century, where the phrase was construed objectively, i.e., so as not to derogate from the principle laid down in *Speight* v *Gaunt* (1883) 9 App Cas 1 that a trustee must act as a prudent man of business would act in his own affairs: *Re Brier* (1884) 26 Ch D 238, CA. The same phrase was used in the Trustee Act 1925, s. 30(1) (now repealed), which Maugham J in *Re Vickery* [1931] 1 Ch 572, however, interpreted literally, i.e., as requiring consciousness of wrongdoing. Maugham J reached this conclusion by relying upon *Re Equitable City Fire Insurance Co. Ltd* [1925] 1 Ch 407, a case which concerned the liability of auditors, not trustees. Maugham J's view conflicted with earlier cases such as *Re Brier*, and effectively made the section a fool's charter. Nevertheless, in *Armitage* v *Nurse* [1998] Ch 241, Millett LJ expressed support for Maugham J's interpretation.

The Trustee Act 1925, s. 30(1) was repealed by the Trustee Act 2000, so that a trustee no longer has the benefit of the statutory exclusion of liability. A trustee may, however, have the benefit of an exclusion of liability clause contained in the trust instrument. The Trustee Act 2000 does not invalidate trustee exclusion clauses; indeed, it effectively provides that the statutory duty of care may be restricted or excluded by the trust instrument (Sch. 1, para. 7). An exclusion clause in the trust instrument may be very wide in scope: the Court of Appeal held in *Armitage* v *Nurse* that such a clause may exclude the liability of a trustee for acts and defaults in carrying out his functions as trustee except those which involve dishonesty. This principle applies even if the trustee is a solicitor and himself prepared the trust instrument: *Bogg* v *Raper* (1998) *The Times*, 22 April, CA. The principle in *Armitage* v *Nurse* was slightly qualified in *Walker* v *Stones* [2000] 4 All ER 412, CA, where it was said that, at least where the trustee is also a solicitor, the test for honesty is not purely subjective. Thus a solicitor-trustee who deliberately acts in breach of trust may be dishonest for this purpose, regardless of his subjective belief, if no reasonable solicitor-trustee could have thought that what he did was for the benefit of the beneficiaries (at p. 443, per Sir Christopher Slade).

The exclusion clause in the trust instrument in the problem will therefore be effective to protect Topaz from liability for breach of trust according to its terms for all acts except those involving 'wilful default' or dishonesty. The question does not state whether Topaz was a solicitor-trustee, but it does not seem that he deliberately acted in breach of trust. In any event, it would not appear from the facts given that he was dishonest, and it may well be that he was not conscious of any wrongdoing. In these circumstances, it seems likely that he will be able to rely on the clause to exclude his liability.

QUESTION 3

By his will, Edward, who died earlier this year, gave £500,000 to his trustees, Sam and Giles, in trust for Edward's daughter, Daphne, for life, remainder to Edward's nephew, Norris. The will gave the trustees an express power to invest in shares quoted on the London Stock Exchange, 'except in shares of Maropet plc'. Sam is a solicitor; Giles is a farmer and an old friend of Edward. Sam and Giles would like to invest part of the trust fund in Old Masters. Norris is a keen environmentalist, and he has written to the trustees asking that they do not make investments in companies which engage in the emission of greenhouse gases.

In the light of these circumstances, advise Sam and Giles:

(a) of their powers of investment;

AND

(b) as to their duties in selecting investments.

Commentary

The law relating to trustee investment has been considerably altered by the Trustee Act 2000, and some of the questions previously set by examiners on this topic are no longer meaningful under the new regime. You should bear this in mind if you look through old examination papers which pre-date that Act. For the most part, the Trustee Act 2000 has (happily!) simplified the law relating to trustee investment. This question deals with those areas which are likely to appear in examination papers following that Act: it covers what qualifies as an investment, and the equitable and statutory duties of trustees relating to the selection and review of investments.

Suggested Answer

(a)   Subject to any provisions in the trust instrument, a trustee may make any kind of investment that he could make if he were absolutely entitled to the trust assets (Trustee Act 2000, s. 3(1)). This power is called 'the general power of investment' (s, 3(2)). The general power of investment does not itself give trustees a power to make investments in land (other than in loans secured on land) (s. 3(3)); trustees are, however, given a separate power to acquire as an investment freehold or leasehold land in the United Kingdom (s. 8(1)(a)).

The general power of investment is additional to any express powers of investment, but is subject to any restriction or exclusion that the trust instrument may contain (s. 6(1)). Had the investment clause in the question provided that the trustees were to be empowered to invest *only* in shares quoted on the London Stock Exchange, the general power of investment would have been effectively excluded. The positive inclusion of a power to invest in shares quoted on the Stock Exchange is not, however, to be treated as an exclusion of the general power of investment. Sam and Giles therefore have the general power of investment, subject only to the restriction on investing in shares in Maropet plc. That this is the intended effect of the statute is apparent from an explanatory note which the Law Commission attached to the clause of its Draft Bill which later became s. 6 of the Trustee Act 2000: Law Commission, *Trustees' Powers and Duties* (Law Com No. 260, 1999).

The older view of an investment is that it is the purchase of property from which interest or income is expected to accrue: *Re Wragg* [1919] 2 Ch 58. More recently, however, it has been accepted that an investment includes any laying out of money with a view to obtaining a return, which suggests that even the purchase of an asset which can produce a return only on sale is included: *Re Lilly's Will Trusts* [1948] 2 All ER 906. The modern view is that investment may include a capital, as well as an income, return: *Cowan* v *Scargill* [1985] Ch 270; *Harries* v *Church Commissioners for England* [1992] 1 WLR 1241, at p. 1246. On this basis, the purchase of Old Masters, which do not themselves produce an income, could today be regarded as an investment. The risk for the trustees, however, is that if such paintings were sold soon after purchase, it might be argued that they were acquired not for investment but for purposes of trading, with the result that the profits of the sale could be liable to income tax.

(b) The Trustee Act 2000 subjects trustees to a statutory duty of care, which applies when a trustee is exercising the general power of investment or any other power of investment, however conferred, or when carrying out his statutory duties in relation to the exercise of a power of investment or to the review of investments (under ss. 4 and 5) (Trustee Act 2000, ss. 1 and 2 and Sch. 1, para. 1).

The duty of care requires a trustee to exercise such care and skill as is reasonable in the circumstances, having regard in particular to any special knowledge or experience that he has or holds himself out as having, and (if he acts as a trustee in the course of a business or profession) to any special knowledge or experience that it is reasonable to expect of such a person (Trustee Act 2000, s. 1(1)). It would appear that this puts into statutory form a distinction which had been previously drawn in the case law, under which a professional trustee (namely a trust corporation) is treated as subject to a higher standard of care than an unpaid (lay) trustee: *Re Waterman's Will Trusts* [1952] 2 All ER 1054; *Bartlett* v *Barclays Bank Trust Co. Ltd (No. 1)* [1980] Ch 515, at p. 534. It would appear from the question that Giles is a lay trustee; he will therefore be judged by the standard of care established in the case law, namely that of the prudent man of business investing for the benefit of persons for whom he feels morally bound to provide: *Re Whiteley* (1886) 33 ChD 347, at p. 355 (Lindley LJ). In investing, therefore, Giles may not take more than a prudent degree of risk: *Learoyd* v *Whiteley* (1887) 12 App Cas 727, at p. 733; *Bartlett* v *Barclays Bank Trust Co. Ltd (No. 1)* [1980] Ch 515, at p. 531. Although he is not a professional trustee, Sam is a professional person, so that it would seem that he will be required to exercise a higher degree of skill in relation to the legal work which he performs for the trust.

In exercising any power of investment, whether under the Trustee Act 2000 or otherwise, a trustee must have regard to the standard investment criteria, and must from time to time review the investments of the trust and consider whether, having regard to such criteria, they should be varied (Trustee Act 2000, s. 4(1), (2)). The standard investment criteria require the trustee to have regard to the suitability of the investment to the trust and to the need for diversification so far as is appropriate to the circumstances of the trust (s. 4(3)). The statutory duty to select suitable investments is two-fold: if, for instance, trustees are considering investing in shares in X plc, they must consider both whether investment in shares is suitable for the trust, and whether shares in X plc are a suitable investment within that class. Diversification is important in order to spread the risk of investment. Sam and Giles might therefore be in breach of trust were they to invest the entire trust fund, for instance, in the shares of one company. The trustees are not, however, guarantors of the success of their investment policy, and so are not liable merely because the investments do not, in the course of time, turn out to have been the most profitable that could have been made: *Nestlé* v *National Westminster Bank plc* [1993] 1 WLR 1260, CA.

Both duties effectively require the trustees to have regard to the particular trust; and the trustees must act even-handedly between the beneficiaries. In the problem, therefore, the investments should be selected so as to provide, so far as possible, both a reasonable income for Daphne for her life, and reasonable capital growth for the remainderman, Norris. The trustees would therefore probably be in breach of trust were they to invest the entire trust fund in Old Masters, since, apart from breaching the duty to diversify, they would be investing in a way that would produce no income for Daphne.

In selecting investments, and having regard to the above, the trustees' duty is to secure the maximum financial return for the trust: *Harries* v *Church Commissioners for England* [1992] 1 WLR 1241, at p. 1246. The consequence is that, in a private trust (such as that in the question), the trustees may not have a policy of ethical investment which would be likely significantly to reduce financial returns. The only exception to this in the case of a private trust is where all the beneficiaries are *sui iuris*, form a closed class and unanimously agree to such a policy: *Cowan* v *Scargill* [1985] Ch 270. Therefore, even assuming Norris is at least 18 years of age, the trustees would probably be in breach of trust in pursuing the ethical policy he proposes unless Daphne expressly agrees to it.

QUESTION 4

Alex died last year. By his will he left his residuary estate to his trustees in trust for his sister, Samantha, for life, remainder to her son, Edwin. The residuary estate comprises the following assets:

    (i)   Rocky, a two-year-old racehorse with many wins to her credit;

    (ii)   an interest in remainder under a trust which will fall into possession on the death of Lionel, who has a life interest thereunder; and

    (iii)   a lease of land in Yorkshire which has 40 years unexpired.

Advise the trustees:

(a)   of their duties to the beneficiaries in relation to these assets;

AND

(b)   whether, and to what extent, the trustees may make advancements to Edwin under the Trustee Act 1925, s. 32.

Commentary

Questions involving the rules in *Howe* v *Earl of Dartmouth* and *Re Earl Chesterfield's Trusts* should appeal to students with an interest in technical details, but wise candidates will not allow the technicalities of the rules to obscure an appreciation of the principles underlying them. It is important to note that the impact of the rules has been affected by the Trustee Act 2000, as virtually all investments are now authorised (the exception being land outside the United Kingdom: s. 8(1)).

The fact that the two parts of the question deal with different areas illustrates the risk that you run if you pick and choose individual topics for revision.

Suggested Answer

(a)   It must be considered whether any of the assets comprising residue fall within the rule in *Howe* v *Earl of Dartmouth* (1802) 7 Ves 137, which is designed to promote equality among beneficiaries. The rule applies (subject to a contrary intention) where residuary personalty is settled by will upon persons in succession; it obliges the trustees to convert into authorised investments such parts as are of a wasting, hazardous, future or reversionary nature, or which consist of unauthorised securities.

The rule is therefore applicable to Rocky, the racehorse, which for a short time might produce a great deal of income, but whose capital value might eventually be no more than horsemeat. The interest in remainder is also subject to the rule: but for the duty to convert, this property would be of no immediate benefit to the life tenant, Samantha.

Under the Trustee Act 2000, s. 8(1), trustees have power to acquire (*inter alia*) leasehold land in the United Kingdom for investment, for occupation by a beneficiary, or for any other reason. They would therefore have power to acquire even a short lease. The rule in *Howe* v *Earl of Dartmouth* cannot therefore apply to the lease of land in Yorkshire. Samantha, the life tenant, will therefore be entitled to all the rent or other income that it produces.

In respect of the racehorse and the interest in remainder, however, the trustees are under a duty not merely to convert, but also to apportion until conversion takes place.

In the absence of a power to postpone sale, Rocky must be valued one year after Alex's death. Whatever income Rocky produces, Samantha is entitled to interest at the rate (subject to the discretion of the court) of 4% per annum on this sum from the date of Alex's death until the conversion is effected. Any shortfall in the actual income in any year must be made good, first out of any surplus in future years and then (if necessary) out of capital when the asset is sold.

Although an interest in remainder is saleable, the uncertainties surrounding the date it will fall into possession, and the amount of inheritance tax that it may have to bear, considerably discount its market value. Generally, therefore, it is better for trustees to retain such interest until it falls into possession. Apportionment is effected under the rule in *Re Earl of Chesterfield's Trusts* (1883) 24 Ch D 643. This requires a reversionary interest to be valued at the date of its sale or (if later) its falling into possession. A proportion of this sum ranks as capital, the balance as income. Let us suppose that the valuation produces a figure of £10,000. The proportion treated as capital is that part of £10,000 which, if invested at 4% interest with yearly rests, would (after deducting income tax at the basic rate) produce the sum of £10,000. Edwin receives that part; the balance goes to Samantha.

   (b)   The power of advancement under the Trustee Act 1925, s. 32, is a power to advance capital money, which therefore excludes money arising by way of income. The statutory power is not applicable to capital monies arising under the Settled Land Act 1925, but that is not relevant in the problem because the trust of the leasehold land in Yorkshire arose only on Alex's death, which was after 1996, since which date no new settlements under the Settled Land Act 1925 can be created. The power is therefore exercisable in respect of all the items of property comprising Alex's residuary estate. Monies raised on the sale (pursuant to the rule in *Howe* v *Earl of Dartmouth*) of Rocky and the interest in remainder could be advanced to Edwin under s. 32, as could any securities (e.g., shares) in which the trustees might invest the proceeds of such sales. Bearing in mind the discounted market value of an interest in remainder, the trustees might be better advised to sell one or more of the other assets. Although the power is to apply only money, in practice the courts have permitted trustees to transfer trust assets, such as land or shares, directly to a beneficiary by way of advancement under the statutory power, rather than requiring the trustees to sell the assets in question to provide the beneficiary with the funds to purchase them for himself: *Re Collard's Will Trusts* [1961] Ch 293.

The power under s. 32 is to advance up to one half of a beneficiary's vested or presumptive share of capital. Since Edwin has a vested interest in the entire capital, the power could extend to a maximum of one half the value of the residuary estate. The written consent of any person with a prior interest (i.e., Samantha) is necessary.

The statutory power is exercisable only for the beneficiary's 'advancement or benefit'. 'Advancement' means establishing the beneficiary in life; 'benefit' is broadly interpreted. Together they mean any use of the money which improves the beneficiary's material situation: *Pilkington* v *IRC* [1964] AC 612, HL. Usually a benefit is a financial benefit (e.g., from tax saving); but it can include even a purely moral benefit. In *Re Clore's Settlement Trusts* [1966] 1 WLR 955, an advancement by way of a gift to charity was held to be for the benefit of a wealthy beneficiary: but the court emphasised that the moral compunction must be that of the beneficiary, not that of the trustees. An advancement may take the form of a sub-trust, and beneficiaries of such sub-trust might even include other persons — such as any children Edwin may have in the future: *Pilkington* v *IRC*. It remains unclear whether an advancement under which the beneficiary is merely a discretionary object suffices. The trustees may make the advancement directly to Edwin, or to Edwin's parent or guardian for Edwin's benefit; but if the advancement is for a specified purpose, the trustees should not pay the money directly to Edwin unless they consider that they can trust him to carry out the prescribed purpose: *Re Pauling's Settlement Trusts* [1964] Ch 303, CA.

QUESTION 5

Mole, who died recently, made the following dispositions in his will:

(a) £10,000 to his son Bill, provided he attained the age of 18;

(b) his shares in Midnight Oil Ltd to his daughter Delia, provided she attained the age of 25; and

(c) his freehold house, Dunromin, to his other daughter Elizabeth, defeasible upon her marrying under the age of 21.

It was further provided that neither of the dispositions to the daughters should take effect until the death of Mole's widow.

Mole's wife has survived him. Bill is now aged 14, Delia is 16 and Elizabeth is 19.

Advise Mole's executors and trustees whether they may (or must) use income to assist Mole's children; and, if so, to what extent.

Commentary

This is a tricky question: the law is extraordinarily complex, and the things asked are very precise. Some examination papers carry at least one treacherous question like this for those who have worked hard and really enjoy the subject. A cool-headed and well-prepared student can earn high marks; a persistent waffler, however, will be skating on very thin ice. If you do decide to attempt this sort of question, it is better to leave it until later in the examination, when you already have at least a couple of good answers under your belt. This is definitely not a question for 'writing yourself in'.

Suggested Answer

It is convenient to deal with each child in turn.

(a) Bill. The Trustee Act 1925, s. 31, provides for the circumstances in which trustees may (or must) pay the trust income to beneficiaries who are not entitled to it under the terms of the trust instrument. In the case of a contingent interest, the section applies only if the limitation carries the intermediate income or interest for the maintenance of the legatee (s. 31(3)).

Since the gift to Bill comprises a sum of money, it is a pecuniary legacy. It is also contingent since it vests only if Bill attains 18. Generally, a contingent pecuniary legacy does not carry the intermediate income: *Re Raine* [1929] 1 Ch 716. However, such a gift does carry interest if (*inter alia*) it was made to a minor by his father. Two requirements must, however, be met. First, there must be no other fund provided for his maintenance: *Re George* (1877) 5 ChD 837. Secondly, the contingency must not be the attaining of an age greater than the age of majority (presently 18): *Re Abrahams* [1911] 1 Ch 108. This latter requirement is clearly satisfied. Assuming that the former is also met, and that there is no expression of a contrary intention in the will, the gift will carry interest and so fall within the Trustee Act 1925, s. 31. This exceptional case is indeed expressly recognised by s. 31(3), which states that the section applies to a contingent legacy made (*inter alia*) by a parent of the legatee if, under the general law, the legacy carries interest for the maintenance of the legatee, and it specifies a rate of interest of 5 per cent (s. 31(3)). Whether such legacy does carry such interest is determined by reference to the cases, including those mentioned above.

Assuming the gift carries such interest, the Trustee Act 1925 imposes a trust to accumulate this income during Bill's minority, but gives the trustees a power to pay to Bill's (surviving) parent or guardian, or otherwise apply for or towards his maintenance, education or benefit, the whole or such part of the income as may be reasonable, whether or not there is any other fund applicable to the same purpose. The trustees must have regard (*inter alia*) to the age of the minor, his requirements, and generally to the circumstances of the case (Trustee Act 1925, s. 31(1)). Accumulations may be applied for the benefit of the minor as if they were income of the current year (Trustee Act 1925, s. 31(2) proviso).

When Bill attains 18, his gift vests and he is entitled to the capital and accumulations. If Bill dies under 18, the gift does not vest and (in the absence of a gift over) it will go on a resulting trust to Mole's estate. Any sums previously paid to or for Bill's benefit under s. 31, however, need not be repaid.

(b) Delia. This gift is a contingent and future specific bequest of personalty. Under the Law of Property Act 1925, s. 175, such a bequest carries the intermediate income from the death of the testator, except so far as such income is otherwise expressly disposed of. There being no such express disposal here, Delia will receive the intermediate income eventually if she attains 25.

This does not, however, mean that the income is in the meantime subject to s. 31; for that section gives way to a contrary intention in the will (Trustee Act 1925, s. 69(2)). The deferring of the gift suggests that the testator did not intend Delia to have the intermediate income until the widow's death. In *Re McGeorge* [1963] Ch 544, the testator specifically devised land to his daughter but stated that the devise was not to take effect until the death of his widow. Cross J held that by so deferring the enjoyment of the property the testator had shown an intention that the intermediate income should not be subject to s. 31, but should be accumulated for 21 years (the relevant period of accumulation) or until the earlier death of the widow. If Mole's disposition indicates a similar intention, the same result will ensue.

If, however, the court does not find a contrary intention from the postponement of the bequest, the application of the income is governed by the Trustee Act 1925, s. 31(1). Thus there is an accumulation trust during Delia's minority, and the trustees have power to apply income for her maintenance or benefit. The position is the same as that in respect of Bill during his minority. When Delia attains 18, the trustees must pay her the income that arises thereafter: this is indicated by s. 31(1)(ii), which gives a beneficiary who at 18 'has not a vested interest in such income' the right to such income. Since her interest is contingent, however, any accumulations made during her minority are not paid to her at 18, but remain part of the capital of the fund subject to her interest vesting at the age of 25.

(c)   Elizabeth. This gift is a future specific devise of property which carries the intermediate income unless it is otherwise expressly disposed of (Law of Property Act 1925, s. 175). As in the case of Delia, however, the postponement of the gift may evidence an intention that it should not carry such income until the widow's death. In support of his decision in *Re McGeorge*, Cross J pointed out that, if such a disposition were to be treated as carrying the intermediate income, an adult devisee with a vested interest would be able to call for an immediate conveyance in disregard of the instruction that the gift be deferred.

There was another ground for the decision in *Re McGeorge*. The daughter in that case (like Elizabeth in the problem) was over 18 and had an interest which, although future and defeasible, was vested. Cross J held that she was not entitled to the income under the Trustee Act 1925, since s. 31(1)(ii) confers the right to income at majority only on a beneficiary who does not then have a vested interest in such income.

On either of these bases, therefore, the result is that the income must be accumulated until the widow's death, or (if earlier) until Elizabeth's interest ceases to be defeasible on her attaining 21 without having already married.

QUESTION 6

(a)   Consider the classes of persons on whose behalf the court is empowered to approve an arrangement under the Variation of Trusts Act 1958.

AND

(b)   In 1988, Mark, a wealthy businessman, settled a large sum of money in trust for such of his two sons, Luke and John, as should attain the age of 30, if both in equal shares, with remainders over in default to their respective issue (if any).

Mark had for several years expressed a desire to retire to the Channel Islands, and last year he went to live on Jersey. His sons, Luke and John, however, who are presently aged 16 and 18 respectively, are at school in Yorkshire and hope to read law at a university in England. Both are presently unmarried and without children. Mark's solicitor has advised him that, on grounds both of administrative convenience and tax-saving, the trust should be transferred to Jersey.

Advise the trustees whether such transfer can be sanctioned by the court under the Variation of Trusts Act 1958; and, if so, of the likelihood that the court's consent will be obtained.

Commentary

The suggested answer to part (b) illustrates the importance of not giving a definite answer to problems likely to turn upon a multiplicity of facts which are not stated. Do not be afraid, in such cases, to indicate what further information you may require. Indeed, sometimes the question will expressly ask you to do this.

Suggested Answer

(a) The Variation of Trusts Act 1958, s. 1, empowers the High Court to approve an arrangement varying or revoking the trusts on behalf of four classes of persons, these being listed in paras (a) to (d) of s. 1(1).

Paragraph (a) comprises minors and other persons who by reason of incapacity are incapable of assenting; the interest of such person can be either vested or contingent. Paragraph (c) applies to persons unborn. Paragraph (d) refers to persons who have an interest under the discretionary trust which will arise under protective trusts where the interest of the principal beneficiary has not yet failed or determined.

The definition of persons falling within para (b) is, however, the most complex. It includes any person (whether ascertained or not) who may become entitled to an interest under the trusts as being at a future date or on the happening of a future event a person of any specified description or a member of a specified class. The proviso however excludes any person who would be of that description or a member of that class if the said date had fallen or the said event had happened at the date of application to the court.

Case law has indicated the scope of para (b). In *Re Suffert's Settlement* [1961] Ch 1, the settlor's daughter had a life interest under the trust together with a general testamentary power of appointment. In default of appointment, the property was to be held for those persons who would be her statutory next of kin if she died intestate and unmarried. The daughter, who was unmarried and aged 61, applied to the court for approval to be given to an arrangement dividing the fund between herself and her statutory next of kin. Buckley J held that he was not empowered to give consent on behalf of the daughter's two cousins because they fell within the proviso. If the daughter had died at the date of application to the court, the two cousins would be her statutory next of kin: they 'would be' persons of that description. Other potential next of kin, however, are not within the proviso, and the court is empowered to give its consent on their behalf. *Re Moncrieff's Settlement Trusts* [1962] 1 WLR 1344 is to similar effect.

In *Knocker v Youle* [1986] 1 WLR 934, it was held that para (b) does not enable the court to give its consent on behalf of persons who have contingent (albeit very remote) interests. This is because the paragraph refers only to persons 'who may become entitled', not to those who already are. *Re Suffert's* and *Re Moncrieff's Settlement Trusts* were distinguishable because prospective next of kin of a living person have no interest in that person's estate, they have merely an expectation (a spes). Riddall, however, has argued that *Knocker v Youle* is wrong, and that the word 'interest' in the first part of para (b) refers to a vested interest: Riddall [1987] Conv 144. This would mean that para (b) would include persons who have merely a contingent interest, provided such contingency is more than one step removed.

It might also be pointed out that s. 1 does not enable the court to give its consent on behalf of persons merely on the ground that they are untraceable. In such cases, however, a *Benjamin* order might be appropriate: *Re Benjamin* [1902] 1 Ch 723.

Lastly, it is provided that, except in the case of para (d), the court shall not approve an arrangement unless it is satisfied that it is for the benefit of the persons on whose behalf approval is given.

(b) An arrangement varying or revoking the terms of a trust under the Variation of Trusts Act 1958 has been held to include the sanctioning of the 'export' of a trust to a foreign jurisdiction. The court has power to consent on behalf of beneficiaries who fall within paras (a) to (d) of s. 1(1). As a minor having a contingent interest under the trusts, Luke falls within para (a).

Moreover, any issue of either son fall within para (c), since these are persons unborn. Consent cannot be given on behalf of John, however, since he no longer falls within any of the paragraphs: he has already attained majority, and has an interest under the trust, albeit contingent. Under the statute, therefore, John's own consent to the export of the trust is required.

The court is not obliged to sanction an application to the court under the Variation of Trusts Act 1958: the court may give its approval 'if it thinks fit'. Furthermore, the court may not approve an arrangement on behalf of persons within paras (a) to (c) unless it would be for the benefit of those persons. In *Re Seale's Marriage Settlement* [1961] Ch 574, the court approved, on behalf of the children, the export of a marriage settlement to Canada, which was the country to which the family had emigrated many years earlier and in which they were permanently settled. The benefit to the children was one of administrative convenience.

By contrast, in *Re Weston* [1969] 1 Ch 223 the Court of Appeal refused to give its consent, on behalf of minor beneficiaries, to the export of a trust to Jersey. Unlike their counterparts in the aforementioned case, the family here had only just moved to Jersey and there was no evidence that they intended to stay there any length of time. The judges involved, however, gave different reasons for their refusal. Stamp J at first instance castigated the arrangement as a blatant piece of tax avoidance: yet tax avoidance is lawful, and most applications under the Act have tax saving as a main object. In the Court of Appeal, Lord Denning MR, in Shakespearian vein, considered that the minors' welfare might be imperiled were they to be uprooted from England. This outweighed any benefit from tax-saving. Harman LJ, by contrast, decided on the ground that Jersey law could not administer trusts; but this opinion was evidently made *per incuriam: Re Windeatt's Will Trusts* [1969] 1 WLR 692. Moreover, in the later case of *Re Chamberlain* (1976, unreported) the court approved an export of a trust to Guernsey where the main beneficiaries were resident in France and Indonesia.

It therefore appears that the export of a trust upon the grounds proposed in the problem will be permitted unless the welfare of unborn or minor beneficiaries is endangered. There is probably little likelihood of endangerment as regards the unborn beneficiaries; but more evidence is needed to assess the impact upon Luke's welfare. Such evidence would include whether it is intended that Luke should cease to be educated in England, or whether he is to remain in the country while the rest of his family move to Jersey.

11 Pension-fund Trusts

INTRODUCTION

For trusts lawyers, both professional and academic, pension funds are an area of increasing importance and interest. Most pension-fund trusts are created by an employer (which it is here convenient to call 'the company') with separate trustees who hold the fund upon trust to pay pensions to retired employees in accordance with each employee's contractual entitlement. Under some schemes (non-contributory schemes) the whole fund is provided by the company alone; but many schemes are contributory in that the employees also make contributions of a specified amount.

Most of these funds take the form of a trust, and there are two principal reasons for this. First, the trust enables the assets of the pension fund to be distinguished from those of the employer company. This offers some safeguards against an unscrupulous employer and makes it more difficult (though, as the Robert Maxwell saga revealed, not impossible) for the employer to treat the pension fund as its own property. Secondly, very important tax exemptions are available to pension funds, but only to those which exist in the form of an irrevocable trust. The Maxwell scandal led to a review of the law relating to pension funds, and to the introduction of special rules to regulate them in the Pensions Act 1995. This Act set up a regulatory authority with supervisory powers over trustees of pension funds, it introduced minimum funding requirements and restrictions on an employer's receipt of surplus while a scheme is on-going, and it requires one third of the trustees to be member-nominated trustees.

Pension funds increasingly feature in courses on equity and trusts. In the context of trusts law, it is possible to identify three important areas: the extent to which the law of trusts is developing special rules for pension funds; the beneficial ownership of a surplus; and the control of the exercise of powers under a pension fund. Each of these areas is covered by one of the three questions and answers in this chapter.

Useful discussions of pension funds generally are to be found in the following books: Moffat, *Trusts Law; Texts and Materials*, 3rd edn, London: Butter-worths, 1999, chap. 13; Hayton, *Hayton and Marshall: Cases and Commentary on the Law of Trusts*, 11th edn, London: Sweet & Maxwell, 2001, pp. 734–76; Martin, *Hanbury and Martin: Modern Equity*, 16th edn, London: Sweet & Maxwell, 2001, chap. 16.

Among the articles on this area, a very readable and valuable one is Pittaway, 'Pension funds — is a separate branch of trust law evolving?', (1990) 4 *Trust Law & Practice* 156. Other notable contributions are: Nobles, 'Don't Trust the Trustee' (1990) 53 MLR 377 and 'The Exercise of Trustees' Discretion under a Pension Scheme' [1992] JBL 261; Moffat, 'Pension Funds: A Fragmentation of Trust Law?' (1993) 56 MLR 471; and Mesher, 'Social security for occupational pensions: is the law of trusts superannuated?' (1993) 46 CLP (vol. 2) 96.

QUESTION 1

To what extent is the law of trusts developing a distinct set of principles for pension-fund trusts?

Commentary

The essential structure could be reduced to the following reasons for distinguishing a pension-fund trust from other trusts:

(a) *Large number of beneficiaries*
potential problem: uncertainty of objects
judicial response: *McPhail* v *Doulton.*

(b) *Large size of many pension funds:* cf. large charitable trusts
potential problem: unduly restrictive investment clause
judicial response: *Mason* v *Farbrother.*

(c) *Essential contractual nature*
potential problem: adequate control of powers
judicial response: *Mettoy* case; *Imperial Group Pension Trust*; *Wilson* v *Law Debenture Trust.*

Suggested Answer

Although pension funds normally adopt the trust form, they differ in a numbr of ways from family trusts. One important difference is in the sheer number of beneficiaries: a family trust is likely to have a small range of beneficiaries, whereas under a pension fund the beneficiaries may be reckoned in the hundreds of thousands. The House of Lords in *McPhail* v *Doulton* [1971] AC 424 recognised the need for trust law (which was largely developed in the context of family trusts) to adapt to take account of the modern large-scale trusts for the benefit of employees. This it did by discarding the 'complete list' test for discretionary trusts. It appears that the House of Lords intended its decision to be of general application, and not to be restricted to pension-fund trusts.

It is therefore evident that the growth in pension-fund trusts has had an impact upon the general law of trusts. What is more difficult to ascertain is the extent to which the law of trusts is developing, or ought to develop rules of special application to these pension-fund trusts. In addition to the large number of beneficiaries, there are other elements which distinguish such trusts from family trusts. Thus some pension-fund trusts contain many millions of pounds — far larger than the majority of family trusts. In the context of trustees' investment policy, Megarry V-C in *Cowan* v *Scargill* [1985] Ch 270 saw no reason to hold that different principles should be applied to pension-fund trusts from those which apply to other trusts. In contrast to this, in *Mason* v *Farbrother* [1983] 2 All ER 1078, the judge considered that the very size of the pension fund involved (£127 million) meant that it had 'something of a public element in it'. He treated this as a special circumstance justifying the court's sanctioning an extension of the trustees' investment powers under the Trustee Act 1925, s. 57, beyond that permitted under the general law at that time. (The courts showed a similar willingness to permit a widening of the investment powers of trustees of very large charitable trusts: see *Trustees of the British Museum* v *A-G* [1984] 1 WLR 418 and *Steel* v *Wellcome Custodian Trustees Ltd* [1988] 1 WLR 167.) The Pensions Act 1995, s. 34(1), gave trustees of an occupational pension scheme the same powers of investment as if they were entitled to the assets absolutely; and similarly wide powers were conferred on trustees of other trusts by the Trustee Act 2000, s. 3(1). Future applications to the court are therefore more likely to comprise attempts to have restrictions on investment imposed by the trust instrument removed. It remains to be seen if the courts will adopt a different approach for pension-fund trusts in these circumstances.

Most important of all, perhaps, is the fact that the beneficiaries of pension-fund trusts (unlike the majority of beneficiaries under family trusts) are not volunteers but provide consideration for their benefits. This was first acknowledged judicially in *Kerr* v *British Leyland (Staff) Trustees Ltd* (1986, unreported) and has been accepted in subsequent cases, notably *Mettoy Pension Trustees* v *Evans* [1990] 1 WLR 1587 and *Davis* v *Richards & Wallington Industries Ltd* [1990] 1 WLR 1511. The consideration may take the form of direct contributions to the fund; but even if the fund is non-contributory, the employees can be treated as furnishing consideration by working for the employer in the expectation that they will eventually receive a pension from the fund. Indeed, pensions are sometimes considered to be a form of deferred remuneration. Since the employees in a pension fund provide commercial consideration for their benefits, a pension-fund trust is therefore an example of a commercial (or at least a quasi-commercial) trust, in contradistinction to the traditional family trust, which is essentially a creature of the settlor's bounty. It appears, however, that the underlying contractual basis of a pension fund does not itself preclude the employees from being entitled to any surplus by way of resulting trust: *Davis* v *Richards & Wallington Industries Ltd*.

It was the contractual nature of the employees' rights that impressed Warner J in the *Mettoy* case that the power to appoint the surplus, although vested in the company rather than the trustees, was a fiduciary power rather than a personal power. Furthermore, as the company was in liquidation and there was nobody who could exercise that power, it was appropriate for the court to exercise it in the most appropriate manner. There is no comparable instance of the court's executing a fiduciary power in the context of a family trust. At first sight, *Klug* v *Klug* [1918] 2 Ch 67, may appear to run counter to this view. In that case, which involved a family trust, one of two trustees (the Public Trustee) wished to exercise the power of advancement in favour of the beneficiary in remainder, but the other trustee objected on grounds which indicated that she had taken improper considerations into account. The court ordered the advancement to be made. It is arguable, however, that the court was not exercising the discretion itself, but was merely giving effect to the wishes of the untainted trustee. The remedy in the *Mettoy* case may therefore, in practice, be available only in the peculiar circumstances of a pension-fund trust.

There is now implicit judicial recognition that established principles of trust law are inadequate to control the exercise of all powers under a pension fund. Thus it is evident that not all powers exercisable under a trust can be fiduciary powers, so that equity is powerless to intervene. New duties in relation to the exercise of powers under a pension-fund trust are therefore being imported from the law of contract. Thus, the employee's right to have the pension fund properly managed, and the correlative duties imposed on those with powers in relation to the fund, are being treated as derived from the employee's contract of employment: see particularly *Imperial Group Pension Trust Ltd* v *Imperial Tobacco Ltd* [1991] 1 WLR 590. Since it is equity which traditionally fills the gaps left in the common law, this might be considered a reversal of roles! It appears, however, that the courts are unwilling to permit the commercial nature of a pension-fund trust to justify a departure from the general rule of trust law, that a beneficiary is not entitled to see documents which reveal the reasons for the exercise of the trustees' discretion: see *Wilson* v *Law Debenture Trust Corp.* [1995] 2 All ER 337.

QUESTION 2

In the absence of an express indication in the trust deed establishing a pension fund or the exercise of any power to deal with surplus funds, it is difficult to ascertain who is beneficially entitled to any surplus that arises. This is largely the fault of trust law itself.

Discuss

Commentary

The question deals with an important aspect of pension-fund trusts: the ownership, subject to any appointment, of any surplus. 'Surplus' means the amount by which the value of the trust's assets exceed its actuarial liabilities. The liabilities are the payments which the fund needs to make to satisfy the contractual entitlements of its pensioner-beneficiaries, these being retired employees currently receiving a pension, and present employees when they eventually retire. So long as the pension-fund trust continues, the surplus is merely actuarial. There is no actual surplus until the trust is wound up, which may occur if the company which created it is taken over or is dissolved on insolvency.

Surpluses began to be amassed in the 1980s, largely owing to higher than expected interest rates and redundancies, which reduced the anticipated demands on the funds. To combat this, the Finance Act 1986 imposed a ceiling on the permitted size of surpluses, so that schemes which operated with excessive surpluses lost the tax advantages. If the company which set up and (at least partly) funded the scheme was beneficially entitled to a large surplus, it could become a target of a 'corporate raid', i.e., an attempted take-over by another company seeking to get its hands on the surplus funds. For primarily these reasons, the issue of the application of surplus funds came to prominence in the 1990s, and, in view of the recession and insolvencies of that period, seems likely to remain important.

Suggested Answer

The need to identify the beneficial ownership in a pension-fund surplus can arise in two sets of circumstances: where the pension fund is continuing, and where it is wound up (which may occur when the company which established it is dissolved or taken over). The trust instrument may specify how, in either event, any surplus is to be applied. Most instruments, however, in order to retain flexibility, do not. Instead, most confer a variety of powers (either on the trustees or the company) to enable them to deal with the surplus. Since, however, the exercise of a power is necessarily discretionary, it is important to ascertain who is entitled to the surplus should there be no exercise of the power, i.e., to ascertain who has a beneficial interest subject to defeasance.

Identifying such beneficial ownership can be difficult, and the Pensions Act 1995 does not provide a solution. Superficially, it might appear that the law of trusts is to blame, since most pension funds (in order both to create funds distinct from the employer's own assets and to take advantage of various tax exemptions) are created as trusts; and, on the recent occasions when the courts have applied principles of trust law, there has been no consistency of result. A deeper analysis, however, suggests that the uncertainties are not wholly a result of trust law, but arise also from the nature of pension funds themselves.

In *Re Courage Group Pension Schemes* [1987] 1 WLR 495, Millett J noted that, under most pension schemes, the employees cannot be asked to increase their contributions, even if the fund is in deficit, and it will be the company which must make good any shortfall. Any surplus is therefore to be treated as the result of overfunding by the company alone, and so would appear to belong (so far as not appointed) to the company beneficially.

A different view, however, was taken in *Mettoy Pension Trustees Ltd* v *Evans* [1990] 1 WLR 1587. There, Warner J thought that, if the company were effectively at liberty to apply the surplus in any way it wished, it was difficult to appreciate why the trust instrument should expressly give it a power to do something it was in any event entitled to do: namely, to apply the surplus to the benefit of the employee-objects. Warner J's judgment seems, therefore, to proceed on the basis that, subject to the exercise of any power of appointment, the surplus belonged beneficially to the employees.

Only a few weeks after judgment was delivered in *Mettoy*, the court was again asked to rule on the application of a surplus in *Davis* v *Richards & Wallington Industries Ltd* [1990] 1 WLR 1511. It is therefore not surprising that *Mettoy* was not cited in the later case, where Scott J adopted a different approach. Here, the pension scheme had been wound up with a surplus of £3 million. Contributions to it were derived from three sources: the company, the employees, and other companies' pension schemes which had joined and whose assets had been transferred (the transferred funds). The scheme had in fact been amended to enable the surplus to be applied to the employees; but the court was asked to decide (*inter alia*) how, in the absence of the valid exercise of such power, the surplus should be held.

Scott J decided that, in the absence of any indication in the trust instrument, there was a presumption that the surplus was held on a resulting trust for those who had contributed to it. He did not think that the fact that the contributions from all sources had a contractual origin under the pension scheme was itself sufficient to exclude any claim under a resulting trust. Under this particular scheme, the company had been required to contribute whatever sums were necessary to enable the trustees to maintain the benefits. The benefits should therefore be treated as having been funded first by the employees' contributions and by the transferred funds, and only secondly by the company's contributions. It was therefore logical to treat the surplus as being provided first by the company's contributions. In effect, the company had made an overpayment, and thereby acquired an equitable right to its repayment; and the device whereby such repayment was effected was the resulting trust. The practical result of this approach (which was similar to that adopted in *Re Courage*) was that the company was entitled to the entire surplus.

Scott J also rejected any claim under a resulting trust by the employees or the trustees of the transferred funds. He gave two reasons. First, the value of the benefits would be different for each employee, depending upon when he joined and how old he was when he left. A resulting trust was unworkable as between the employees, and the court would not impute to the employees an intention that would lead to such a result. Secondly, the scheme was established to take advantage of various tax exemptions, and the relevant legislation placed a ceiling on the amounts that could be returned to employees. A resulting trust for the employees would have breached these requirements, and equity would not therefore impute an intention to the employees that any part of the surplus derived from their contributions should be returned to them under a resulting trust. A resulting trust of the transferred funds was rejected on similar grounds. Scott J therefore held that any part of the surplus derived from either of these two sources was to devolve as *bona vacantia*.

In *Air Jamaica Ltd* v *Charlton* [1999] 1 WLR 1399, at p. 1412, however, Lord Millett, giving the advice of the Privy Council, expressed the view that Scott J's reasoning in the *Davis* case was erroneous. Lord Millett said that evidence that the employees did not intend to retain a beneficial interest could not prevent them having an interest under a resulting trust.

There is, therefore, a conflict of authority as to where, subject to the exercise of any power of appointment, the beneficial interest in any surplus in fact lies. This, however, may not be the fault of trust law itself: in the absence of an expressed indication in the trust or statutory intervention, there appears to be no obviously 'correct' solution. Where the pension fund is wound up, the allocation of a surplus will usually be determined by the exercise of a power, and it has been held that the mere fact that a surplus on winding up might be attributable to overpayments by the employer is not a sufficient reason for the trustees to refuse to exercise the power so as to allow the surplus to go to the employer: *Thrells Ltd (1974) Pension Scheme* v *Peter Lomas* [1992] PLR 1.

Where the pension fund is still continuing, any surplus is merely actuarial: the extent of the surplus depends upon which of a variety of methods of calculation the actuary employs, and there can be no certainty that the surplus will continue or that it will not, in a future year, turn into a loss. It may therefore be inappropriate to seek to identify the ownership of a surplus in a continuing fund. There is much to be said for Knox J's observation in *Re London Regional Transport Pension Fund Trust Co. Ltd* (1993) *The Times*, 20 May that 'the question of whether a continuing fund is in surplus or in deficit cannot be answered with any precision, ... and the concept of ownership of a surplus is even more uncertain than that of ownership of the fund as a whole'.

QUESTION 3

Consider the extent to which the court can control the exercise of a power to appoint a surplus under a pension-fund trust.

Commentary

Most pension-fund trusts confer a variety of powers upon the trustees or the company (or the trustees with the consent of the company) to enable them to deal with any surplus. Examples of commonly found powers are: a power to amend the trust deed or the rules made under it in order to increase pensions or other benefits to the employees and pensioners beyond their contractual entitlements; a power to enable the company (and, more rarely, the employees) to take a 'contributions holiday' (i.e., to reduce or suspend its contributions to the fund in the event of there being an excessive surplus); and a power to make a payment out of the pension fund to the company. The power of the court to control the exercise of the power derives originally from equity, which means that the manner of the exercise of the power can be controlled only if it is a fiduciary power. Recent case law, however, has revealed the existence of duties derived from the law of contract. The suggested answer deals with duties of both types.

Suggested Answer

If the power to appoint a surplus is vested in the trustees of the pension-fund trust, it is inevitably a fiduciary power, which means that the trustees must actively consider exercising the power, consider fairly the respective claims of the objects of the power, and avoid a conflict of interests. In the past, however, the trustee of the pension scheme was sometimes the employer company itself; and other schemes must (since the Pensions Act 1995) provide for employees to be represented on the board of trustees. Where the trustee may exercise a discretion in a way which may benefit himself, there is a conflict of interests. The strict application of the no-conflicts rule to pension-fund trusts would mean that no trustee who was himself a beneficiary under the pension fund would be permitted to benefit from the exercise of the trustees' power. Similarly, no company trustee could exercise a power as trustee to apply any part of the surplus to itself, or take a contributions holiday; and any employee-trustee would have to be excluded from any discretionary benefits awarded by the trustees to employee-beneficiaries generally. Furthermore, the application of the no-conflicts rule would enable the court to intervene to prevent the trustees from exercising their power in a way which would benefit all or any of their number.

There are conflicting judicial opinions on the question whether the no-conflicts rule is strictly applicable to trustees of pension schemes. In *Re William Makin & Sons Ltd* [1993] OPLR 171, Vinelott J considered that the rule did so apply, on the basis (which he expressed in *British Coal Corporation* v *British Coal Superannuation Scheme* [1995] 1 All ER 912) that it was 'outrageous' that a person with a power to distribute a fund among a class which includes himself should be able to apply any part of it for his own benefit. In *Re Drexel Burnham Lambert Pension Plan* [1995] 1 WLR 32, however, Lindsay J considered that the no-conflicts rule should not apply with all its harshness to trustee beneficiaries who, like the trustee-employees in the case before him, had not deliberately placed themselves in a position of conflict in the sense of 'pushing themselves forward to be trustees but rather were selected as persons able and willing to serve their colleagues in such a way': ibid., at p. 42. Where, as in *Drexel* itself, the trustees had not placed themselves into the position of conflict, the exercise of their discretion in a way which benefited themselves would be subject to the same 'jealous and scrupulous' examination as would be appropriate to a purchase by a trustee of the beneficial interest of a beneficiary. Lindsay J expressly left open the question, however, of whether the no-conflicts rule could be overcome by an express provision in the trust deed. The no-conflict rule in fact ceased to apply to trustees of pension funds who are also members of the scheme, under the Pensions Act 1995, s. 39. The rule continues to apply to non-member trustees, however.

Any power vested in the trustees of the fund will almost invariably be construed as conferred on the trustees *virtute officii*, and therefore as fiduciary in nature. If, however, the power is vested in a third party, equity would normally consider it to be a personal, rather than a fiduciary, power. The application of this equitable presumption to pension funds, however, would mean that where (as is not infrequently the case) the power to appoint a surplus is vested in the company-employer, the court would be unable to control in any way the exercise of that power, provided it was exercised within the defined class of objects. This would mean that where the company was itself one of the objects of the power, it would be entitled to forget about the power or to release it, or to exercise it spitefully or capriciously; and there would be nothing to prevent it from exercising the power (e.g., to appoint any surplus) in favour of itself. In view of the special nature of a pension-fund trust — particularly the element of contractual entitlement of the employee-beneficiaries — the courts have striven to assert some power to control the exercise of the company's discretion in such a case.

First, although equity normally presumes that a donor of a power does not intend to put the donee into a position of conflict, the *Drexel* case (*supra*) would seem to suggest that a power conferred upon a third party (in practice, the employer-company) can still be treated as a fiduciary power (and as such susceptible to judicial control) even though the donee might itself benefit from its exercise (or, if entitled in default of exercise, from its non-exercise).

Thus, in *Mettoy Pension Trustees* v *Evans* [1990] 1 WLR 1587, there were several factors which led Warner J to construe as fiduciary in nature, the power vested in the company (not itself a trustee of the fund) to appoint a surplus. These included the desirability of preventing a company's pension-fund surplus from being raided by another company in a take-over, and the fact that a pension-fund trust is of a commercial nature: the beneficiaries are not volunteers but provide consideration for their pensions — they might be thought to have earned a right to have the company properly consider the exercise of the power in their favour.

In the *Mettoy* case itself, the pension fund was brought to an end (with a surplus of £9 million) when Mettoy was compulsorily wound up in 1983. Mettoy had a power to apply any surplus in increasing the benefits to the beneficiaries. Warner J's finding that the power was of a fiduciary nature meant that it was not a beneficial asset of Mettoy's, so that Mettoy's liquidator could not exercise it by applying the surplus in favour of the company's creditors. Indeed, Mettoy's liquidator could not exercise it in favour of the pensioner-beneficiaries either, since this would put him into a position of conflict (i.e., as trustee of the power, whose duty is to the beneficiaries, and as liquidator of the company, whose duty is to the creditors). In these circumstances, Warner J held that the court would itself exercise the fiduciary power — and he called for further evidence which would indicate the most appropriate manner of doing so. This is the first reported instance of a court executing a fiduciary power in the manner which Lord Wilberforce had explained in *McPhail* v *Doulton* [1971] AC 424 was possible in relation to discretionary trusts.

Secondly, the donee of a power under a pension scheme (whether himself a trustee of the fund or a third party) may owe duties to the employee-beneficiaries of the fund in relation to the exercise of that power which derive, not from equity (and so are not dependent upon the power's being construed as fiduciary), but rather from the common law: namely, the implied duties which arise by virtue of the contract of employment. These other duties (such as to act in good faith, and to exercise the power for its proper purpose and not for a collateral purpose) are similar to the particular duties which are imposed by equity on the donee of a fiduciary power. Provided these duties are fulfilled, there is no conflict in the exercise of the power resulting in a benefit to the donee of the power.

Thus in *Imperial Group Pension Trust Ltd* v *Imperial Tobacco Ltd* [1991] 1 WLR 590, Browne-Wilkinson V-C held that, as the employee-beneficiaries were not volunteers, the company's power to withhold consent to an amendment to a pension scheme had to be exercised in good faith. The company was not entitled to use its power to induce members to transfer to a new scheme. The duty of good faith implied into the contract of employment itself was therefore to be implied into the contract underlying the pension-fund trust. Similarly, in *British Coal Corporation* v *British Coal Superannuation Scheme* at p. 926, Vinelott J stated that a company with a power to amend its pension scheme must exercise the power so as to fulfil the legitimate expectations of the members and pensioners; but, provided it does so, it may exercise the power so as to reduce or suspend its own contributions.

The emergence of these duties is not, however, without problems: since the duties are necessarily expressed in general terms, there may be practical difficulties for the company to know whether it is doing what is necessary to comply with them, particularly where the fund is still continuing so that the surplus is purely actuarial.

Set against this, however, there appear to be serious problems for employees who suspect that the donee of the power (whether a trustee of the pension fund or the company) has breached its duties in relation to the power. The problem is that it has been held that, like the beneficiaries under an ordinary family trust, the employee-beneficiaries cannot, in the absence of evidence of bad faith, compel the trustees to disclose the reasons for their decisions: *Wilson* v *Law Debenture Corp.* [1995] 2 All ER 337. In the view of Rattee J, the fact that the employees were not volunteers did not justify a departure from the general principle established in *Re Londonderry's Settlement* [1965] Ch 918.

Although the Pensions Act 1995 requires the body of pension-fund trustees to include employees, the beneficiaries of a pension-fund are not a homogeneous group — there will be different classes of beneficiaries, for example present employees, former employees and existing pensioners — and, for the trustees properly to exercise their fiduciary powers, they must consider the different classes of objects. Furthermore, in the apportioning of a surplus between the continuing and outgoing members, the trustees should consider the members' legitimate expectations that the discretion will be exercised in their favour: *Re London Regional Transport Pension Fund Trust Co. Ltd* (1993) *The Times*, 20 May. The decision in *Wilson* v *Law Debenture Corp.* will considerably restrict the practical ability of individual employees or groups of employees, dissatisfied with the share of surplus allocated to them, to ascertain whether such allocation has been properly carried out.

12 Breach of Trust

INTRODUCTION

This chapter includes real and personal remedies against trustees and other persons into whose hands property has passed in breach of trust. Questions are usually predictable. This topic often occurs chronologically at the end of a course and may, therefore, be reasonably fresh in the student's mind — always a bonus.

A question concerning the process of tracing is often popular and an important first step is to read *Re Diplock* [1948] Ch 465, where the Court of Appeal dealt thoroughly with the fundamental principles relating to equitable tracing. You should also read *Boscawen* v *Bajwa* [1996] 1 WLR 328, where the Court of Appeal indicated that aspects of the reasoning in *Re Diplock* are in need of reappraisal in the light of the significant developments in the law of restitution which have taken place in the last 50 years.

Here comes a difficulty. You need to know the extent to which tracing is permitted at law before you can embark on an examination of equitable tracing. So, you have spent the best part of the academic year studying equity and now you are expected to exhibit a familiarity with the common law. That, after all, smacks of real life which is not always conveniently departmentalised. It may be that your course covers the law of obligations and you have dealt with the common law and equity side by side. On the other hand, your lecturer may be an equity lawyer who feels unhappy with common law concepts. You should, therefore, know from the content of your course what is expected of you.

To what extent could you be expected to deal with the personal common law action of conversion or the action for money had and received in a course on equity? The answer is, probably, not at all. It is likely that you will only need to be able to deal with the tracing process at law rather than concern yourself with the precise nature of the claim. You should also bear in mind that, although the House of Lords' decision in *Lipkin Gorman* v *Karpnale Ltd* [1991] 2 AC 548 concerned only tracing at common law, their Lordships' observations on the defence of change of position are very broad, and are likely to be held applicable to tracing in equity also: *Boscawen* v *Bajwa* (though see Lord Millett's dicta in *Foskett* v *McKeown* [2001] 1 AC 102).

For additional reading (and you will find numerous articles referred to in the textbooks), look at Goff and Jones, *The Law of Restitution*, 3rd edn, London: Sweet & Maxwell, 1986.

QUESTION 1

The only restriction on the ability of equity to follow assets is the requirement that there must be some fiduciary relationship which permits the assistance of equity to be invoked. (per Millett J, *Agip (Africa) Ltd* v *Jackson* [1990] Ch 265)

Discuss, in the light of this quotation, the requirement that there must be some fiduciary relationship before tracing in equity is permitted.

Commentary

The central issue in this question is the requirement of a fiduciary relationship, so the answer requires a thorough discussion of the case law on this point. The crucial thing for the candidate is to ensure that the answer does not deteriorate into one of the 'write all you know' type. Related ideas can therefore be explored, but only to the extent that they throw light on the central issue.

The suggested answer explores the question in the following manner. First, it puts the requirement into context by briefly setting out what all the requirements are to trace in equity. Secondly, it examines the background and emergence of the requirement since the Judicature Acts, and mentions cases in which such requirement has been accepted or criticised. Thirdly, it compares the need for a fiduciary relationship with the need for an equitable (or perhaps a legal) proprietary right, looking in particular at the issue of theft from a legal beneficial owner. Fourthly, it looks at the ways in which the courts have treated the requirement flexibly: in not insisting that it necessarily exist between claimant and defendant, and in treating such relationship as arising in the case of mistaken payments.

Suggested Answer

There are certain requirements which must be satisfied before a claimant may follow assets in equity. These are: there must be an equity to trace; the property must be traceable; and the result must not be inequitable. The issue in the question is whether the first of these requirements, the equity to trace, imports the need for a fiduciary relationship.

Before the Judicature Acts 1873–75, the courts of common law and the Court of Chancery applied their own distinctive rules relating to tracing. Just as tracing at common law was available only to a person who had a proprietary right at law, so tracing in equity was available only to a person who had a proprietary right in equity. Following those Acts, it might have been thought that equitable tracing would be available to a beneficial legal owner where common law tracing proved inadequate. This indeed appears to have been recognised in *Banque Belge Pour L'Etranger* v *Hambrouck* [1921] 1 KB 321, CA. In *Re Diplock* [1948] Ch 465, however, the Court of Appeal expressed the view that, in order to be able to trace in equity, it was not sufficient for the claimant merely to have an equitable proprietary right, there also had to be a fiduciary relationship. In *Westdeutsche Landesbank Girozentrale* v *Islington LBC* [1996] AC 669, the House of Lords seemed to accept the correctness of this proposition. Other cases, however, reveal some judicial reluctance to accept such a requirement. Doubts were expressed by Millett LJ in *Bristol and West Building Society* v *Mothew* [1998] Ch 1, at p. 23; and in *Foskett* v *McKeown* [2001] 1 AC 102, Lord Millett (as he now is) stated that he could see no logic in the requirement. These observations may indicate that the House of Lords might at some future time wish to reconsider *Re Diplock*. The requirement for a fiduciary relationship in order to trace in equity remains, however, for the present at least.

Where the claimant has an equitable proprietary right, there will be a fiduciary relationship. The classic example of this is, of course, the trust, whether express, implied or constructive. A trust is not, however, a prerequisite: a person who entrusts property to a fiduciary, for instance, will retain an equitable proprietary interest sufficient to enable her to trace. Thus, in *Re Hallett's Estate*

(1880) 13 Ch D 696, one Mrs Cotterill paid money to her solicitor to invest on her behalf; instead he paid part of this into his personal bank account. It was held that, in these circumstances, Mrs Cotterill was entitled to trace her money in equity. The same principles apply to all fiduciary relationships, such as those between a company and its directors, between a principal and agent, and between partners in a business *inter se*.

It is clear, however, that a fiduciary relationship is not itself sufficient to enable the claimant to trace. Tracing is, after all, the process of identifying the claimant's property or its product in a third party's hands, so there can be no right to trace if the claimant has no proprietary right to the assets in question. In the *Westdeutsche Landesbank* case, the House of Lords held that the bank retained no proprietary interest in money which it had paid to the defendant local authority under an interest rate swap arrangement which was *ultra vires* the local authority. The claimant would therefore have had no right to trace such money in equity. On the other hand, it may be that the requisite proprietary right need not be equitable. In *Aluminium Industrie Vaasen BV* v *Romalpa Aluminium Ltd* [1976] 1 WLR 676, it was held that, where a fiduciary relationship existed, even a legal owner (with no distinct equitable proprietary right) could trace in equity.

Because no fiduciary relationship exists in respect of property vested in a beneficial legal owner, it might appear that tracing is not available to such owner if the property is stolen from him by a thief. If the property stolen is money and is mixed by the thief in his own bank account, the victim, whilst possessing a personal remedy against the thief, cannot claim any legal proprietary remedy against the money in the account. In such circumstances, however, the House of Lords has accepted that, once the victim's legal title to the money passes (upon mixing in the account), a constructive trust is imposed upon the thief, and it is this trust which gives rise to a fiduciary relationship enabling the victim to trace in equity into the mixed fund: see *Lipkin Gorman* v *Karpnale Ltd* [1991] 2 AC 548 (Lord Templeman); and the *Westdeutsche Landesbank* case (Lord Browne-Wilkinson).

The case law provides other illustrations of the courts' willingness to interpret the requirement for a fiduciary relationship flexibly. It does not, for example, matter that such relationship does not exist between the claimant and the person against whom the tracing claim is brought. In *Re Diplock* itself, money was wrongfully distributed by the executors of a will to a number of charities. It was held that the next of kin, who should have been entitled to such money, were entitled to trace into the hands of the money's innocent recipients. The right of the next of kin to trace arose from their equitable right against the executors to have the estate properly distributed. In that case, therefore, the fiduciary relationship was between the next of kin and the executors.

Another example of the court's flexible approach is in relation to payments made under a mistake. A fiduciary relationship, giving rise to a right to trace in equity, can also arise where the defendant receives the claimant's property as a result of a mistake. In *Chase Manhattan Bank NA* v *Israel-British Bank* (London) Ltd [1981] Ch 105, the plaintiffs, as a result of a book-keeping error, wrongly made a double payment of $2 million into the account of the defendant bank. At that time, the common law action of money had and received did not apply to money paid as a result of a mistake of law, which that was (but this is no longer so: see *Kleinwort Benson Ltd* v *Lincoln City Council* [1999] 2 AC 349, HL). The plaintiffs therefore needed to be able to trace in equity. It was held that the mistaken second payment gave rise to a fiduciary relationship, which gave the plaintiffs a right to trace. The House of Lords in the *Westdeutsche Landesbank* case has since doubted that the fiduciary relationship arose at the time of the mistaken second payment; rather, their Lordships considered that it arose only when the defendant's conscience was affected, i.e., when it became aware of the mistake two days later. The decision in *Chase Manhattan* nevertheless remains good law in so far as it illustrates that the fiduciary relationship needed to trace does not need to be a pre-existing one.

QUESTION 2

Brown is a solicitor and a trustee of the Rainbow Trust. His co-trustee, Grey, is not a solicitor, but is a member of the Rainbow family. Grey is content to leave the entire management of the trust to Brown. Under the terms of the trust, Leone has a life interest, and the capital is held for Azure and Grey in equal shares.

In 1985, Brown invested half of the trust fund in the family company, Rainbow Ltd, which he understood to be an authorised investment within the terms of the trust deed. In fact, the trust deed expressly prohibited the trustees from investing more than one fifth of the trust fund in Rainbow Ltd. When Rainbow Ltd went into insolvent liquidation in 2000, the trust's total investment in that company was lost. All the other investments which Brown made have been very successful, however, and during the period he has been administering the trust a healthy capital growth has been achieved.

Between 1988 and 1995, Brown made advances of capital sums out of the trust to Leone, which comprised breaches of trust. Brown did not realise that these payments were in breach of trust, as he did not check the terms of the trust deed, which he kept in his office safe.

Advise Azure.

Commentary

This question covers breach of trust by trustees where they fail to comply with the terms of the trust. Distinctions between professional and non-professional trustees need to be considered, and between active and non-active trustees.

The question is not difficult but requires a knowledge of the statutory provisions imposing liability and providing defences. Discussion of the case law dealing with the possibility of setting off a profit made by successful investments against losses sustained by an improper investment is required, however, to achieve a good mark.

There is only one devious point hidden in the question and that relates to the limitation period. The clue to look out for is the careful use of dates. If they are not relevant, the examiner would probably have simply set the events in the previous year.

Suggested Answer

The basic principle is that trustees who commit a breach of trust which results in a loss to the trust estate are personally liable to the beneficiaries to make good the loss. Brown's excessive investment in Rainbow Ltd and the wrongful advances of capital were both in breach of the terms of the trust deed. Brown is therefore prima facie liable to make good such losses to the trust fund. The liability of trustees is personal, not vicarious: *Townley* v *Sherborne* (1643) J Bridg 35. Grey is not therefore vicariously liable for Brown's breaches of trust. Grey may be personally liable for his own breach, however, in failing to participate in the management of the trust and merely leaving matters in the hands of his co-trustee: *Bahin* v *Hughes* (1886) 31 Ch D 390. Equity does not, after all, countenance a sleeping trustee.

The investment in Rainbow Ltd is a breach of trust to the extent that the amount invested exceeded the one fifth limit imposed by the trust instrument. The measure of the trustees' liability is the loss caused to the trust. In this instance, the onus would be on Azure to establish that there is a loss which would not have occurred but for the breach: *Target Holdings Ltd* v *Redferns* [1996] 1 AC 421, HL, at p. 440. Unless there are circumstances which indicate that the trustees were in breach of trust in investing in Rainbow Ltd at all, it would seem that the trustees' liability would be limited to the loss of the excess over one fifth only.

Brown has, however, invested the remaining assets profitably. Normally, a gain made in one transaction may not be set off against a loss suffered in another. This is the rule established in *Dimes* v *Scott* (1828) 4 Russ 195, where the trustees retained an unauthorised investment for longer than the prescribed period. When the investment was eventually sold, the trustees were able to invest extensively in Consols, as the price had dropped. This resulted in a greater gain for the remaindermen. The trustees were nevertheless held liable for the loss caused by the retention of the unauthorised investment without being allowed to set off the gain.

If the gain and the loss were made in a single transaction, though, then the rule is reversed. In *Fletcher* v *Green* (1864) 33 Beav 426, the proceeds of sale of an unauthorised investment were invested in Consols, the value of which then rose. It was held that the trustees were entitled to take advantage of such rise. The difficulty, as these cases illustrate, is often in determining whether the gains and losses occur in the same or in separate transactions. In *Bartlett v Barclays Bank Trust Co. Ltd (No. 1)* [1980] Ch 515, the trustees had engaged in a sequence of speculative investments. One of these, the Guildford project, was successful; but another, the Old Bailey project, was a disaster. The bank pleaded that it should be permitted to set off the profit from one against the loss on the other. Brightman J allowed them to do so, expressing the view that it would be unjust to deprive the bank of the element of salvage in assessing the cost of the shipwreck. In the question, Brown and Grey would be able to set off the gains only if they could show that the activities which produced such gains were so connected to the losses as to form part of one transaction. On the facts as stated, there is no evidence of such connection, and so the trustees are unlikely to succeed.

A claim brought by a beneficiary against a trustee for breach of trust must be brought within six years from the date on which the right of action arose (Limitation Act 1980, s. 21(3)). There is a proviso to the subsection that time does not start to run against a remainderman until his interest falls into possession. As the advances made by Brown were in breach of trust, they would not cause Azure's interest to fall into possession for the purposes of the Limitation Act: *Re Pauling's Settlement Trusts* [1964] Ch 303, CA. Azure's interest falls into possession only on the death of Leone, and as the question suggests that Leone is still alive, it would appear that time has not yet even started to run against Azure. He will not, however, be permitted to bring any claim against the trustees if it is shown that he participated in, or consented to, the breach, or if it can be shown that he later acquiesced in the breach: *Re Pauling's Settlement Trusts*.

A trustee who would otherwise be liable for breach of trust may be relieved if he can show that he acted honestly and reasonably and ought fairly to be excused (Trustee Act 1925, s. 61). It is unlikely that the court would grant relief under this section to a person who is professionally involved with the management of trusts, such as Brown. It is the trustee who has the onus of showing that he acted honestly and reasonably: *Re Stuart* [1897] 2 Ch 583. There are no general principles in applying the statute; every case turns on its own circumstances: *Re Turner* [1897] 1 Ch 536. Nevertheless, it might be surmised that if Grey left everything to Brown and never asked for explanations, he would probably not be considered to have acted reasonably, and he might not even count as honest for this purpose: *Re Second East Dulwich Building Society* (1899) 79 LT 726. A trustee may also be able to escape liability by relying on an express exclusion clause in the trust instrument; the question does not indicate, however, whether the Rainbow Trust contained any such clause.

The fact that Brown is a solicitor and Grey apparently a layman may be a relevant factor in determining the liability of Brown and Grey *inter se*: if it can be shown that Brown exercised a controlling influence over Grey, the latter might be entitled to an indemnity from the former (*Re Partington* (1887) 57 LT 654). It seems unlikely, however, that an indemnity could be claimed by a non-participating trustee. Apart from this, it might be possible for Grey to claim a contribution from Brown under the Civil Liability (Contribution) Act 1978, although there is no reported case law as yet to indicate what the attitude of the courts might be where such a claim is brought by a passive trustee. Rights of indemnity or contribution between the trustees do not, however, affect the personal liability of each to Azure; so that if each of the trustees is personally liable, Azure could recover the full amount of the loss from either of them, leaving it to that trustee to make a claim against his co-trustee.

Leone received the advances in breach of trust. Leone has therefore been unjustly enriched, and she will be liable to repay to the trust the sums advanced to her if they can be traced into her hands, unless she can rely on the defence of change of position. The trustees' personal liability will be reduced to the extent of any sums so recovered from her. If, however, Leone can establish such a defence (so that she can show that she is an innocent volunteer who has, for example, spent the money so that it cannot be traced), *Re Diplock* [1948] Ch 465 suggests that she will not be personally liable to repay the advances, since she did not receive the money from the personal representatives of an estate in the course of administration. The modern principle of unjust enrichment nevertheless suggests that she should remain personally liable, since she has still had the benefit of the sums she received (as where she spent them on a holiday). If Leone is held personally liable to repay, her liability is reduced to the extent that such sums can be personally recovered from the trustees (*Re Diplock*, at p. 503). If, on the other hand, Leone instigated or requested the breach, the trustees are entitled to impound her beneficial interest by way of indemnity: *Chillingworth* v *Chambers* [1896] 1 Ch 685; Trustee Act 1925, s. 62. The trustees will also be entitled to withhold payments of income from Leone in order to repair the breach: cf. Re *Balfour's Settlement Trusts* [1938] Ch 928.

If it were to be shown that Grey had participated in the breach of trust, he will be required to indemnify Brown to the extent of his beneficial interest under the trust, which would effectively give Brown a partial indemnity: *Chillingworth* v *Chambers*.

QUESTION 3

George was appointed the sole executor of Harriet's will. Harriet died last year leaving her entire estate, worth £130,000 after payment of debts, to her cousin Albert in Australia. George died recently. Albert has only just learned of this and has discovered that George, believing that as executor he was entitled to the estate beneficially and knowing that he was terminally ill, has made the following dispositions of the estate:

(a) £40,000 of the estate was contributed to the purchase of a house by George's daughter, Peggy. The house was purchased for £60,000 and Peggy contributed the remaining £20,000. The house is now worth £80,000.

(b) George settled £40,000 on trust for his son Felix as part of a marriage settlement on the occasion of his marriage to Matilda.

(c) George used £20,000 to buy a valuable antique Grecian urn which he gave to his service club.

(d) George used £20,000 to finance his gambling habits and this has all been lost at the Spend Casino.

(e) George gave the remaining £10,000 to his housekeeper May. May paid this into her current account, in which there was a balance of £5,000, but has since drawn out £10,000.

Advise Albert whether he has any claim against the recipients of Harriet's estate.

Commentary

This problem raises a number of different permutations of the tracing remedy. Most problems raised in this field relate to the issue of tracing in equity. The limitations of the remedy of tracing at common law need to be known.

The issue of the up-and-coming defence of change of position is also raised and merits some discussion of the important House of Lords decision in *Lipkin Gorman* v *Karpnale Ltd* [1991] 2 AC 548, although this case is concerned with tracing at common law.

Suggested Answer

The right to trace is available at common law if the claimant retains the legal title to the property. Here, tracing at law is not available because George, the legal owner, has disposed of the property and the legal title has passed. It is necessary, therefore, to consider the availability of the remedy in equity.

(a)   Peggy is presumably an innocent volunteer. The trust funds have been mixed with her money. The mixed funds have been used to purchase a house. The value of the house has now risen.

Albert is the true beneficiary, and therefore has an equitable proprietary interest. £40,000 of the trust property is in the hands of an innocent volunteer and has been used for the acquisition of property. An equitable proprietary remedy may be available which will enable Albert to trace the property.

In equity, where the trust property has been transferred in breach of trust to an innocent volunteer who has mixed it with her own, the trust and the volunteer share *pari passu* in the property purchased with the mixed fund: *Sinclair* v *Brougham* [1914] AC 398, HL, *Re Diplock* [1948] Ch 465, CA. They will share the profits and the capital in the proportions in which they contributed.

The right to trace may be lost where it would produce an inequitable result. In *Re Diplock* it was held that where trust money was spent on altering or improving land then it would be inequitable to force the innocent volunteer to sell the land to satisfy a charge on it. Peggy has used the money to buy land. It might be argued, therefore, that her circumstances have changed as a result of the receipt of the trust money, thus rendering it inequitable for the remedy to be enforced against her. This would, however, mean that Peggy would be unjustly enriched. In the light of *Boscawen* v *Bajwa* [1996] 1 WLR 328, the most appropriate solution would be for the court to defer Albert's right to enforce the equitable charge until Peggy has had a reasonable opportunity to raise and pay the amount due, e.g., by mortgaging the house.

If the proprietary claim fails, then an equitable claim in personam can be brought for the principal sum of £40,000 without interest. However, Peggy will only be liable to the extent that the money cannot be recovered directly from George's own estate. The claim in these circumstances is limited to claims arising out of the administration of estates and is subject to the primary liability of the executor: *Re Diplock*.

(b) £40,000 was settled on trust under a marriage settlement for Felix. He is within the marriage consideration and, therefore, not a volunteer. Where trust property has been transferred to a bona fide purchaser of a legal estate for value and without notice of the equitable interest, the property is taken free from the claims of the beneficiaries. However, Felix has acquired merely an equitable as opposed to a legal interest and does not receive the protection of 'equity's darling'.

Alternatively, and especially if the tracing remedy does not satisfy Albert's loss, he may recover the loss (or the balance) in a claim in personam. In this case, Albert should look to the personal remedy against George's estate in the first instance, but may recover the balance from Felix in a claim in personam.

(c) The service club is a volunteer as it has given no consideration for the urn. Presumably it is also innocent. Equitable tracing is, however, available against an innocent volunteer if the property can be traced into the volunteer's hands. The trust money has been exchanged for the urn with no mixing of other funds. The club have the identifiable proceeds of the trust money. Albert can therefore trace in equity into the urn and obtain an order to restore the urn, being property acquired with the £20,000.

(d) £20,000 of trust property was dissipated by George on gambling at the Spend Casino.

The right to trace is lost where the property has ceased to be identifiable. Where the money has been dissipated, therefore, it can no longer be identified and cannot be traced. However, the money has passed into the hands of the Spend Casino, which is a volunteer, as no valuable consideration is given: *Lipkin Gorman* v *Karpnale Ltd* [1991] 2 AC 548. However, a casino stands the risk of losing or winning when they permit someone to place bets. The defence of change of position was considered in *Lipkin Gorman* v *Karpnale Ltd*, a case which was concerned with legal tracing only. In *Lipkin Gorman* v *Karpnale Ltd*, it was held by the House of Lords that a casino was entitled to set off any winnings made by the gambler on the basis that they had changed their position by paying such winnings to him. Change of position was not a complete defence and the club were held liable in an action for money had and received for the net amount he had lost gambling at the club. It was stated, per curiam, by the House of Lords, that it is right to recognise the defence of change of position in good faith in restitution claims, based on the unjust enrichment of the defendant. The House of Lords, however, left the development of this doctrine to future cases. So, although it is likely that future courts will develop this doctrine, there is presently no direct authority for this defence to be raised by the Spend Casino in a claim to trace in equity.

The Spend Casino will also be subject to a claim in personam under *Re Diplock*, as confirmed on appeal in *Ministry of Health* v *Simpson* [1951] AC 251, HL. This will be for the amount which Albert has been unable to claim from George's estate and will be limited to the principal sum without interest.

(e) £10,000 of trust money has been mixed in May's current account with £5,000 of her own money. Where trust money is mixed with that of an innocent volunteer, tracing in equity is available. However, May has withdrawn £10,000. As the account is a current account, the rule in *Clayton's case* (1816) 1 Mer 572, first in, first out applies. The rule in *Clayton's case* is a rule of convenience and applies unless it is impracticable or would result in injustice (*Barlow Clowes International Ltd (in liquidation)* v *Vaughan* [1992] 4 All ER 22. If the prima facie rule is to apply here, then, as May had £5,000 of her own money in the account, she is presumed to draw that out first, followed by £5,000 of trust money. The remaining money is, therefore, trust money.

If the £10,000 withdrawn has been used to buy an investment, Albert will be able to claim a charge on the investment and rank *pari passu* with May. If, however, the £5,000 trust money cannot be traced (if, for example, it has been dissipated), Albert will be left to pursue a claim in personam as discussed previously.

QUESTION 4

On 1 January 1996, Tonto, who was trustee of the Una Charitable Trust, in breach of trust paid into his bank account £10,000 of the charity's money. There was already £6,000 of his own money in his account. One week later he bought shares to the value of £5,000 and withdrew this amount from his account. The next day, he drew out £3,500 which he used to buy a boat. On 1 March 1996, he paid into the account in breach of trust £5,000 belonging to the Duo Trust Fund, of which he was also trustee. The next day he drew out £5,000 which he used to pay debts which he had incurred in his business. The following day he withdrew a further £5,000 which he gave to his daughter, Dora, which she used as a deposit on a house she was buying.

The boat has now been destroyed in a hurricane. The shares are now worth £6,000.

Tonto has just been declared bankrupt. Advise the beneficiaries of the two trusts.

Commentary

This question deals with the mixing of monies in a bank account. Once money or other property has been mixed, it is not possible to trace at common law. The question therefore requires an application of the rules for tracing in equity. The answer takes account of the significant decision of the Court of Appeal in *Boscawen* v *Bajwa* [1996] 1 WLR 328.

It is important to be aware that different rules apply to the mixing of trust monies with a trustee's own money, and the mixing of the monies of two trusts that are both treated as innocent volunteers.

Where there is a series of transactions involving payments into and out of a bank account, as here, it is essential to work the transactions through in draft form first, calculating the amounts remaining in the bank account and to whom they belong after each transaction. You should also apportion the rights to any property purchased from the mixed account according to whose money has been used for its purchase.

You should, of course, explain which rule you are applying in each transaction, so that a kind-hearted marker will be able to give you credit for legal knowledge even if you slip up on your arithmetic!

Suggested Answer

As Tonto is bankrupt, a personal claim against him for breach of trust is likely to be of little value to the Una Charitable Trust ('Una') or to the beneficiaries of the Duo Trust ('Duo'). Una and Duo should therefore first try to trace their funds into the property to which the funds have been applied.

The first transaction involves the mixing in Tonto's bank account of Tonto's own money and money belonging to Una. Tracing at law is not possible as the money has been applied by its legal owner, Tonto; and, in any event, money or other property cannot be traced at law once it has been mixed. Tracing is, however, possible in equity, as Tonto is a trustee and therefore in a fiduciary relationship (*Re Diplock* [1948] Ch 465), and property can be traced in equity even after it has been mixed.

The shares which Tonto buys for £5,000, paid for from the account, are prima facie deemed to have been purchased out of his own £6,000 in the account, on the basis that a trustee is deemed not to be acting in breach of trust: *Re Hallett's Estate* (1880) 13 Ch D 696. If this is the case, the shares belong to Tonto, and the money remaining in the account belongs as follows:

Tonto   £1,000

Una   £10,000

If the same principle is applied on the purchase of the boat, then the boat represents £1,000 of Tonto's money and £2,500 of Una's money. The bank account then has no money of Tonto's left in it, and there is £7,500 of Una's money remaining.

The rule in *Re Hallett's Estate*, however, is displaced where the trustee, having purchased an investment, subsequently dissipates the balance in the account, which, on the application of *Re Hallett's Estate*, would mean that the beneficiary's money would have been dissipated. In such circumstances, *Re Oatway* [1903] 2 Ch 356 held that the beneficiary is entitled to treat the investment as having been purchased first out of the trust monies, so as to enable the beneficiary to trace into the investment. Hayton has cogently argued that the rule in *Re Oatway* exemplifies the underlying principle that a trustee should not be permitted to allocate profitable transactions to himself, as this would allow him to benefit from his own wrongdoing: Underhill & Hayton, *Law Relating to Trusts and Trustees*, 15th edn, 1995, David J. Hayton (ed.), London: Butterworths, 1995. The fact that some money of Una remains in the bank account should not, therefore, affect Una's right to trace into the shares, which, in view of the boat's destruction, it would obviously be better advised to do.

The remedy granted in *Re Oatway* itself was an equitable charge over the investment to the value of the trust monies used in its purchase. That case did not deal with the position in the event of the investment's increasing in value. It would, however, appear to follow from dicta in *Re Tilley's Will Trusts* [1967] Ch 1179 (where trust money had been mixed with the trustee's own), that Una should be able to benefit from the entire increase in value, i.e., to claim that the shares are held for it upon a constructive trust.

Assuming that Hayton's view is applied, the money remaining in the bank account immediately after the shares have been purchased belongs as follows:

Una   £5,000

Tonto   £6,000

The rule in *Re Hallett's Estate* is then applied to the purchase of the boat, which is therefore bought entirely from Tonto's own money. After the purchase of the boat, the money remaining in the bank account is as follows:

Una   £5,000

Tonto   £2,500

The rest of this answer proceeds on the basis that Hayton's approach to the application of *Re Oatway* represents the law.

Tonto's payment into the account of £5,000 belonging to Duo means that there is then £12,500 in that account. When Tonto subsequently withdraws the first £5,000 from the account, the withdrawal first comprises £2,500 of Tonto's own money (*Re Hallett's Estate*). As between innocent volunteers, the appropriation of withdrawals from an active bank account is governed by the rule in *Clayton's Case* (1816) 1 Mer 572, whereby withdrawals are treated as made in the same order as payments in, i.e., first in, first out. As Una and Duo are both innocent volunteers, the balance of £2,500 withdrawn is treated as Una's money. The second withdrawal of £5,000 therefore comprises the remaining £2,500 of Una's money, and £2,500 of Duo's. This leaves £2,500 in the bank account which can be traced by Duo.

Assuming that the creditors are bona fide purchasers without notice, Una cannot trace its £2,500 applied in the discharge of Tonto's debts into their hands. Una can, however, claim to be subrogated to the creditors' claims against Tonto: *Boscawen v Bajwa* [1996] 1 WLR 328 (CA). If the creditors' claims were secured, e.g., by a mortgage over Tonto's assets, Una would be able to claim an equitable charge over those assets to the extent of £2,500. If, however, the creditors' claims were unsecured, there is no advantage to Una, as a personal claim would not give it priority over Tonto's creditors in Tonto's bankruptcy.

Assuming that Dora is an innocent volunteer, Una and Duo can prima facie trace the monies which she has received into the house she has bought. In *Re Diplock*, however, the Court of Appeal held that, where an innocent volunteer had applied trust monies in building an extension to its existing premises, tracing would not be permitted as this would produce an inequitable result, i.e., the plaintiff could compel a sale of the entire premises. That principle, however, seems to be giving way to a broader principle that tracing will be permitted unless the defendant can establish the defence of change of position. In *Lipkin Gorman* v *Karpnale Ltd* [1991] 2 AC 548, the House of Lords held that such a defence was available to a tracing claim; *Lipkin Gorman* itself concerned tracing at common law, but it has been suggested by Millett J that such a defence is also available in equitable tracing: *Boscawen* v *Bajwa* (supra). More recently, however, in *Foskett* v *McKeown* [2001] 1 AC 102, Lord Millett (as he now is) suggested that the defence of change of position is available only where the basis of the claim is unjust enrichment. Where the claimant uses the tracing process to vindicate a property right, by contrast, the only defence is that of the bona fide purchaser for value.

The most appropriate remedy might be for the court to grant Una and Duo an equitable charge over the house, but to defer their right to enforce it for a reasonable time in order to enable Dora to raise (e.g., by mortgaging the house) the amount necessary to satisfy the equitable charge. If the house has increased (or fallen) in value, Dora, Una and Duo, all being innocent volunteers, share the increase (or the loss, as the case may be) rateably: *Sinclair* v *Brougham* [1914] AC 398 (HL); *Re Diplock* (supra).

If Dora is indeed an innocent volunteer, no personal claim will lie against her: *Ministry of Health* v *Simpson* [1951] AC 251. If, however, she receives the £5,000 with constructive notice that it is trust money, she will be personally liable as a constructive trustee to account for it under the principle of knowing receipt: *Agip (Africa) Ltd* v *Jackson* [1990] Ch 265 (Millett J.).

13 Equitable Doctrines

INTRODUCTION

The maxims of equity are the general principles upon which the Chancery Court developed this system of law and reflect the desire to be fair and even-handed between litigants. The maxims underlie the equitable doctrines and remedies. Their origins are to be found in the history of property law but they are sometimes applied to more modern situations and not always very happily. The application of conversion to trusts for sale of land led to some surprising results and the Trusts of Land and Appointment of Trustees Act (TLATA) 1996 converted all trusts for sale of land existing on 1 January 1997 (when the Act came into force) into trusts of land to which the doctrine does not apply. (There is one very limited exception to this which is referred to in Question 2(a)(iii) in this chapter.) Although it is still possible to create a trust for sale of land, there is little point in it, as the power to postpone sale overrides any provision to the contrary (s. 4(1)), and s. 3 abolishes the application of the doctrine of conversion to a trust for sale of land.

Questions on the doctrines of equity may well be general essay questions which will draw on your overall knowledge of the subject. It would be unwise to attempt these types of questions perhaps, unless you feel you have read generally and widely enough on the background of equity. Problem questions involving the more modern applications of the doctrines are a possibility if your lectures have covered these areas.

In deciding how much attention to give to these more general areas of equity, you should look at past examination papers and consider the emphasis given to equity itself by your lecturer. Although all courses on trusts will include some background of equity, some lecturers will not regard it as worthy of examination questions, whilst other lecturers may set questions on it. You will only know which type of course your lecturer favours by looking at the past examination questions and listening to your lecturer!

QUESTION 1

Equity looks on that as done which ought to be done.

Discuss critically the applications of this maxim in the equitable doctrine of conversion.

Commentary

The equitable doctrine of conversion is an anachronism which can produce unfortunate results in its present day applications. It probably has more significance in land law than in trusts, although it is still capable of affecting interests on succession. The material for this type of question is more likely to be found in a book on equity rather than a book on trusts, and some reference may well be made to it in books on land law e.g., Maudsley & Burn, *Land Law — Cases & Materials*, 7th edn: London: Butterworths, 1998.

It is essentially only something which would be examined on a course which covers equity as well as trusts.

Suggested Answer

Although equity did not have the same rigid rules of precedent as the common law, the Court of Chancery did have certain principles which it applied in administering equity. These became known as the 'maxims' of equity, and 'equity looks on that as done which ought to be done' is one of these. Its application is evident in several areas of equity and it underlies the doctrine of conversion.

The doctrine applies wherever there is an obligation to convert property into another form. Equity will then notionally convert the property before the actual conversion takes place. This has the curious result that realty may sometimes be regarded as personalty, and vice versa, in the eyes of equity. This was significant on the passing of property on an intestacy before 1926, when realty devolved upon the heir and personalty to the next of kin, and may still be relevant after 1925 in the case of a will leaving realty to one person and personalty to another.

Jeykll MR gave the reason for the doctrine in *Lechmere* v *Earl of Carlisle* (1733) 3 P Wms 211 as the fact that a *cestui que trust* should not be prejudiced by a trustee's possible delay in dealing with trust property in accordance with his obligations. It has received some unfortunate extensions however, in certain areas, which have produced criticisms from the judges, and it was abolished as regards trusts for sale of land by s. 3 of the TLATA 1996.

The doctrine of conversion still applies, however, to a contract for the sale of land. As soon as there is an enforceable contract, equity will impose a constructive trust on the vendor. From the contract, the vendor's interest is treated as being in the proceeds of sale which, if the vendor dies before completion, are payable to the persons entitled to his personalty. The purchaser, who is regarded as having a beneficial interest in the land, should therefore insure it. The position as to insurance may of course be varied by the terms of the contract for sale, and the Standard Conditions applicable to domestic conveyances provide that insurance of the property shall remain the responsibility of the vendor until completion.

In *Re Sweeting (deceased)* [1988] 1 All ER 1016, the doctrine was applied to a conditional contract where the condition was not fulfilled until after the testator's death. An unfortunate extension of its application is the rule in *Lawes* v *Bennett* (1785) 1 Cox 167, which decided that the doctrine applies retrospectively when an option to purchase is exercised after the grantor's death. Moreover, if the option is granted after a specific devise of the property by will, on exercise of the option the devise is adeemed and the property, which becomes personalty retrospectively, passes to the residuary legatee: *Weeding* v *Weeding* (1861) 1 J & H 424.

A duty to convert property also arises under the rule in *Howe* v *Earl of Dartmouth* (1802) 7 Ves 137. The rule aims at achieving fairness as to investments between a life tenant and a remainderman. It requires trustees of a residuary personalty fund which is left in succession to convert any wasting assets, or future assets not yielding an income, into authorised investments, unless the will reveals a contrary intention. The income from any such part of the fund before conversion is apportioned between the life tenant and the remainderman.

A strict application of the doctrine of conversion can produce some unfortunate results, and it is hardly surprising that the courts have sought to avoid it in some circumstances.

QUESTION 2

James, who died earlier this year, appointed Tina and Tom as executors and trustees of his will and devised all his realty to his son Sam and all his personalty to his daughter Doris. Advise the executors as to who is entitled to the following properties owned by James:

(a)(i) 'The Beeches', held by James and his wife Wynne upon trust for sale for themselves as tenants in common.

(ii) Would your answer differ if James and Wynne had held 'The Beeches' as joint tenants?

(iii) Would your answer differ if James had died before 1 January 1997?

(b) 'The Larches', which James contracted to sell to Peter, subject to Peter obtaining planning consent for an extension, shortly before he died. Peter has now obtained planning consent.

(c) 'The Firs', upon which he had granted an option to purchase to Frank. Since James died, Frank has given notice to Tina and Tom of his intention to exercise the option.

Would your answer differ if the will had included a specific devise of 'The Firs' to Sam?

Commentary

This question requires a knowledge of some of the circumstances in which the doctrine of conversion applies.

Like all questions in parts, it is probably unwise to attempt it unless you know the answer to at least two parts of it! If you have revised this topic, however, it is a fairly straightforward question, with almost arithmetical answers. You should achieve at least a pass if you can apply the principles, although a more detailed knowledge of the cases would be required to pass well.

Suggested Answer

(a)(i)   Wherever there is co-ownership of land, this must take effect behind a trust. Before 1 January 1997, s. 34 of the Law of Property Act 1925 imposed a statutory trust for sale. Because a trust imposes a binding obligation on trustees and 'equity looks on that as done which ought to be done', the equitable doctrine of conversion operated to convert property held on a trust for sale to personalty. In the eyes of equity, there was a notional sale and the property was regarded as money.

On or after 1 January 1997 when the TLATA 1996 came into force, co-ownership takes effect behind a trust of land under the Act, and any trusts for sale existing at that date became trusts of land. It is still possible expressly to create a trust for sale (as here), but the requirement to sell can be overridden (s. 4(1), TLATA 1996) and it will take effect as a trust of land under the Act. Section 3 of the Act abolishes the doctrine of conversion as regards any trust for sale of land (with one exception referred to in **(iii)** below).

James and Wynne will therefore hold the legal estate to 'The Beeches' as joint tenants at law on a trust of land under TLATA 1996, for themselves as tenants in common in equity. The right of survivorship does not apply to a tenancy in common and James's share of 'The Beeches' will therefore pass under his will to his son Sam as realty.

(ii)   If James and Wynne held 'The Beeches' as joint tenants, the position as regards the legal estate is the same, and co-ownership takes effect behind a trust of land under TLATA 1996. The right of survivorship applies to a joint tenancy at law or in equity, however, so that James's equitable interest in 'The Beeches' will pass to Wynne and not under James's will at all.

(iii)   Although s. 3 of the TLATA 1996 abolished the application of the doctrine of conversion to a trust for sale of land, a saving was made by the section for a will such as James's where the testator died before the Act came into force. If James had died before 1 January 1997, therefore, at his death the doctrine of conversion would have applied to the trust for sale on which 'The Beeches' was held, and his share would have passed under his will as personalty to Doris.

The position would have been the same even if there had been no express trust for sale but one had been imposed by reason of co-ownership by s. 34 of the Law of Property Act 1925.

This provision can now be relevant only in tracing title, and in practice, wills leaving personalty to one person and realty to another are rare (except perhaps in examination questions!). A testator is much more likely to specify the property he is leaving by name ('The Beeches') in his will.

(b) As soon as a valid and enforceable contract to sell property exists, equity regards the beneficial interest as having passed to the purchaser, and the vendor holds the legal title as a constructive trustee for the purchaser. Because the contract is enforceable by equity, equity regards the transaction as a notional sale. The interest of the vendor is therefore in the proceeds of sale, which are personalty.

In *Re Sweeting (deceased)* [1988] 1 All ER 1016, conversion applied to property subject to a conditional contract for sale when the condition was fulfilled after the testator's death.

The proceeds of sale of 'The Larches' will therefore go to Doris as personalty.

(c) The application of the doctrine of conversion to contracts for the sale of land was extended by the rule in *Lawes v Bennett* (1785) 1 Cox 167 to options to purchase. As soon as an option to purchase land is exercised, the property becomes personalty in the hands of the vendor because there is a binding obligation to sell it. This is still the case, even if the option is made exercisable after the death of the grantor (*Re Isaacs* [1894] 3 Ch 506). Therefore, as soon as Frank gives notice to Tina and Tom of his intention to exercise the option, it is regarded as personalty in their hands and will again go to Doris.

However, if the will makes it clear that the devisee of property is to take all the testator's interest in it, then the devise may operate to override the rule in *Lawes v Bennett*. Moreover, it is relevant whether the option was granted before or after the devise in the will. If it was granted before the devise, then there may be a presumption that the testator intended to give the whole of his interest in the property to the devisee, including any rights under the option. In *Calow v Calow* [1928] Ch 710, a devise of land or 'the proceeds of sale of the land' was held to survive a subsequent contract to sell the land completed after the testator's death. Conversely, if the option was granted after the devise, then the option is regarded as overriding the devise: *Re Carrington* [1932] 1 Ch 1.

If James' will was made before the option to purchase was granted, then the effect of Frank's notice to Tina and Tom to exercise the option is to operate the doctrine of conversion retrospectively. 'The Firs' becomes personalty in their hands and will go to Doris.

If James's will was made after the option was granted, however, then it is likely that the option will be regarded as a right attaching to the property, and 'The Firs' will pass, together with the right, to Sam as realty.

QUESTION 3

(a) Two sisters, Amy and Bertha, were joint tenants of a house. Amy, who died recently, by her will purported to leave the house to Bertha and their brother Cyril in equal shares. There was also a bequest in the will of valuable jewellery worth at least half of the value of the house to Bertha. Advise Bertha and Cyril.

(b) John, who died recently, made a will in which he gave a legacy of £5,000 to Bill. Bill had lent John £5,000 secured by a charge on John's house. There is a sum of £3,000 outstanding on this debt. Advise Bill as to whether the debt will be satisfied by the legacy.

Commentary

The first part of this question is on the application of the doctrine of election, and the second part on a possible application of the doctrine of satisfaction.

Both of these doctrines have their origins in equity's desire to be fair to the children of a family in the distribution of family wealth. The doctrines were extended, however, beyond the family circumstances and the doctrine of satisfaction particularly, in its application to creditors to whom a legacy was left. There are few recent cases on the doctrines although they are still occasionally applicable today.

This is not a subject to cover unless your lecturer directs you to do so or deals with it in your lectures.

Suggested Answer

(a) The doctrine of election means that a person who receives a benefit from a transaction from which he also suffers a loss must elect to take with the transaction or against it; that is, he may elect to take the benefit and suffer the loss, or not to accept the benefit at all. It usually applies to a will and arises where property is left to A and some of A's property is left by the same will to B. A cannot accept the gift under the will unless he compensates B from his own property. It is irrelevant that the testator has made a mistake as to the ownership of A's property which he has purported to leave to B.

Because Amy and Bertha were joint tenants of the house and the right of survivorship applies to a joint tenancy, the house automatically passes to Bertha on Amy's death. Amy is therefore leaving to Cyril property which is not hers to dispose of. In *Re Gordon's Will Trusts* [1978] Ch 145, where a mother and son owned a house as joint tenants and the mother devised it to her trustee upon trust for sale and left furniture and £1,000 to her son, Buckley LJ accepted that the doctrine of election could apply to those gifts to the son.

In that case, other property given in trust for the son was not freely alienable by him, which in fact prevented the application of the doctrine to it. The jewellery in this question would appear to have been given outright to Bertha, however, so it would seem that the doctrine would apply.

Bertha will therefore have to elect to take with the will, in which case she may keep the jewellery but must convey half of the house to Cyril, or against it, in which case she may keep the whole of the house but must compensate Cyril by letting him have the jewellery. She will be obliged to let him have the whole of the jewellery, however, and not just jewellery to the value of half of the house.

Hanbury and Martin's *Modern Equity*, 15th edn, London: Sweet & Maxwell, 1997, criticises the doctrine of election as 'too uncertain an instrument of equity', pointing out that the ultimate donee of the elector's property will always benefit, whereas the person put to their election may not benefit at all. This would seem to be the position here. (Note that the doctrines have been omitted from the latest (16th) edition 2001 to allow for coverage of more relevant and topical areas.)

   (b) The doctrine of satisfaction evolved in order to ensure, as far as possible, an equal distribution of family wealth among the children of a family. It was applied in certain circumstances to adeem a legacy left to a child who had previously received a portion (a sum of money to set him up in life).

It also applies where a legacy is left to a creditor, the underlying maxim for this being that 'equity imputes an intent to fulfil an obligation'. It must be possible to presume from the circumstances that the testator did intend to pay the debt with the legacy and, like all presumptions, it is rebuttable. Certain technical rules have developed to rebut the presumption.

First, the legacy must be as beneficial to the creditor as the debt (see *Re Van den Bergh's Will Trusts* [1948] 1 All ER 935). As Bill's loan was secured by a charge on John's house, this would not be the case.

Secondly, the doctrine applies only if the will was made after the debt was incurred. We are not told the dates of the will or the debt.

Thirdly, it will not apply if the will includes a clause (which is frequently included in wills) directing the testator's executors to pay the testator's debts and funeral and testamentary expenses. In these circumstances, both the debt and the legacy will be payable.

For all these reasons, it is possible that the doctrine of satisfaction will not apply to the legacy in John's will, and Bill will be able to recover his debt from the estate and also take his legacy of £5,000.

14 Equitable Remedies

INTRODUCTION

Equitable remedies are available in all fields of law, so do not assume that you will be confined to discussing cases involving trusts. Contract and commercial law, labour law, tort and breach of confidence are all areas which may be used to consider the application of an equitable remedy. Although you are not being examined on your knowledge in these fields, you will clearly need to have some background knowledge. Since equity and trusts is normally taught towards the end of a degree course this should not present too much of a problem. If it happens to occur earlier in your course then do not panic, your examiner will probably take this into account.

During your course of study some controversial or notorious case may arise where equitable remedies are sought. A claim may be brought based on the Human Rights Act 1998 in respect of the right to respect for private and family life (as in, for example, *Venables and Thompson* v *News Group Newspapers* [2001] 1 All ER 908, [2001] 2 WLR 1038, and *Douglas and Zeta-Jones* v *HELLO! Ltd* [2001] 2 WLR 992, [2001] 2 All ER 289); a breach of confidence claim may be brought in a case involving national security such as the *Spycatcher* case (*A-G* v *Guardian Newspapers Ltd (No. 2)* [1990] 1 AC 109), or an international fraud may receive public attention. It is likely that your examiner will frame a question round such a case. So, keep abreast of current case law, particularly if it features on the national news. If your lecturer starts referring you to newspaper reports as an example of the topicality of the subject, take the hint and read up the material. It is very gratifying for your lecturers when they can prove to you how relevant to the modern world their subject is. If they can, they will try to reflect it in the examination.

The most likely remedies to be examined are specific performance and injunctions. They can occur as either essay or problem questions. The question might deal more narrowly with types of injunctions, such as freezing injunctions or search orders, where there have been a number of recent developments. Rescission and rectification are less commonly examined, but listen to your examiner for pointers on this one. For that reason the sample questions in the chapter concentrate on specific performance and injunctions.

As equitable remedies are discretionary you will need to bear in mind general equitable principles, for example, the maxims of equity, when answering the questions. As usual, the area is mainly case law except for the provisions of the Supreme Court Act 1981.

QUESTION 1

The Draconian and essentially unfair nature of [search] orders from the point of view of respondents against whom they are made requires, in my view, that they be so drawn as to extend no further than the minimum extent necessary to achieve the purpose for which they are granted, namely the preservation of documents or articles which might otherwise be destroyed or concealed. (per Scott J in *Columbia Picture Industries Inc.* v *Robinson* [1987] Ch 38)

Discuss critically.

Commentary

A quotation of this sort can be followed by various commands: 'comment', or 'examine', or, as in this question, 'discuss'. Sometimes, as here, you are required to perform the test 'critically'.

Whatever the form adopted by your examiner you are required to do two things for a degree-level answer to this question. First, you must show you know what the procedure entails. So, in this question you must explain what the search order is all about. You will be expected to cite the relevant authorities.

Secondly, you must be critical. The key is to read the quotation. This may seem obvious, but there is a great temptation in the exam room to read and digest only key words. In this question the key words are 'search orders'. An answer which simply describes the search-order procedure will achieve a pass, but little more. What is required is a critical analysis of the current use of the procedure.

The quotation gives the lead. You should explain in what respects the procedure is considered by the judge to be 'Draconian'. The quotation is provocative so your answer can be argumentative, even bullish. Give both sides of the argument, then come down on one side and give reasons for your decision. Provided you have argued your case well, you will not lose marks if your examiner happens to disagree with your verdict.

As with all discussion questions, beware of losing your way. Plan your arguments in advance. Prepare a checklist of the points to be made, then tick them off as you make them. A question of this sort gives you the opportunity to show off your skills in arguing a case, provided you have a sound knowledge of the law involved.

This type of question may also occur as an assessment which would require a deeper analysis of the literature. For example, more should be made of the article by Dockray and Laddie (1990) 106 LQR 601 and the judgment of Nicholls V-C in *Universal Thermosensors Ltd* v *Hibben* [1992] 1 WLR 840. The application to the European Court of Human Rights in *Lock International plc* v *Beswick* [1989] 1 WLR 1268, noted in the article by Dockray and Laddie, should also be considered in the light of the implementation of the Human Rights Act 1998.

Suggested Answer

Search orders have sometimes been described as civil search warrants, enabling the applicant to enter on the respondent's premises, search and take relevant evidence.

Since their initial use, originally in *EMI Ltd* v *Pandit* [1975] 1 WLR 302, and subsequently in *Anton Piller KG* v *Manufacturing Processes Ltd* [1976] Ch 55 from which they derived their previous name '*Anton Piller* orders', these orders have been extensively used. They now have a statutory basis in s. 7 of the Civil Procedure Act 1997.

Their popularity has ensured that the injustice which they were created to remedy has been ameliorated. However, applicants have not always been entirely honest when seeking this remedy; they have not always come to equity with clean hands. Concern has been expressed, both on the Bench and by academic writers, that such orders are being abused. In *Universal Thermosensors Ltd* v *Hibben*, Nicholls V-C laid out a series of guidelines for the use of these orders. He recognised that they can be both a virtue in eliciting evidence which would otherwise not have seen the light of day, and a vice in that the procedure is open to abuse. These guidelines are now laid out in *Practice Direction* [1996] 1 WLR 1552.

Search orders are sought where there is a risk that vital evidence may be lost or destroyed. Their use has been particularly appropriate in cases where the defendant is suspected of infringing the claimant's intellectual property rights or of breaching trade secrets. They have also been used in one reported case within the field of family law (*Emanuel* v *Emanuel* [1982] 1 WLR 669), to enable the wife's solicitors to enter the husband's home and inspect documents relating to his financial means.

In order to bring such a case, a claimant needs evidence which might be in the hands of the defendant. It might consist of confidential documents or material such as videotapes. In the *Anton Piller* case, the defendants were the plaintiff's selling agents. The plaintiffs believed that the defendants were selling confidential information about their electrical equipment and plans to their competitors. However, to prove this they needed access to documents kept at the defendants' premises. The Court of Appeal granted an order which permitted them to enter the defendants' premises and inspect the documents.

It is crucial that the application is made without notice. If the other side knew of the application the risk is that the evidence would be destroyed forthwith. Surprise is a key element of the procedure. Herein lies the danger. The judge, at the hearing without notice, must rely exclusively on the word of the applicant.

In the first place, the judge may be required to determine to what extent any particular scientific or technical knowledge is the subject of patent or copyright, or is merely legitimately accepted scientific research. As Hoffmann J said in *Lock International plc v Beswick* [1989] 1 WLR 1268, 'It may look like magic but turn out merely to embody a principle discovered by Faraday or Ampère'.

Secondly, an unscrupulous applicant might abuse the power in a commercial situation by seeking to crush a competitor by the use of oppressive tactics. In *Lock International plc v Beswick*, the *Anton Piller* order was carried out by five representatives of the applicant. These were solicitors or employees of the applicant. They were, however, accompanied by 11 or 12 police officers who were armed with a search warrant in respect of alleged criminal activities of the respondent.

On appeal (noted (1990) 106 LQR 173), it was said that what had happened was regrettable, and it was unfortunate that the judge had not been informed of the involvement of the police.

Three conditions for the grant of the order were laid down in *Anton Piller KG v Manufacturing Processes Ltd* by Ormrod LJ:

(1) There must be a very strong prima facie case.
(2) There must be actual or potential damage of a very serious nature.
(3) There must be clear evidence that the defendant has in his possesion incriminating documents or things and a real risk that they might be destroyed before an application with notice can be heard.

Lord Denning MR added to these the condition that the order must do no real harm to the defendant. It would seem, however, that the fact that disclosure might expose the defendant to the risk of violence from his associates is not a defence (*Coca-Cola Co.* v *Gilbey* [1995] 4 All ER 711).

These conditions are more onerous than the conditions laid down in *American Cyanamid Co.* v *Ethicon Ltd* [1975] AC 396 for the issue of interim (formerly known as 'interlocutory') injunctions. This reflects the concern of the courts to protect the respondent from an abuse of process. The procedure should not be used as a means of finding out what proceedings can be brought (*Hytrac Conveyors Ltd* v *Conveyors International Ltd* [1983] 1 WLR 44). In other words, the material sought should be specific and should support the cause of action proposed by the claimant for the trial of the main claim. Fishing expeditions are not permitted. The orders are not, in fact, search warrants. They are precisely limited.

When applying for the order, the applicant must make a full disclosure to the court. There is clearly a potential weakness in a procedure which only hears one side of the case. Therefore, there is a particularly strict duty for a full and frank disclosure of all relevant facts. As Scott J pointed out in *Columbia Picture Industries Inc.* v *Robinson* [1987] Ch 38, the procedure constitutes an apparent breach of the rule of natural justice that citizens should not be deprived of their property without a fair hearing.

In carrying out the order the applicant should be accompanied by a solicitor. Documents or other evidence may be inspected and removed according to the terms of the order. They may not be used for any other purpose unless the respondent has consented or the court has so ordered. If damage is caused to the respondent then the applicant may be obliged to pay damages which could be exemplary in nature.

Two cases have sought to limit the scope of search orders: *Tate Access Floors Inc.* v *Boswell* [1991] Ch 512 and *Rank Film Distributors Ltd* v *Video Information Centre* [1982] AC 380. The former case emphasises a requirement for the claimant to make a full disclosure. In the latter case it was held that the privilege against self-incrimination could be raised by a defendant. This decision was abrogated by the Supreme Court Act 1981, s. 72, in cases relating to intellectual property. Future challenges to this may arise as a result of the implementation of the Human Rights Act 1998.

In *Universal Thermosensors Ltd* v *Hibben*, Nicholls V-C set out seven points of procedure. The defendant must have the opportunity to get legal advice, so the order should be served at a time that enables this to happen. If the defendant is a woman alone in a private house, the claimant's solicitor must be a woman, or accompanied by a woman. A detailed list of items removed should be prepared at the premises and checked by the defendant. The defendant should be restrained from communicating with others, apart from a lawyer, only for a limited period of time; a week is too long. Orders at business premises should be executed in the presence of an officer or employee. The claimant should not use the opportunity for a general search of the defendant's papers. The order should be served and supervised by an experienced solicitor independent of the claimant, who should submit a written report to the defendant and to the court at a subsequent hearing with notice.

The courts are clearly concerned to ensure that the procedure is not abused. As an equitable remedy, the search order has shown the willingness of the courts to adapt well-established remedies to new situations. The maxim that equity will not allow a wrong to be without a remedy is still valid today, yet the dangers of the procedure are acknowledged by the courts that developed it. Concern over abuse of search orders has been expressed both by the judges and the legal profession as a whole. While such orders provide a valuable remedy, the balance must be maintained between the potential parties to a claim. Although it is unlikely that this remedy will disappear, it is likely that, in future, judges will need very cogent evidence before granting search orders.

QUESTION 2

Lex Ltd produces videos and tapes of lectures and accompanying notes for the purpose of teaching law to overseas students by distance learning. Ten staff are employed on a full-time basis. Portia, a senior member of staff, and author of a leading textbook on European law, is employed on a five-year contract to develop new materials within her field. Her contract requires her not to work for any other firm of law tutors during the period of her contract and for one year thereafter. Portia is a member of the National Union of Law Teachers (NULT).

Negotiations over conditions of service between Lex Ltd and its staff have now broken down. The following circumstances have occurred:

(a) Portia, who has three years left to run on her contract, has written a letter of resignation to Lex Ltd. She has accepted an offer of employment at the Cambridge base of the tutorial firm, Law sans Larmes, which has its headquarters in Brussels.

(b) All the materials that Portia had been working on have disappeared from the office, and Lex Ltd fears that they may now be in the possession of Law sans Larmes. The company has also discovered that its current students have received advertisement material from Law sans Larmes, and believes that Portia took a list of clients with her. It also believes that Law sans Larmes have bank accounts in Cambridge and Brussels, and that fees received are transferred on a regular basis to the Brussels account.

(c) After conducting a ballot in which the majority of members voted in support of industrial action, NULT has called a strike at Lex Ltd's premises as a result of the breakdown in negotiations. Picketing is taking place on a daily basis.

Advise Lex Ltd of any equitable remedies it may have in these circumstances.

Commentary

This problem question has a variety of points in it and mixes both specific performance and injunctions. They are, however, quite straightforward and not too difficult to spot. You should be able to score a good 2(i) if you work methodically through the various remedies, explaining their availability in each instance. For a first-class answer, some critical analysis of their usage would be necessary.

Suggested Answer

(a) Portia is in breach of her contract of employment with Lex Ltd. An employment contract, that is, a contract *of* service, cannot be enforced specifically against an employee (Trade Union and Labour Relations (Consolidation) Act 1992). This statutory provision stems from the equitable principle that such contracts should not be turned into 'contracts of slavery' (per Fry LJ in *De Francesco* v *Barnum* (1890) 45 ChD 430 at p. 438). A claim for damages would provide an adequate remedy since, although Portia is a leading author and a senior member of staff, it is likely that she could be replaced.

Lex Ltd may, however, wish to enforce the express negative stipulation in her contract restraining her from working for anyone else during the remaining period of her contract. Earlier case law indicates that a claim for an injunction to this effect would be successful. In *Lumley* v *Wagner* (1852) 1 De G M & G 604, an opera singer broke her contract which required her to sing at the plaintiff's theatre for three months. The remedy of specific performance was refused but an injunction preventing her singing at any other theatre during the contractual period was granted. This was followed in *Warner Bros Pictures Inc.* v *Nelson* [1937] 1 KB 209 where the actress, Bette Davis, was prevented from working for a rival film company in breach of a no-competition clause.

However, these cases have been modified where it appears that to grant the remedy would mean that the defendant was prevented from working in any capacity (*Whitwood Chemical Co.* v *Hardman* [1891] 2 Ch 416). In *Rely-A-Bell Burglar and Fire Alarm Co. Ltd* v *Eisler* [1926] Ch 609, an injunction was refused which would have enforced compliance with a stipulation by an employee not to enter into any other employment during the term of his contract. In effect, the defendant would be required to work for the plaintiff or starve. It is considered unrealistic to expect an individual with a particular talent to work in an entirely different capacity. *Warner Bros Pictures Inc.* v *Nelson* was disapproved in *Warren* v *Mendy* [1989] 1 WLR 853, a case where an injunction preventing a boxer from seeking financial services from anyone other than his manager was refused. The principle was stated that an injunction will not be granted if its effect is to prevent a person from working for anyone other than the plaintiff. In *Page One Records Ltd* v *Britton* [1968] 1 WLR 157, 'The Troggs', a group of musicians, appointed the plaintiff company to act as their agent for five years, and agreed not to engage any other person to act in that capacity. An injunction enforcing the negative stipulation was refused since the practical effect would have been to oblige the group to continue to employ the plaintiff company.

The case of *Warner Bros Pictures Inc.* v *Nelson* is clearly difficult to reconcile with the later cases of *Page One Records Ltd* v *Britton* and *Warren* v *Mendy*. One significant difference is the length of the contracts: in *Warner Bros Pictures Inc.* v *Nelson* the term of the contract was for not more than 20 weeks, while in *Warren* v *Mendy* it was for two years. Issues of mutual trust and confidence are also relevant.

The negative stipulation in Portia's contract is that she has expressly agreed not to work for any other firm of law tutors in the UK during the contractual period. If an injunction were to be granted, then, in effect, she would be obliged to resume employment with Lex Ltd, notwithstanding that a decree of specific perform-ance would be unlikely to be available. Such a result is contrary to the principles expressed in the later cases and an injunction is, therefore, likely to be refused.

The principle would remain the same whether the injunction was sought against either Law sans Larmes or Portia.

(b) Lex Ltd may seek an injunction to prevent Portia taking its latest teaching materials. There is a right in equity to restrain an abuse of confidential information. This does not necessarily rely on an employment relationship.

Knowledge of the list of customers is critical to Lex Ltd's commercial enterprise and would also amount to confidential information. An interim injunction could have been sought to prevent this information being divulged (*Robb* v *Green* [1985] 2 QB 315). However, the information has already been acted upon, and equity will not act in vain. In the *Spycatcher* case (*A-G* v *Guardian Newspapers Ltd (No. 2)* [1990] 1 AC 109), the final injunction was refused. The information had already been published worldwide and the injunction would have been futile. A claim for damages against Law sans Larmes might be appropriate if a profit has been made (*Seager* v *Copydex Ltd (No. 2)* [1969] 1 WLR 809).

If Lex Ltd fears that the teaching materials have also been taken, it may seek a search order against both parties (formerly called an *Anton Piller* order after the case of *Anton Piller KG* v *Manufacturing Processes Ltd* [1976] Ch 55). This would permit the company's agents to inspect the evidence at the premises of Law sans Larmes and at Portia's home. The application is made without notice where there is a risk that the evidence might be destroyed before a claim could be brought. The application must be made, and the order served, in accordance with the procedures established in *Universal Thermosensors Ltd* v *Hibben* [1992] 1 WLR 840. In particular, as the defendant is a woman, the order must be served by, or in the presence of, a woman.

Lex Ltd must show a very strong prima facie case and actual or potential damage of a very serious nature. It already has evidence that the information is in the hands of Law sans Larmes and the damage to its business could be irreparable.

Lex Ltd is clearly concerned that if it sues Law sans Larmes for damages the latter may be unable to satisfy the claim if assets are transferred abroad. It may, therefore, consider seeking a freezing injunction under the procedure established in *Mareva Compañía Naviera SA* v *International Bulkcarriers SA* [1975] 2 Lloyd's Rep 509. This is an order which prevents the defendant from transferring assets abroad. It is usually obtained without notice and could be sought at the same time as the search order.

The principles in *American Cyanamid Co.* v *Ethicon Ltd* [1975] AC 396 must be satisfied. Further to the Supreme Court Act 1981, s. 37(3), the injunction may be granted to prevent the defendant removing the assets from the jurisdiction of the court or dissipating them in some way.

Lex Ltd must show that it has a good arguable case and will be required to give an undertaking in damages in the event that it is unsuccessful at trial. In addition, it must comply with the guidelines originally established in *Third Chandris Shipping Corp.* v *Unimarine SA* [1979] 2 All ER 972. The remedy will only be available where there is good reason to believe that assets will be moved out of the jurisdiction or otherwise disposed of so as to defeat the claim.

Some of the assets of Law sans Larmes appear to be in Brussels. Lex Ltd may consider the possibility of seeking a freezing injunction which covers not only the English bank account, but also the Brussels account. The Court of Appeal have affirmed in the cases of *Babanaft International Co. SA* v *Bassatne* [1990] Ch 13, *Republic of Haiti* v *Duvalier* [1990] 1 QB 202 and *Derby & Co. Ltd* v *Weldon* [1990] Ch 48, that there is no geographical limit to the jurisdiction of the court. However, an injunction in this form would not be available where it may adversely affect third parties and where its effect may be oppressive to the defendant.

(c)   In order to obtain an interim injunction against the union to prevent picketing, Lex Ltd must first show that there is a serious question to be tried according to the principles in *American Cyanamid Co.* v *Ethicon Ltd.* Secondly, it must show that it would suffer irreparable damage if the injunction is not granted and the dispute continues. Lex Ltd may decide to seek an injunction without notice. This is permitted under the Trade Union and Labour Relations (Consolidation) Act 1992, provided that all reasonable steps have been taken for the defendant to be notified and heard.

The Trade Union and Labour Relations (Consolidation) Act 1992, as amended, provides that the court shall have regard to the possibility of the defendant establishing a defence of immunity to tortious liability under the 1992 Act. This modifies the *American Cyanamid* principles to the extent that Lex Ltd may have to show a prima facie case. This is particularly important in cases of this type where the outcome of the claim for an interim injunction pending trial may be decisive. In *NWL Ltd* v *Woods* [1979] 1 WLR 1294, where an interim injunction was sought restraining industrial action, the merits of the case were considered on an interim basis pending trial.

QUESTION 3

To what extent have the requirements for interim (formerly known as 'interlocutory') injunctions laid down by the House of Lords in *American*

Cyanamid Co. v *Ethicon Ltd* [1975] AC 396 been followed by subsequent cases?

Commentary

This essay question requires a discussion of the way in which the leading case, *American Cyanamid Co.* v *Ethicon Ltd*, changed the rules relating to interim injunctions, and the further development of those rules in subsequent cases. It is one of those colourful areas where Lord Denning MR has robustly defended a certain position, and where other developments have occurred in particular fields.

As with all essay questions, the way to a high mark is to launch into a critical analysis of the case law. You would not be asked a question of this sort if the case law were straightforward.

One of the difficulties in dealing with a question of this sort in an exam is what to put in and what to leave out. You could spend all the allotted time dealing with search orders and freezing injunctions. It is preferable, however, to deal with the central issue: that is, should the defendant be required to establish a prima facie case? Then show, by example, the extent to which this point has moved from the position established in the leading case.

This also is a question which could be encountered as an assessed essay, in which case you will have much more scope to expand the examples and refer to the literature, for example, Christine Gray, 'Interlocutory Injunctions since Cyanamid' [1981] CLJ 307.

Suggested Answer

The House of Lords in *American Cyanamid Co.* v *Ethicon Ltd* [1975] AC 396 established new criteria for the granting of an interim (formerly kown as an 'interlocutory') injunction.

Prior to *American Cyanamid* it had been necessary for the plaintiff to show a prima facie case before the injunction would be granted. See, for example, *J. T. Stratford & Son Ltd* v *Lindley* [1965] AC 269. In addition, it had to be shown that the balance of convenience supported the grant. So, if the plaintiff could show that damage would be suffered which could not be compensated by an award of damages at the trial, then, once a prima facie case was made out, the injunction would be granted. This meant that frequently the issues which were to be heard at the trial of the action were rehearsed at the hearing of the motion for the injunction.

In *American Cyanamid* the House of Lords disapproved of the court conducting a trial on affidavit evidence, when the essential purpose of an injunction is to preserve a party's position until trial. They decided that it was no longer necessary to establish a prima facie case at the interim proceedings. Provided that it could be shown that there was a serious question to be tried, then the remedy would be granted. Subject to this, the main test was the balance of convenience between the parties. The balance of convenience would be tested primarily by the adequacy of damages. If the balance of convenience was not clearly established then the *status quo* would be maintained. There is only one qualification made, which is that in individual cases special factors might have to be considered. The House of Lords did not classify these special factors.

One of the difficulties encountered with this approach is that frequently the claim never comes to trial. Litigation is expensive, and a party against whom an injunction has been made may feel sufficiently discouraged to settle or drop the case. So the decision to grant the injunction at the interim hearing may dispose of the claim and the issues may never be fully aired. Under the former position, this did not matter. If a prima facie case had to be made out, then the evidence would be presented and cross-examined.

An example of this occurs in trade disputes. The strength of the workers' case often lies in their ability to withdraw their labour. If an injunction is sought barring them from strike action then, on the *American Cyanamid* principles, the balance of convenience will invariably be in favour of the employer. This was recognised in the Trade Union and Labour Relations (Consolidation) Act 1992, and the court is to have regard to the likelihood of the defendant establishing the defence of immunity to tortious liability.

A further statutory modification to the principles in *American Cyanamid* is made in the Human Rights Act 1998. Where an interim injunction is sought to restrain publication before the trial, this may potentially affect the right to freedom of expression protected under Article 10 of the European Convention on Human Rights. Thus, s. 12 of the Act provides that publication before trial should not be restrained unless the court is 'satisfied that the applicant is likely to establish that publication should not be allowed'. In any event, even if s. 12 is satisfied, the 'balance of convenience' argument may still prevail (*Douglas and Zeta-Jones* v *HELLO! Ltd* [2001] 2 WLR 992, [2001] 2 All ER 289).

However, these statutory modifications to the *American Cyanamid* principle are exceptions. Criticism of the application of the principle has been left to the judges in later cases.

In *Fellowes & Son v Fisher* [1976] QB 122, the Court of Appeal had differing views on the application of the *American Cyanamid* principles. The majority of the court refused an injunction to prevent a breach of a restrictive covenant in an employment contract, on the ground of the balance of convenience. Lord Denning MR, however, refused the injunction on the ground that no prima facie case had been made out. He stated that *American Cyanamid* did not apply because the facts of *Fellowes & Son v Fisher* fell within one of the exceptional cases outlined by Lord Diplock where special factors could be considered.

In *Hubbard v Pitt* [1976] QB 142, Lord Denning MR again took a different approach from the rest of the Court of Appeal. An injunction was granted by the majority of the court to restrain protesters obstructing access to the premises of an estate agent. The majority took the view that there was a serious question to be tried and the balance of convenience supported the grant. They did not require that a prima facie case should be made out. Lord Denning MR, dissenting, argued that a prima facie case was required and that the case fell outside *American Cyanamid* because 'special factors' applied. These 'special factors' related to freedom of speech and the right to demonstrate.

Thus Lord Denning MR has relied on the reference to 'special factors' to take cases outside *American Cyanamid* and rely on the former rule that a prima facie case must be established.

Other cases where special factors have prevailed include *Smith v Inner London Education Authority* [1978] 1 All ER 411. Here the defendant was a public body and it was held that in such cases the interests of the general public must be considered. In libel cases where the defendant intends to plead justification, an interim injunction is unlikely to be granted on *American Cyanamid* principles.

Trade disputes are dealt with by statute. The Trade Union and Labour Relations (Consolidation) Act 1992 provides that the defendant in an application for an interim injunction may prove a prima facie defence under the statute. In *NWL Ltd v Woods* [1979] 1 WLR 1294 Lord Diplock observed that *American Cyanamid* was not dealing with a case where the grant or refusal of the injunction would dispose of the action. He stated that in such a case the consideration of the balance of convenience should take into account the likelihood of success had the case gone to trial.

There are two areas in which there have been important developments in the field of interim injunctions. These are the search orders and freezing injunctions, formerly known as *Anton Piller* and *Mareva* orders (named respectively after *Anton Piller KG* v *Manufacturing Processes Ltd* [1976] Ch 55 and *Mareva Compañía Naviera SA* v *International Bulkcarriers SA* [1975] 2 Lloyd's Rep 509).

Search orders have been described as being of a 'Draconian nature' permitting a claimant to enter the defendant's premises and inspect evidence which it is believed may be removed or destroyed. They are available without notice so that the defendant is not forewarned. Ormrod LJ laid down three conditions, the first of which was that the claimant must have an extremely strong prima facie case. This is an exception to the *American Cyanamid* principles. Search orders are mandatory in nature. The courts are less willing to grant a mandatory order without an indication of the strength of the claimant's case.

Freezing injunctions are available to prevent a defendant moving assets or otherwise disposing of them in order to make the pursuit of the main claim fruitless. The claimant must have a legal or equitable right to protect and have a good arguable case.

The jurisdiction to grant search orders and freezing injunctions is now contained in the Supreme Court Act 1981, s. 37.

Thus, there are various situations where the principles in *American Cyanamid* have been refined or distinguished to meet the particular case.

QUESTION 4

(a) Amelia, a sculptress, agrees with Belinda to make a bust of Belinda, a world renowned child actress, for £500. When the bust is completed, Cindy, a film buff and fan of Belinda, offers Amelia £1,000 for it. Amelia, who is in severe financial difficulties, accepts Cindy's offer.

Advise Belinda on the availability of any equitable remedies for breach of contract in these circumstances.

(b)   Delia took a long lease of the top flat on the 14th floor of a tower block being built two years ago. The service contract requires Easimoney Ltd, the freeholder, to undertake external building repairs, to have the outside of the windows cleaned once a month, and to install a lift within a reasonable period of time.

A recent gale has dislodged some tiles from the roof, and rain now leaks into Delia's flat. Despite Delia's repeated requests, the roof has not been repaired. The windows are never cleaned and the lift has not been installed.

Advise Delia of any equitable remedies that might be available to her.

Commentary

This is a straightforward question requiring a knowledge of the rules relating to specific performance. It is a good illustration of the need to read the question. For example, the claimant in part (a) is a child. This is not simply to add local colour to the question but is designed to raise the issue of mutuality. If you miss this point, your marks go down.

The second part of the question requires you to know the application of specific performance to contracts requiring supervision and construction contracts. You have to know the case law. Of particular importance is the decision of the House of Lords in *Co-operative Insurance Society Ltd* v *Argyll Stores (Holdings) Ltd* [1998] AC 1. (See also P. Luxton [1998] Conv 396.) If you can answer the first part, but know nothing about the cases relevant to the second, then it is too risky to tackle this question. A superb answer to the first part but zero on the second will barely earn you a pass.

However, if you have specific performance at your fingertips, then this question is fairly uncomplicated if you pick up all the points.

Suggested Answer

(a)   The equitable remedy of specific performance is discretionary. It will not be available where damages provide an adequate remedy, or where the claimant has acted in an inequitable manner. Neither will the court grant the remedy unless it can be enforced; equity will not act in vain. If it is unjust to the defendant to grant the remedy, it will not be awarded.

Normally, contracts for the transfer of personal property will not be specifically enforced. They can usually be compensated for adequately by an award of damages. However, if the item of property has some particular rarity, or beauty or uniqueness, such as King Canute's hunting horn (*Pusey* v *Pusey* (1684) 1 Vern 273), then specific performance may be granted.

There is statutory authority for the remedy contained in the Sale of Goods Act 1979, s. 52. This enables the court to grant specific performance of a contract to deliver specific or ascertained goods where it is just to do so.

The contract between Amelia and Belinda is for personal property, a bust of Belinda. In order for the remedy of specific performance to be granted there must be something unique about the property. In *Cohen* v *Roche* [1927] 1 KB 169, a contract for the sale of eight Hepplewhite chairs was not specifically enforceable. The chairs were not considered to be of any special value or interest. On the other hand, a contract for the sale of a ship was enforced in *Behnke* v *Bede Shipping Co. Ltd* [1927] 1 KB 649, where the ship was of 'peculiar and practically unique value to the plaintiff'.

The bust of Belinda is unique: there is only one in existence. It is a case which falls within the ancient jurisdiction of cases such as *Pusey* v *Pusey*, where the goods are distinguishable because of their rarity, rather than *Cohen* v *Roche*, where the goods, though rare and valuable, are still no more than ordinary commercial articles.

However, Amelia is in severe financial difficulties, and, for that reason, accepts the offer from Cindy. Since the remedy is discretionary, the court would consider whether it is equitable in the circumstances to grant Belinda specific performance of the contract against Amelia. Where a hardship would amount to an injustice (if Amelia could show that it would put her out of business) then the court may be reluctant to award specific performance of the contract (*Patel* v *Ali* [1984] Ch 283).

Neither will the court act in vain. An equitable remedy will be granted only if it can be complied with by the defendant. In *Jones* v *Lipman* [1962] 1 WLR 832 the defendant attempted to defeat a contract for the sale of land by transferring the land to a company he had set up for this express purpose. The court awarded specific performance because the company was a sham. Normally specific performance would not be granted against a defendant who no longer owned the property. If Amelia has already delivered the bust to Cindy, then Cindy will take free of Belinda's claim to specific performance, assuming Cindy is a bona fide purchaser without notice. In these circumstances, Belinda will have to rely on the remedy of damages for breach of contract.

For specific performance to be awarded, it must be available to either party. If there is a lack of mutuality, there is a discretion to refuse the remedy. In *Flight v Bolland* (1824) 4 Russ 298, a minor was refused specific performance as it would not have been available against him. There is judicial authority for the viewpoint that the time to determine mutuality is at the time of the trial, not the contract. In *Clayton v Ashdown* (1714) 2 Eq Ab 516, it was held that where a minor attained majority at the time of the trial the remedy would be available. This principle was confirmed by the Court of Appeal in *Price v Strange* [1978] Ch 337.

There are, therefore, various grounds on which the court may refuse to exercise its discretion to award specific performance in favour of Belinda.

(b) Delia is seeking specific performance of her landlord's covenants. The general principle is that the court will not grant specific performance of a contract where constant supervision would be required: 'Specific performance is inapplicable where the continued supervision of the court is necessary in order to ensure the fulfilment of the contract' (Dixon J, *J.C. Williamson Ltd v Lakey and Mulholland* (1931) 45 CLR 282, at pp. 297–8). Equity will not act in vain and the court is unable constantly to supervise the performance of a contract. In practice, this means that if the court might have to give 'an indefinite series of rulings in order to ensure the execution of the order', the court will not grant the remedy (*Co-operative Insurance Society Ltd v Argyll Stores (Holdings) Ltd* [1998] AC 1). It will not, therefore, enforce a contract where such supervision would be necessary.

There are, however, exceptions to this principle and the courts, in some of the modern cases, are more willing to grant specific performance even where there are potential problems relating to supervision.

The earlier case of *Ryan v Mutual Tontine Westminster Chambers Association* [1893] 1 Ch 116 shows the application of the general principle. The lessor of a flat covenanted to appoint a caretaker who would be in constant attendance and would undertake cleaning and general portering duties. A caretaker was appointed but he was frequently absent. The Court of Appeal refused to grant specific performance as it would be unable to supervise the performance of the covenant. It awarded damages instead.

However, in *Posner* v *Scott-Lewis* [1987] Ch 25, specific performance of a similar covenant to employ a resident porter was awarded. The court held that if the obligation was sufficiently defined and the degree of supervision was not unacceptable, then, if the plaintiff would suffer greater hardship, the equitable remedy would be awarded.

Similarly, if the order can be defined with precision, so that the defendant knows exactly what is to be done, then the court will be more likely to grant the discretionary remedy (*Morris* v *Redland Bricks Ltd* [1970] AC 652, at p. 666, per Lord Upjohn).

The strength of the claimant's case is also a relevant factor given the equitable nature of the remedy (see Spry, *Equitable Remedies*, 5th edn, (1997)).

In *Co-operative Insurance Society Ltd* v *Argyll Stores (Holdings) Ltd* [1998] AC 1, a case concerning the enforcement of a covenant in a commercial tenant's lease to continue running the business, Lord Hoffman distinguished between orders which require a defendant to carry on an activity and orders which require him to achieve a result. In the former case, which might involve an order to carry on running a business over an extended period of time, the possibility of repeated applications for rulings on compliance with the order may arise. Whereas in the latter case, where a result is to be achieved, however complicated, the court may simply look at the finished result and rule on whether compliance has been effected. So cases such as *Wolverhampton Corporation* v *Emmons* [1901] 1 KB 575, concerning a building contract, and *Jeune* v *Queens Cross Properties Ltd* [1974] Ch 97, concerning repairing covenants, are exceptions to the general principle because they involve the achievement of a result — a building, or specific repair.

The terms in Delia's lease are threefold. The first is to install a lift. In *Wolverhampton Corporation* v *Emmons* [1901] 1 KB 515, the Court of Appeal established three requirements: the building work must be clearly defined; damages would be an inadequate remedy; and the defendant has possession of the land. It would seem that these requirements are satisfied. The building work is clearly defined except that the time-limit is vague. However, the court is unlikely to be unwilling to specify what would constitute a reasonable time. Since the work would have to be undertaken on part of the block of flats which is in the landlord's possession, it would be impossible for Delia to carry out the work herself. Damages would, therefore, be an inadequate remedy.

This exception was extended to landlords' covenants to repair in *Jeune* v *Queens Cross Properties Ltd* [1974] Ch 97. The Landlord and Tenant Act 1985, s. 17, now provides that specific performance of a landlord's repairing covenant may be granted. This overrides any equitable principles restricting the remedy. Delia would therefore be able to seek specific performance of the covenant to repair in respect of the damage to the roof caused by the gale.

The covenant to have the windows cleaned highlights the problem of supervision. Clearly, such a contractual obligation is ongoing and would require constant superintendence. However, applying *Posner* v *Scott-Lewis*, the work is clearly defined. If an order is issued requiring the landlord to appoint a firm of window-cleaners to carry out the work, then the supervision required is no more than the appointment of the porter in *Posner* v *Scott-Lewis*. This falls into the category defined by Lord Hoffmann in the *Co-operative Insurance Society* case, as the achievement of a result. Damages might be an adequate remedy in that they would enable Delia to employ a window-cleaner herself. However, to employ a window-cleaner to clean the exterior of the windows on the 14th floor is not practicable and the court would no doubt take the view that it would cause greater hardship to Delia than to the landlord. Therefore, Delia has a reasonable prospect of success in enforcing this covenant.

15 Pick 'n' Mix Questions

INTRODUCTION

Your examination paper may contain one question which mixes a number of different topics. This may be upsetting at first sight. You may have carefully revised several topics which are covered in the question only to discover that it includes one topic which you thought safe to leave out. Assuming that each section in the question bears equal marks (and that is a reasonable assumption unless there is any contrary indication) then it is probably unsafe to tackle it in these circumstances. Most (if not all) questions in the paper will be discrete and you will find the question on charities or administration of trusts or whatever your favourite topic may be, without any difficulty. Once you have identified it then you are away.

However, the possibility of a mixed topic question is another reason why you should read the questions carefully before starting to write. A question might include two sections on charities, then a section on a private purpose trust with a question mark over its validity, and a concluding section on a gift to an unincorporated association. One question spotted in a university exam paper contained four problems: a secret trust; certainty of objects; certainty of intention, and wound up with the doctrine of election — not a pretty sight. If you glance at the question, think 'charities', and plough into it, only to discover 20 valuable minutes later that you have to deal with a subject about which you know nothing, you have wasted a great deal of effort and lost, probably, a class or worse.

Needless to say, if you know each of the topics then you do not have a problem. In fact, if your luck holds and you are thoroughly familiar with the case law for each point, this question may be a dream ticket.

Three questions have been selected to illustrate these points. Question 1 mixes charitable trusts, discretionary trusts and covenants to settle. Question 2 mixes constitution of trusts, *donationes mortis causa* and certainty of words and objects. Question 3 mixes the three certainties, secret trusts and trusts of imperfect obligation.

The main advice is: do not be taken by surprise by a pick 'n' mix question. Suspend disbelief: just because section (a) is on secret trusts does not mean the other sections must also be on the same theme. READ THE QUESTIONS CAREFULLY.

QUESTION 1

Four years ago Alpha transferred £100,000 to Beta 'upon trust to provide, at his discretion, grants for law students in the United Kingdom, absolute preference to be given to my relatives'. One year ago, Alpha covenanted with Beta to transfer to Beta, upon the same trusts, any property he (Alpha) might subsequently acquire under the will of Gamma. One month later Gamma died, and in his will he bequeathed 10,000 shares in Delta Ltd to Alpha.

Alpha died last month, without having taken steps to transfer the shares in Delta Ltd to Beta. In his will Alpha gave all his property to his niece, Omega.

Discuss.

Commentary

The separate parts of the question are not intrinsically difficult, but the higher marks will be obtained by a student who can show how the different areas interact.

Suggested Answer

It is first necessary to consider who is entitled to the shares in Delta Ltd. As sole beneficiary of Alpha's will, Omega is entitled to the shares if they formed part of his estate at his death. They will not comprise part of such estate if they are the subject-matter of a fully constituted charitable trust. Alpha, however, never transferred the legal title to the shares to the trustee, Beta, as he had covenanted to do. Furthermore, there is no evidence that he did everything necessary to be done by him in order to perfect the transfer in equity: see *Milroy* v *Lord* (1862) 4 De GF & J 264 and *Re Rose* [1952] Ch 499, CA. The trust therefore, remains incompletely constituted in respect of the shares. There is no evidence that valuable consideration has been supplied for the creation of the trust. As regards the shares, therefore, the trust is an incompletely constituted voluntary settlement. Equity will not compel Alpha's estate to transfer the shares to Beta, since equity will not assist a volunteer: *Re Plumptre* [1910] 1 Ch 609. The person entitled to the shares is, therefore, Omega.

Nevertheless, even though the shares are not themselves bound by the trust, it is still necessary to consider whether Beta can sue Alpha's estate for damages for breach of covenant. It has been argued that a covenantee of a voluntary covenant should be able to sue for damages for its breach and hold such damages in trust for the volunteers: see Elliott (1960) 76 LQR 100. The courts, nevertheless, are opposed to such a claim. In *Re Pryce* [1917] 1 Ch 234, the court would not direct the covenantees to sue, and in *Re Kay's Settlement* [1939] Ch 329 it positively directed them not to sue. There is no objection to such a claim if the covenantee is suing in respect of her own loss as beneficiary, as in *Cannon* v *Hartley* [1949] Ch 213; but this is not the situation in the problem. By contrast, in *Fletcher* v *Fletcher* (1844) 4 Hare 67, the court held that there was already a perfect trust of a chose in action: viz, the benefit of the covenant itself. This suggests that if Alpha intended the benefit of the covenant to comprise trust property, Beta will be obliged to sue Alpha's estate for damages for breach of covenant and to hold the substantial damages which he will recover upon the trusts declared. There is, however, no evidence that this was Alpha's intention.

An alternative explanation was proffered in *Re Cook's Settlement Trusts* [1965] Ch 902 by Buckley J. He considered that, whilst it might be possible to create a valid trust of the benefit of a covenant concerning property in existence and owned by the settlor at the date of the covenant, it is not possible to create a trust of the benefit of a covenant which relates to after-acquired property. If this view is followed, there can be no trust of the covenant in the problem.

Since the covenant was entered into only one year ago, it is enforceable by a third party whom the covenant purports to benefit, unless it appears that the parties intended otherwise (Contracts (Rights of Third Parties) Act 1999). If the specified purpose is charitable, this raises the question whether such a covenant is enforceable by the Attorney-General. This seems unlikely, since he is not a person who is intended to benefit from the covenant. It also seems unlikely that the persons who might benefit under a charitable trust would have a personal right of action under the 1999 Act, since such persons do not have a beneficial interest under a charitable trust. The conclusion must be that the 1999 Act does not operate in relation to voluntary covenants to transfer property in favour of charity.

Even if a trust of a chose in action has been created, Beta will not hold it upon the trusts declared unless these are valid trusts. A trust to provide grants for law students is itself a valid charitable purpose within the second head of Lord Macnaghten's classification in *Pemsel's Case* [1891] AC 531: namely, for the advancement of education. The problem is whether the expression of an 'absolute preference' for Alpha's relatives denies it charitable status. For a trust to be charitable it must be for the public benefit. This means (*inter alia*) that a sufficient section of the community must be capable of benefiting. Where the beneficiaries are defined by reference to a personal nexus, which includes a family relationship, the trust is not charitable: *Re Compton* [1945] Ch 123, CA. Furthermore, in the context of the advancement of education, an indirect benefit to the public is insufficient: *Re Compton*.

Nevertheless, it was held in *Re Koettgen's Will Trusts* [1954] Ch 252, that provided the primary class is a sufficient section of the community, a preference for a private class will not destroy the trust's charitable nature. This case has not, however, met with general approval (see *IRC* v *Educational Grants Association Ltd* [1967] Ch 993, CA). Thus, the trust will not be charitable if the preference is not limited (as in *Re Koettgen's Will Trust*) to 75% of the trust income. Secondly, it will not be charitable if the preferred class has priority: *Caffoor* v *ITC* [1961] AC 584, PC. In the problem the words used are 'absolute preference', which may suggest a priority. If so, the trust will fail to achieve charitable status on both grounds.

If it is not charitable, can the trust be valid as a private discretionary trust? It would probably satisfy the test for certainty of objects, since it would appear to be possible to say of any given person whether or not they are a law student in the United Kingdom: *McPhail* v *Doulton* [1971] AC 424, HL. It would probably also not fail for administrative unworkability, since the description of objects probably does form something like a class: *McPhail* v *Doulton*. Nevertheless, unless (which is unlikely) it can be construed as a trust for immediate distribution of capital, it would be void for perpetuity. Assuming this to be so, the benefit of any chose in action would be held by Beta on a resulting trust for the benefit of Alpha's estate. In practice, this means that the covenant is simply unenforceable.

If the purported trust is void, the money which Alpha transferred to Beta is also held on a resulting trust for Alpha's estate. Omega is therefore entitled to it.

QUESTION 2

Discuss, with reference to decided cases, whether any of the following words create a valid trust. Indicate any problems which may have to be overcome before a trust can be imposed in these cases.

(a)   Look, I am giving this cheque to our baby.

(b)   The money in my deposit account is as much yours as mine.

(c)   I hereby give to my executors and trustees £500,000 on trust to apply the said sum at their absolute discretion for the maintenance and support of red haired women in London.

(d)   It is my dying wish, Marjorie, that you should have my London flat. Here are the deeds and the keys, put them in your bag. My solicitor will sort out the details when I am dead.

Commentary

This question contains a mixed bag of problems relating to the constitution of a trust. It draws heavily on particular cases, which can make it very unattractive if you are not familiar with the exact case. In that sense, it is not a very sporting question. Many examiners try to avoid questions which rely on the student's knowledge of a particular case, preferring to test the understanding of general principles. However, if you are faced with a question of this type, and you know the relevant cases, then it can be a gift. Avoid the temptation of starting your answer with an immediate reference to the case. For example, do not start with: 'This is a *Jones* v *Lock* problem . . .'. Instead, state the issue raised by the question, then the general rule with exceptions, and then illustrate your answer with cases. Some questions of this sort can subtly vary the facts of the case. Watch out for those!

Suggested Answer

(a)   In order for a trust to be created there must be a clear manifestation of an intention to create a trust. Where the settlor makes a declaration of self as trustee, the trust is fully constituted. Where the settlor is to be one of co-trustees, the declaration constitutes the trust and it is not necessary for the property to be transferred into the names of all the trustees to give effect to it (*Choithram (T.) International SA* v *Pagarani* [2001] 1 WLR 1, PC).

The statement made implies a gift not a trust. The gift is imperfect since a cheque is merely an order to a banker; therefore, even if the cheque is handed to baby when the words are spoken, no property right is thereby transferred beyond the paper on which the cheque is written. In *Jones* v *Lock* (1865) LR 1 Ch App 25, an attempt was made to argue that, in effect, the donor had made a declaration that he was a trustee of the cheque for the beneficiary. It was held that a failed gift will not be construed in equity as evidence of an intention to declare a trust. Likewise, in *Pappadakis* v *Pappadakis* (2000) *The Times*, 19 January, it was held that an invalid assignment which did not identify the assignee who was to hold on trust could not operate as a declaration of trust.

Although there is present an intention to benefit the donee, there is no intention present to hold the property as trustee. This was confirmed in *Richards* v *Delbridge* (1874) LR 18 Eq 11, where words written on a lease which indicated an intention to give the lease to the grandson of the leaseholder were held ineffective at common law to effect the transfer. Since they were words indicating a gift, they were ineffective in equity to operate as a declaration of trust.

The gift will be perfected only when, and if, after presentation of the cheque, the funds are transferred to the credit of the payee's account.

(b)   This statement again raises the issue of certainty of intention to create a trust. In this situation the holder of the deposit account has not made an attempt to transfer the account into joint names. It may be arguable, according to the circumstances of the case, that the account holder has manifested an intention to hold the account on trust by conduct. The words are not sufficient in themselves, but, coupled with the conduct of the parties, they may be. For example, in *Paul* v *Constance* [1977] 1 WLR 527, where money was put into an account in the sole name of Mr Constance, his assurances to Mrs Paul that the money in the account was owned jointly were held sufficient to indicate an intention by him to hold the account on trust for them jointly. In *Re Vandervell's Trusts (No. 2)* [1974] Ch 269, where money from a settlement was used to purchase shares in exercise of an option, it was held that the conduct of the trustees in using this money and paying dividends into the settlement constituted sufficient evidence of an intention to create a trust even though no specific words had been used. Compare *Choithram (T.) International SA* v *Pagarani* [2001] 1 WLR 1, where words which indicated an outright gift were construed in the context of the case as words of a gift to be held on the trusts of a settlement already constituted by the donor.

The decision in *Paul* v *Constance* was applied in *Rowe* v *Prance* [1999] 2 FLR 787, where a boat, which was held in the sole legal ownership of the defendant, was considered to be held on trust for the claimant and defendant in equal shares. The defendant had always referred to the boat as 'our boat' and had assured the claimant (his partner in an extra-marital affair) that her interest in the boat was her security.

There must, however, be a clear intention evinced, whether by words and/or conduct, to create a trust. In *Re B (Child: Property Transfer)* [1999] 2 FLR 418, where a house, further to a consent order, was transferred to the mother 'for the benefit of the child', no trust was created for the child. The relationship between mother and child had broken down.

Therefore, although it is difficult to state that the words are sufficient on their own to create a trust, coupled with other conduct there may be sufficient certainty of the requisite intention.

(c) In this gift there is a clear intention to create a trust. However, the issue is whether a gift to red haired women in London is sufficiently certain to be carried out by the trustees. The trust appears to be discretionary. The test for certainty of objects in a discretionary trust was outlined in *McPhail v Doulton* [1971] AC 424, HL, where it was held that the test was the same as that established for powers in *Re Gulbenkian's Settlements* [1970] AC 508, HL. The test is 'Can it be said with certainty that any given individual is or is not a member of the class?' The question is concerned with whether the concept is clear, rather than with any evidential difficulties. So, in *Re Baden's Deed Trusts (No. 2)* [1972] Ch 607, the question was whether the words 'relatives' and 'dependants' were conceptually certain.

The problem of definition arises, therefore, in respect of red haired women. Can it be said whether any given person is or is not a member of the class? The problem is not, in this case, in proving whether a person is or is not within the class. Instead, the difficulty lies in defining the term 'red haired'. Whereas all people may agree whether certain individuals are red haired, there may be some borderline cases where the trustees could not decide. The concept of what constitutes red hair may, therefore, be so unclear that it is impossible to carry out the trust.

Another problem might arise in relation to the width of the class. If a discretionary trust is so wide that it is administratively unworkable, this may invalidate it. In *McPhail v Doulton*, Lord Wilberforce suggested that a discretionary trust for the residents of Greater London might be so wide that it was unworkable. This was followed in *R v District Auditor, ex parte West Yorkshire Metropolitan County Council* (1986) 26 RVR 24 (QBD), where a discretionary trust was purportedly created for the inhabitants of the county of West Yorkshire. The description of objects was considered to be so large that the trust was invalidated for administrative unworkability. This would be different if the gift was construed as a mere power (see *Re Manisty's Settlement* [1974] Ch 17).

The difficulties inherent in validating this gift to red haired women indicate a capriciousness in the mind of the donor. While there is no general principle that a donor may not act capriciously (*Bird* v *Luckie* (1850) 8 Hare 301), where the gift involves the exercise by a trustee of a fiduciary obligation, the position is different. The difficulties, in the first instance, of defining red hair, and secondly, in the potential width of the class, indicate an element of caprice which may cause a court to invalidate a gift on that ground alone (see *Re Hay's Settlement Trusts* [1982] 1 WLR 202).

(**d**) It appears from the wording that this is a death bed gift. In order to effect a transfer of land at common law there should be a deed (Law of Property Act 1925, s. 52). There would appear to be no deed transferring legal ownership in this case. Neither does there appear to be any consideration given. Marjorie is, therefore, a volunteer. The normal principle is that equity will not assist a volunteer in enforcing an imperfect gift.

However, there are some exceptions to this and one in particular, the principle of *donatio mortis causa*, may assist Marjorie. There are three conditions which must be satisfied before this exception will be allowed. The gift must be conditional on death, it must be made in contemplation of death and the donor must give the donee control over the gift (see *Cain* v *Moon* [1896] 2 QB 283).

Here, the question indicates that the gift is made in contemplation of death and it is not difficult to raise the presumption that it is, therefore, conditional on death (*Wilkes* v *Allington* [1931] 2 Ch 104). The donor states that the formalities will be dealt with after death. The subject-matter of the gift is land. Until recently, it was thought that it was not possible for land to be the subject of a *donatio mortis causa* (*Duffield* v *Elwes* (1827) 1 Bli (NS) 497). However, the Court of Appeal decision in *Sen* v *Headley* [1991] Ch 425 dispelled these doubts. In that case, someone who already had the keys of a house was given a bunch of keys including one to a steel box in the house containing the title deeds. It was held that the donor had parted with dominion over the house and the title deeds in circumstances otherwise satisfying the conditions for a *donatio mortis causa* and the gift was completed. It would, therefore, seem that as Marjorie has the keys, giving her physical control, and the deeds, this would be sufficient to give rise to the application of the rule that gifts made in contemplation of death are enforceable despite a lack of the appropriate formalities.

QUESTION 3

Sam, who died recently, appointed Tick and Tack as the executors and trustees of his will and made the following dispositions:

(a)   £50,000 to my sister Doris absolutely, feeling sure that she will give her son a reasonable amount.

(b)   £30,000 to Tick and Tack for purposes of which I will inform them.

(c)   My freehold property 'Dunroamin' to Tick and Tack upon trust to sell and to hold the net proceeds of sale for such worthy causes as they shall think fit.

Sam left his residuary realty to his son Percy and his residuary personalty to his daughter Mavis.

Advise Tick and Tack as to the validity of these dispositions, and as to who should benefit if any of them fail.

Commentary

This is a question which requires a fairly detailed knowledge of different parts of an equity and trusts syllabus. You may be lucky and find that you remember the relevant law and cases, but unless you feel fairly confident of doing well on two of the three parts, you might be wise to leave it alone. It is a question on which you might scrape a pass if you know some law, but would find it difficult to score well.

Hard-pressed examiners like to be able to see clearly which part of a question they are marking. It will help the examiner, therefore, if you number each part of your answer and leave a space between the different parts.

Suggested Answer

(a)   It is unlikely that the words in the disposition to Doris are sufficiently obligatory to attach a trust to the property in the hands of Doris. Such words are precatory words and, since *Lambe* v *Eames* (1871) 6 Ch App 597 and the Executors Act 1830, the courts will not lean in favour of a trust: they simply construe the words in the context of the instrument to ascertain if a trust obligation is imposed. In *Mussoorie Bank* v *Raynor* (1882) 7 App Cas 321, the words 'feeling confident' were held to be precatory and failed to impose a trust, and the words 'feeling sure' used here would probably similarly fail. Doris would therefore, take the gift beneficially.

Even if the words were sufficiently certain to impose a trust, a 'reasonable amount' would be too uncertain as regards subject-matter. Although the court held in *Re Golay's Will Trusts* [1965] 1 WLR 969, that a 'reasonable income' was capable of objective determination by reference to a person's life style, a reasonable amount in this case would not seem to have any objective criteria by which it could be assessed, and it would therefore fail.

(b) This disposition could be an attempt to create a half secret trust if it is found to have the necessary element of obligation. Although the words 'upon trust' are not used, it seems fairly clear from the face of the will that Tick and Tack are not intended to take the disposition beneficially.

In the case of a half secret trust, the half secret trustees must accept the trust before the execution of the will. This does not appear to have happened, as Sam refers to a future communication. Although communication of the identity of the beneficiary at any time before death would be sufficient for a fully secret trust, there are dicta in *Blackwell* v *Blackwell* [1929] AC 318, HL, and it was accepted in *Re Bateman's Will Trusts* [1970] 1 WLR 1463, that this must be before the execution of the will in the case of a half secret trust. The reason given for this is that a communication after the will would allow the testator to change his mind and effectively make testamentary dispositions without complying with the Wills Act 1837. This is criticised as failing to take account of the fact that the secret trust arises from its acceptance by the trustees quite independently of the will.

Even if there has already been a communication of the purposes which Tick and Tack have accepted, it will still be invalid as there would then be an inconsistency on the face of the will, which is fatal to a half secret trust: *Re Keen* [1937] Ch 236. The will clearly refers to a future communication and evidence of a prior communication would be inconsistent with it.

(c) This will impose a trust of land under the TLATA 1996. Even where the trust is expressed as a trust for sale, the power to postpone sale cannot be abrogated (s. 4(1)). It is a matter for Tick and Tack whether they decide to sell Dunroamin or keep it for the beneficiary under the trust. There would appear to be a discretionary trust as regards the proceeds of sale, but the trust is a purpose trust. There are no objects of the trust who can, if necessary, enforce it against Tick and Tack. Moreover, a trust must be sufficiently certain for a court to enforce it if necessary and 'worthy causes' would be too vague. In *Re Atkinson's Will Trusts* [1978] 1 WLR 586, it was held that it would be impossible to confine worthy objects to charitable objects, so there is no possibility of this taking effect as a charitable trust. Although charitable trusts are purpose trusts, they are valid as they are enforceable by the Attorney-

General. A non-charitable purpose trust fails, however, for certainty of objects, and also if it infringes the rule against perpetual trusts. This trust will therefore fail.

The disposition in (a) will go to Doris beneficially if there is no certainty of intention to create a trust. If there is such certainty, but the purported trust in favour of Doris's son fails for uncertainty of subject-matter, Doris similarly takes the entire legacy beneficially as it is only the trust grafted onto it which fails (*Curtis* v *Rippon* (1820) 5 Madd 434). The dispositions in (b) and (c) fail completely, however, and will result back to the testator's residuary estate on failure.

The pecuniary legacy in (b) is personalty and will go as residuary personalty to Mavis. The doctrine of conversion, which applied to a trust for sale under the Law of Property Act 1925, was abolished by s. 3 of the TLATA 1996, and Dunroamin would go to Percy, who is entitled to the residuary realty.

Index